BUILD YOUR OWN HOME

By reading this book, you are taking
your first steps on the ladder to
success and, in just a few months,
you could be sitting in your dream
home counting the savings you have
made. More importantly, you will
feel confident that your home has
been built where you want it, to a
high specification, using quality
materials, and with the inspirational
design elements you selected. The
process is easier than you might
think and more personally and
financially rewarding than you could
ever imagine.

Thank you for buying one of our books. We hope you'll enjoy it, and that it will help you to build the home of your dreams.

We always try to ensure our books are up to date, but contact details seem to change so quickly that it can be very hard to keep up with them. If you do have any problems contacting any of the organisations listed at the back of the book please get in touch, and either we or the authors will do what we can to help. And if you do find correct contact details that differ from those in the book, please let us know so that we can put it right when we reprint.

Please do also give us your feedback so we can go on making books that you want to read. If there's anything you particularly liked about this book – or you have suggestions about how it could be improved in the future – email us on info@howtobooks.co.uk

Good luck with building your own home.

The Publishers
www.howtobooks.co.uk

Please send for a free copy of the latest catalogue:

How To Books
3 Newtec Place, Magdalen Road,
Oxford OX4 1RE, United Kingdom
email: info@howtobooks.co.uk
http://www.howtobooks.co.uk

howtobooks

The Daily Telegraph

BUILD YOUR OWN HOME

The ultimate guide to
managing a self-build
project and creating
your dream house

Tony Booth
& Mike Dyson

howtobooks

Published by How To Books Ltd,
3 Newtec Place, Magdalen Road,
Oxford OX4 1RE, United Kingdom.
Tel: (01865) 793806. Fax: (01865) 248780.
email: info@howtobooks.co.uk
http://www.howtobooks.co.uk

First published in 2003
Reprinted 2003

British Library Cataloguing in Publication Data
A catalogue record for this book is available from the British Library

Cover design by Baseline Arts Ltd, Oxford
Produced for How To Books by Deer Park Productions
Typeset by Pantek Arts Ltd, Maidstone, Kent
Printed and bound by Cromwell Press, Trowbridge, Wiltshire

Contents

Contents

Part Three – Internal Works ... The Fun Part!   159

List of Illustrations

Preface

Many people contemplate building their dream home. This book explains the process stage by stage, and is designed to help *you* turn *your* dream into reality, whatever your experience or level of skill.

This is not a do-it-yourself manual: it will not show you how to build a door frame or construct roof trusses. It will, however, guide you through the fundamental elements of the self-build programme, from identifying and assessing a suitable building-plot to arranging finance and contractors. It deals with architects and designers, surveyors, labourers and tradesmen. We explain how to obtain planning permission and where to find appropriate insurance protection whilst construction is under way.

Essentially, this book provides you with the practical knowledge required to go beyond your aspirations, to take that first step and start building the perfect home. You do not need to be a qualified draughtsman or a competent electrician; if you have enough drive and enthusiasm, you will succeed.

Self-build is an established alternative for many people in other parts of the world, particularly in the USA and Canada, and the practice has spread rapidly across Europe in recent years. With the advent of escalating house prices and a desire for better quality and choice, more people in the UK are joining this growing trend. As a direct result, high-street lenders have developed finance packages for the self-builder and there is also much more guidance and support available.

Constructing your own home is not just a stimulating, satisfying and ultimately rewarding experience, it makes good financial sense too. Savings on a new house, built to a standard specification and bought from a named developer, are between 30 per cent and 73.3 per cent, depending upon the degree of personal involvement in the work. Currently, that means a potential saving of between £69,274 and £169,261 on the average cost of a detached home in the UK (Land Registry, 1st Quarter 2003 data). Some keep or reinvest the saving, whilst others choose to spend it on better quality materials, innovative or hi-tech installations or more luxurious fittings than they could otherwise have afforded. But savings don't stop once the property is built. Running costs for lighting and heating can also be reduced considerably, and there are significant tax benefits too.

At the end of the day, you acquire the home *you* want, rather than one forced upon you from a limited variety, designed and constructed by a builder whose only motivation is to profit from your purchase. Instead of having to fit into a house, you can finally make a house fit you!

The choice is yours. If you have sufficient confidence and enough free time to commit to the project, you may want to undertake most of the construction work yourself, from laying the foundations to pinning down roof-tiles. Alternatively, you can hire a labour-force and simply act as site-manager. You can do as much or as little as you want and, whatever the degree of involvement, the finished product will be one you have designed. It will be tailor-made to fit your lifestyle and circumstances.

By reading this book, you are taking your first step on the ladder to success and, in just a few months, you could be sitting in your dream home counting the savings you will have made. More importantly, you will feel confident that your home has been built where you want it, to a high specification, using quality materials and with the inspirational design elements you selected. The process is easier than you might think and more personally and financially rewarding than you could ever imagine.

Tony Booth and Mike Dyson

E-mail: tony_booth@btopenworld.com   Website: www.tonybooth.info
Website: **http://buildingyourownhome.users.btopenworld.com**

Acknowledgements

Many thanks to Chris Park for proofreading yet another book. His expertise and attention to detail have benefited us greatly and transformed our pages into much easier to read text. I would also like to thank the self-building community, who have related stories of their own projects with such infectious enthusiasm and pride. Their dedication is both remarkable and inspiring.

Tony Booth

To my wife Karen, who has mixed concrete, tiled bathrooms and prepared dinner parties to celebrate our completion. We have shared the same dream and gained in strength by doing so.

Mike Dyson

Part One
Before You Begin

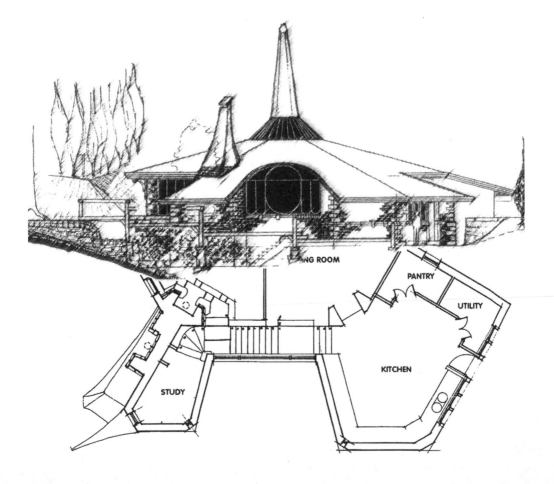

Chapter 1
Why Do It?

This chapter covers:

- the financial incentive

- the guarantee of quality

- using personal skills

- maximising property value

- personal satisfaction

- creating a unique home

Building your own home is an ideal dream for most people. It conjures up thoughts of perfection, splendour and excellence in a world where such qualities seem increasingly deficient. By reading this, you have already started a process that could ultimately turn that dream into a reality, provided you have, and can maintain, sufficient motivation and staying power. The disadvantages are few and far between, whilst the advantages are bountiful. There will be obstacles to overcome and compromises to make along the way, but these will pale into insignificance once the job is done and you are sitting in your new home, contented and proud of a dream fulfilled.

Different people will be stimulated by the self-build option for different reasons. It is useful to identify the primary incentives before proceeding so they can act effectively as energisers. These objectives will propel you forward when the going gets tough or when stumbling blocks are encountered. They are your pot of gold at the end of the rainbow, your ultimate reward, the things that will encourage you and keep you sustained. Having clear and defined reasons for undertaking the task will help instil and maintain an essential quality within you: *a strong and resolute determination to pursue the goal.*

THE FINANCIAL INCENTIVE

The expectation of those undertaking a self-build project is that it will cost less than buying from a traditional development builder. If anything, this assumption only partly discloses the full extent of potential savings. Much depends on the amount of personal time and work you can invest in the project. If you are able to do most of the physical work and act as your own labour force, the profit-margin can double and even treble, eventually supplying you with a home to be proud of *and* a substantial financial asset to keep or sell.

Bear in mind that, when assessing the price of houses being built for sale, a speculative developer works on an economic ratio of two-thirds materials and labour to one-third profit. Builders are actually earning much more today than ever before because, in recent years, labour costs have increased beyond the proportionate cost of materials. They are currently in the region of 40 per cent materials to 60 per cent labour. Therefore, if you are prepared to undertake a large amount of the self-build work yourself, the entire project will produce even greater returns. For example, the average price of a detached house in England and Wales is around £230,900 (2003, 1st Quarter, Land Registry data) and made up of:

£76,966 profit for the builder +
£61,573 materials +
£92,361 labour

The self-builder can potentially save 100 per cent of the profit and labour elements: a whopping total of £169,327 using our example. He can realise it immediately by selling the property or, alternatively, he can invest all or part of this sum in higher quality materials, fittings and installations. The latter option will, of course, increase the value of the property even more.

If you are currently wondering how much time and effort you can afford to put into building your own home, consider for a moment that every hour you can contribute to the process will add value to the property. You will, in effect, be earning money for yourself. Once you begin to calculate the cost of your project, you will find that evenings and weekends given up will actually be earning you as much, if not more, than your daily employment provides. The more time and effort you can put in, the greater the financial rewards will be!

You can opt to maximise the profit or increase the quality of workmanship and materials. Many will choose to blend the two according to circumstances. In any event, it is financially a *win-win* result! You may decide your intention is to build the home of your dreams, one you will enjoy living in for many years to come. Alternatively, it may be a property built purely for selling so that funds can be raised to build or buy an even bigger or better home elsewhere. The extent of the speculative and commercial nature of your self-build scheme is up to you. It is, however, wise to consider this aspect carefully in advance because it will influence the design and scale of the project you undertake, the funds you will need and the quality of materials you employ.

In addition, there are vast ranges of options available to finance the project, and the method chosen will also have an impact on the end profit-margin. For example, instead of a stand-alone self-build scheme, some may opt for a community-based or shared programme of building, where financial resources and skills are pooled together. Although there is generally less individual control under such schemes, they do offer an alternative way of raising the finance needed and mean that others will be available to share the workload and responsibilities. We will discuss the subject of raising funds and alternative schemes more fully in later chapters.

At this stage, it really doesn't matter which route you take to fund the project, it is enough to know that the end result is certain – with careful control, you will acquire a house of greater value and quality than would otherwise be possible and have an asset through which even larger funds can be raised, if required.

THE GUARANTEE OF QUALITY

'If you want something doing well, do it yourself.' This adage is true when applied to self-build. No one will provide more care or attend more fully to your needs, requirements and standards than yourself. Builders must approach the construction of residential property within the confines of commercialism. They are restricted by time and motivated by profitability. You are free to adapt such limitations according to need and therefore can determine the amount of time and money spent on achieving the quality you desire.

When building your own home, you retain full control of cash flow and resources. This enables you to direct the entire operation according to circumstance, and change the nature of work undertaken during any specific period. For example, labour-intensive tasks could be confined to those times when cash flow has been interrupted or when additional funds are awaited. These periods are excellent opportunities to make quality enhancements to the structure, something that few builders would ever consider undertaking. Conversely, the purchase of materials can be made as cash flow improves or as funds are released. Funding can also switch between injections of cash from earned income (which will keep the rate of borrowing low) and staged loan release. This provides a degree of flexibility that you can exploit according to the situation.

It is the ability to control all aspects of the venture that gives you the advantage over a commercial builder. By undertaking as much of the labour-intensive work as possible yourself, you will save money that can then be used to finance better quality materials. And quality does not only pertain to what you see on the outside, it also applies to the robustness of the structure and the degree of visual appeal created once the house is complete. Neither is it limited to materials alone. It also relates to how those materials are fixed together to form the basic construction shell. Most houses are built to a minimum standard and at speed because this increases the builder's profit when the job is finished. As a direct result, the buyers of many new homes complain of:

■ floorboards that bounce and squeak;

■ paper-thin walls with little sound insulation;

■ cracking plasterboard joints;

■ leaking pipes and showers;

■ poor joinery work;

■ inappropriately positioned sockets, switches and radiators.

Most of these problems are associated with a feeble construction behind the façade. As a self-builder, you can go beyond these minimum standards to create a home that not only looks good on the outside, but one that is sturdy and stable on the inside too. Improving the quality of the interior surfaces, such as tiled floors, the standard of timbers and joinery, feature fittings and fixtures, will considerably increase the desirability of the property and its value in the marketplace. At completion, you have a superior home, built to a high standard and with quality materials – not one that falls apart as soon as you start living in it.

USING PERSONAL SKILLS

Half the battle in deciding whether to build your own home is, quite simply, having enough desire and ambition. If these are available in sufficient quantities, all things can be achieved. Your own personal skills are paramount to the success of the venture and in reducing the cost involved. By taking a serious and realistic look at yourself, you can identify strengths that will help you achieve your goal and recognise those areas where professional help is going to be needed. Consider the following:

■ Are you an avid DIYer who has acquired skills through adapting, altering or repairing earlier properties? Is your level of competence high enough to tackle all of the jobs involved?

■ Are you prepared to learn new skills that can later be employed during the construction of your property?

■ Are you a good organiser? Do you enjoy managing the time and deployment of others?

- Are there abilities accumulated in your working life that can be used in the project? These might, for example, include accounting skills, interior design flair, plan drawing, surveying work, carpentry, plumbing, electrical, gardening, tiling, painting or decorating.

- Are you a visionary? Do you have the ability to see the potential in something even though it may not currently exist? Can you adapt easily to changing circumstances and 'think on your feet' when the need arises?

- Do you have good interpersonal skills? Are you a good communicator? Can you orchestrate and motivate a workforce to produce consistently good results?

It is likely you will have some of the attributes necessary to undertake the self-build project. Others may have to be learned. The more skills you can acquire yourself, the less you will need to procure from others and, in direct proportion, the greater your profit-margin will be at completion. Begin this process by examining your strengths and recognising your weaknesses, then decide how practical it is to gain the additional skills necessary to improve final profitability.

Maximising property value

Your property value will be enhanced by the very fact that you have chosen to build the house yourself. The buying public are becoming increasingly aware of self-build homes and recognise that these dwellings usually benefit from having a higher specification than others on the market. They tend to be constructed carefully with better materials and, importantly, with attention to detail. The value is often also augmented because the property is unique. Although it may be comparative in size to neighbouring homes, it is likely to have a style and appeal all of its own.

However, when planning your scheme, it is vital to consider the all-important subject of 'over-building'. This term refers to a property that is out-of-keeping with those around it. A design that is not sympathetic with its locality or which is too big for the plot on which it has been built, is likely to lose value rather than gain it. There is no point in creating a four-bedded detached home with double-garage, if the site is suited to a more modest construction. Put simply, it will never attract a value worthy of its design if it is inconsistent with others around it.

Constructing with the buying public in mind *can* increase the property's value. Consider carefully the elements and features that house buyers find attractive and absorb these into the design so that, when you eventually come to sell the property, it will have instant appeal and attract wider attention. Developers invariably research this subject thoroughly before constructing new homes. You can learn from them by visiting show-homes in the area, assess the features they have incorporated in their designs and transfer some or all to your own project.

PERSONAL SATISFACTION

There is no greater satisfaction than achieving something you set out to do. But, in building your own home, the levels of satisfaction go deeper and last longer. Imagine the delight in being able to control the environment in which you and your family live. To have the space and rooms you always wanted, to enjoy a landscaped garden that meets your needs, with standards of workmanship reminiscent of craftsmen rather than tradesmen. In addition, self-build intensifies personal satisfaction because you will:

- employ skills previously practised merely as a hobby to their full potential;
- develop new skills which can be used to your advantage in the future;
- experience a journey of discovery and learn more about yourself and what you are capable of achieving.

CREATING A UNIQUE HOME

Designing and building your own home is the only opportunity you will ever have to acquire the property you always wanted. This doesn't just apply to the house and its internal layout, but also how it fits on the site and the direction it faces. You will determine which windows in your home will enjoy the best views and design the layout of the external aspects. You are not just going to customise your home, you are going to design and plan it from scratch and you will stay in control throughout. If you decide that something would look better if it was done in a different way, you can do it at any stage during the construction process.

You can choose all the building materials, fittings, fixtures and finishes, and create as much storage space as you need. You can incorporate hi-tech installations and energy conservation equipment, create automatic lighting systems to satisfy security and mood, build a laundry room and sauna, a home office, wine cellar, children's den or a games room. You can have a second bathroom, a shower-room, Jacuzzi and guest washroom. You could even build a second sitting room and enjoy a quiet haven away from the noise of the TV, hi-fi and computer games. If funds permit and space is available, you could even build an indoor heated swimming pool.

The house you will eventually live in will be one that meets all your needs. There will be no reason to compromise or complain about a lack of space or an inadequate number of power-sockets. Your home will satisfy everyone involved because you will have created it with your own requirements in mind. It will fit your lifestyle and the demands of you and your family like a glove. No other property will compare to the one you design and construct. Only by building it yourself can you prove you *can* get *everything* you always wanted in a home.

Summary

- Identify the main incentives to keep you motivated throughout the self-build project.

- Decide whether the intention is to build a home for yourself or one that will be sold for maximum profit.

- Assess your own transferable personal skills and plan to enhance or add to them so that building costs can be reduced.

- Be cautious of over-building on a small site.

- Be aware that your intended design should be sympathetic with the environment and any other properties in the neighbourhood.

- Identify the needs of you and your family so that you plan a home that will be unique and satisfying to all.

Useful Internet Websites

www.selfbuildanddesign.com
From the magazine *Self Build & Design*, this site provides valuable information covering the entire subject matter.

www.selfbuildit.co.uk/glenns_build.htm
Read the experiences of a self-builder. His diary of events runs from the day he envisaged building his own home to finally completing the construction.

http://groups.yahoo.com/group/Build_it_yourself
Join almost 3,000 online self-builder members and discuss your plans, ask questions and benefit from the knowledge and experience of others.

Chapter 2
Personal Qualities

This chapter covers:

- dedication to the job
- patience
- negotiating skills
- an ability to enthuse others
- flexibility in the building schedule

It has been said that *attitude* determines *altitude*. In other words, by thinking positively all things are achievable. In terms of self-build, this process involves recognising or acquiring such personal qualities as enthusiasm, determination and perseverance; it also means stealing time-out to sit back and take stock of the work schedule and assess progress, as well as being sufficiently flexible to modify plans when problems are encountered. Throughout the operation you must maintain your own motivation and encourage others so that jobs are completed, allowing work to continuously move forward.

DEDICATION TO THE JOB

According to the dictionary, 'dedication' means 'giving oneself wholly to a worthy purpose'. At the outset, building your own dream home may seem a goal worth investing all your time, money and effort in, but enthusiasm can diminish as the project proceeds and particularly during periods of difficulty. Maintaining your dedication is crucial, not only at the outset but also throughout the entire venture, otherwise work will slow down and finishing the job will become an uphill struggle. More importantly, getting behind in the schedule of work will result in increased costs for the finished dwelling. There are several exercises that will help you along the way:

- Make a list of the three most important reasons why you are undertaking the task. Keep this handy and refer to it every now and then: it will help to remind you of your goal. One self-builder stuck his list to the door of his mobile home and made a point of reading it each day before going to the building site. This helped him keep going – even when the *going* got tough.

■ Keeping good accounts will not only benefit you when calculating costs, it will also help you to recognise the amounts you are saving as you proceed. Having sight of a rising profit margin can be very inspiring and will help drive you towards the finish line.

■ To be completely dedicated to a single purpose, you must be able to devote enough time to it and be free of other distractions. Some obligations may be insurmountable, for example those concerning work and family, but others may be within your control. If you give time to a residents' association, charitable trust, social group, sports club or some other type of committee, think now about whether your involvement can be reduced so you can do more on the self-build project.

If you have real doubts about your ability to completely build your own home, consider the alternatives before resorting to traditional home-buying methods. You may, for example, join a collective, or purchase an off-the-shelf self-build dwelling. Only you know the degree of personal time and commitment you are able or prepared to give. Assessing this (realistically) at the outset will help you to stay dedicated to the project and prevent you from losing interest in it as time progresses.

PATIENCE

Patience is a virtue, so they say, and you are going to need it by the bucket-load. You will find yourself always waiting for someone or something. This may be a delivery, a contractor or just simply some dry weather for exterior work to continue. Although frustrating, it is important not to get annoyed or disheartened by matters that delay you but which are ultimately outside your control. It was Albert Einstein who said with considerable insight, 'In the middle of every difficulty lies opportunity'. So, try to plan for these eventualities by having a list of alternative tasks that can be undertaken. This will employ your thoughts more constructively and convert what would otherwise be wasted time into a productive commodity.

Patience can also be improved by building into your schedule of work two essential elements that together will help to reduce stress during the construction period:

■ a percentage unit of time to allow for delays;

■ a surplus amount of free time for relaxation and recreation away from the site.

These will help you stay focused, keep your enthusiasm high and provide a welcome breathing space.

NEGOTIATING SKILLS

We all use negotiation in our daily lives to one degree or another. For some of us it is in the workplace: making deals, resolving problems and conflicts, people and time management, selling, marketing and promoting. For others, it is in the home: compromising with the kids over Christmas presents, deciding where to go on holiday, allocating household chores or buying the weekly groceries. All these tasks involve basic skills that you will need to employ during the self-build project. They include:

■ listening to what others are saying and asking for;

■ communicating your own needs so others recognise and understand them;

■ having alternative plans available in the event of conflict;

■ knowing when and how much to compromise;

■ ensuring there is always mutual gain to satisfy all parties involved.

You will need to negotiate with your family over how much should be spent on the venture and, in some cases, promote the advantages of long-term gain over short-term spending. The amount of time devoted to construction will also become an issue, particularly if others feel you are neglecting them or failing to undertake the general day-to-day household tasks. You will also need to negotiate with suppliers, the bank, labourers and tradesmen, to ensure you get best value and a high quality of service.

Be aware that negotiation rarely involves a single issue. There are always two or more sides involved and each will have their own set of needs and goals. Identify what others want, decide what it is worth in return, set your limits, but be prepared to compromise. If your first plan fails because others are intractable, look for an alternative, be creative in your options and never give way more than you intended or can afford.

AN ABILITY TO ENTHUSE OTHERS

If you can maintain your own confidence in the project, it will become infectious, enthusing all others involved. The *right attitude* is a powerful trait and a fundamental driving force. It will spread and inspire those around you to produce the best results throughout the construction period. Transferring your own enthusiasm to the architect will encourage him to be creative; labourers will work harder and faster for you; banks will become more flexible; and your family will cope with the inevitable inconveniences that self-build inflicts, and be more sympathetic if things go wrong.

FLEXIBILITY IN THE BUILDING SCHEDULE

Even the best-laid plans can go wrong! Unexpected obstacles can rise from nowhere to cause delays and, whilst you may not be able to prepare for every eventuality, having a flexible schedule of work will help ease the frustration. Whilst it is essential to have a structured plan with target dates for the completion of each phase, you must guard against making it too rigid, otherwise the slightest problem will stop you in your tracks. Having a schedule and trying to keep to it is one thing but, by being stubborn and unyielding within it, you will simply irritate others and alienate them. Even worse, it will restrict their ability to help you find a solution to the problem.

Prevention is often better than trying to find a cure, so keep your plans realistic and don't assume your workforce will operate at the same breakneck speed as yourself: their priorities are likely to differ considerably from your own. Recognise their abilities, learn about their requirements and ask about other commitments they may have. Try to devise a diary of work that meets the needs of all involved. You can never hope to satisfy everyone all of the time, but a demonstration of flexibility will pay dividends in the long term. Bear in mind that stress and frustration are just as contagious as confidence and enthusiasm. If you are happy and contented, your workforce will be too!

SUMMARY

- Hold on to your vision and be realistic about how much of the self-build project you can undertake yourself.

- Be patient and always have alternative tasks that can be completed rather than allowing work to stop.

- Build time-buffers into your schedule that will allow for delays and relaxation periods away from the project.

- Recognise the negotiating skills you currently use in your daily life and employ them during construction.

- Help reduce stress and build confidence and enthusiasm amongst those around you by controlled flexibility.

USEFUL INTERNET WEBSITES

www.buildstore.co.uk

A superb site providing inspiration for every self-builder. Find plots of land, mortgages; read other people's experiences; get details of architects, designers and other professionals in your area.

www.negotiatelikethepros.com

Improve your skills by reading about the red flags and warning signs that impede good negotiation.

www.buildingcentre.co.uk

A useful range of information for the self-builder including inexpensive guides on products, regulations, research and technical data.

Chapter 3

Living Arrangements

This chapter covers:

- practical considerations

- keeping the existing home

- rented accommodation

- living on site

- family considerations

Planning the management of the self-build venture is essential: it will reduce stress and anxiety and allow you to concentrate effectively on the construction process. A fundamental factor is deciding where you will live during the building phase. You must take into account not only the finance you have available and your proximity to the plot of land, but also the impact it will have on your family and their day-to-day lives. Their support and involvement is crucial to your success and therefore any decisions should be made jointly and with their full approval.

To ensure the project remains profitable, you will need to balance the natural desire to indulge yourself with comfortable and convenient accommodation against an equal need to be frugal in your spending of funds.

PRACTICAL CONSIDERATIONS

Although you may not yet have identified a specific plot of land on which you intend building your new home, it is likely you have a vague idea of the area you envisage it will be. From this starting-point, you should now devise several organisational strategies to satisfy each of the opportunities presented to you. These will be dependent upon the specific location of the building site and the financial resources available. Examine all the options and plan a stratagem now rather than later because, once the plot is identified, you must act quickly to secure it. Considerations will include:

■ the distance of the site to

  (i)   your existing home,

  (ii) your place of work,

  (iii) your partner's place of work,

  (iv) your children's school or college;

■ the amount of security the site will require according to the degree of personal supervision you are able to provide;

■ the finance available to you, for example there may be a need to sell your existing home so that sufficient initial capital is raised to buy land and materials;

■ the anticipated period it will take to complete construction;

■ the time taken to travel from your living accommodation to the site and back again, bearing in mind that time will become a precious commodity once building work begins;

■ the commitments and responsibilities you have to your family and the impact the self-build project will have upon their lives;

■ the expectation of significant events occurring during the venture, for example planning to have additional children or proposing a major career change could be detrimental to both your finance and ability to dedicate time to the project.

KEEPING THE EXISTING HOME

The ideal situation is to retain your existing home whilst building the new one, particularly if you are intending the latter to be an investment property you will sell for profit upon completion. However, speculators should bear in mind that VAT can only be avoided if you live in the new home for twelve months (see Chapter 7), so if the motive is entirely profit driven it may be worth you forming a limited company prior to building. Keeping the existing home will:

■ prevent disruption to the normal family routine;

■ provide a comfortable sanctuary away from the chaos and turmoil of the self-build site;

■ preserve a financial asset that can later be used to support the venture in an emergency, should funds fall short of expectations.

That said, the ideal is not always attainable or expedient. Keeping the existing home might impose additional financial pressures that you could well do without. The decision will depend on the length of construction, the resolve to employ subcontractors for most of the work, and whether you can afford to remain living where you are. It will also depend on your definition of 'building your own home'. In other words, are you having a house built or are you truly building it yourself?

The majority of self-builders are enthusiastic, single-minded and adventurous individuals who are prepared to put all of their physical and financial resources into achieving the end result. This usually means liquidising most of, if not all, your assets at the start of the project to ensure a viable financial package can be put together. Unless you are building within your existing garden boundary, remodelling your current home or are building on a plot of land you already own, you will most likely have to consider alternative living arrangements whilst the building work gets under way.

The advantages of keeping your existing home are self-evident. Some of the disadvantages might include:

- the impetus to carry out work and complete tasks may diminish owing to an 'out of sight out of mind' philosophy;

- upkeep and running costs will be doubled, particularly once the roof is attached and the dwelling becomes habitable;

- providing security for the site in your absence will be a major consideration;

- the loss of time getting to and from the site could become onerous, particularly if it is intended for part of the work to be undertaken during the winter months, when dry weather and daylight are often in short supply.

RENTED ACCOMMODATION

If you decide the best course of action is to sell your existing home to help finance the new one, the next decisions to take are *where* to move and *what* to move into. Again, these will depend on personal and family circumstances. For example, it may be more important for your children to be close to their school than for you to be close to the building site. Alternatively, if their examinations are a few years away, it may be beneficial for them to move and settle into a different school now, rather than later when the new home is built.

Rented accommodation is likely to be a preferred option for many, particularly for those who are reticent about living on-site in a caravan or other similar temporary accommodation. However, renting property is not always a prudent option, as money paid out is effectively 'lost'. Renting does not provide any financial return for the tenant – the longer you stay in the accommodation, the less capital you will have available to invest in building your new home. It is, therefore, crucial to consider the length of time you expect construction will take, as this will directly affect the quantity of funds you will need to meet rental payments.

In addition, you must be careful not to get tied to a restrictive 'term-certain' tenancy agreement that extends too far beyond completion of the new building. For example, an 'Assured Shorthold' agreement that is signed with a landlord for a year's term guarantees that you cannot be evicted from the accommodation for a full twelve months (providing you keep to the terms). This is known as 'security of tenure'. However, it also means that you will be legally liable for the full cost of rent payments for the entire year, even though your circumstances may demand that you leave early (that is, prior to the end of the contracted term). Although a landlord *can* accept a tenant's request to terminate a tenancy agreement early, he does not have to do so. It is, therefore, vital that a careful judgement of the expected construction period is made to ensure alternative accommodation costs are minimised and money is not wasted on lost rent.

Be aware of the following when considering rented accommodation:

■ Look for unfurnished property so that you can move your own furnishings into it, rather than pay for additional and unnecessary storage.

■ If you are starting your project during late autumn or early winter, negotiate a reduction in the rent. Tenants are in short supply during this period, and landlords will usually accept lower rents, rather than suffer a loss of income by having a property stand empty.

■ Always read the tenancy agreement carefully before signing it: you must ensure you fully appreciate what you are agreeing to and what you will become liable for. If there is a clause you do not understand, ask for it to be explained or receive guidance from a Citizens Advice Bureau.

■ The best arrangement for someone whose period of occupation is difficult to determine at the outset, is a flexible tenancy with secure terms. This could take the form of an Assured Shorthold with an initial fixed-term of six months (or twelve months if you are absolutely certain of needing at least this period of time). Once the initial term reaches expiry, ask the landlord if you can continue occupation under a 'Statutory Periodic' tenancy. This has exactly the same conditions and rent as the prior Assured Shorthold but with one difference: it runs usually from month to month (or whatever the periodic nature of rent payments are), and provides the tenant with the right to give notice of one full rental period (usually four weeks) to bring the tenancy to an end at any time. This element of flexibility can be exploited by the self-builder to his full advantage as the construction nears completion. The only drawback with Statutory Periodic tenancies is that the landlord has an equal right to bring the tenancy to an end by issuing two months' written notice. However, it is rare for landlords to employ this right when they have good tenants who are paying rent in full and on time.

LIVING ON SITE

Those wishing to undertake a considerable amount of the physical work themselves, or whose nerves will be eased by being in close proximity to the construction, will invariably take the option to live on site. The advantages to this include being able to use your time, the most valuable commodity, to its full potential. You will be able to start work whenever you like, regardless of traffic congestion, appointments at home and other distractions, which would ordinarily prevent you from getting to the site and starting work.

You will also be able to enjoy the comforts of home while at work. This includes a hot meal to sustain you through the day, a shower and change of clothes if you are feeling grubby, social interaction with your family when they are at home and somewhere warm to go to if the weather turns nasty. You can also leave work whenever you like without having to think about a bus, train or car journey. Just as important is the opportunity you will have for contemplation. Sometimes you will need simply to sit and consider the stage you are at. These periods of 'thinking time' are best done at the site where you can see the building taking shape and assess whether things are going according to plan. From your own home base, you can view the work undertaken to date and plan the next stage. The ability to do this on site will improve your creative potential and also help keep you on, or even ahead of, schedule.

Security is an inherent responsibility for all building plot supervisors. By having a continuous on-site presence, you will deter unwanted visitors, vandals and thieves. You will also help reduce the chance of accidents occurring through children getting in and playing with potentially dangerous equipment and materials. A further benefit of living on the plot is likely to be reduced site insurance premiums.

As time progresses, there will be an escalation in the number of deliveries. These will include building materials such as ready-mixed concrete, timber, bricks, sand and cement, in addition to hired or purchased tools and equipment. It is rare for deliveries to arrive on time, and havoc can be caused if they are taken away because no one was available to receive them. Time will be lost and work may have to be suspended as a result. By living on site, you can be certain of being available to meet deliveries, check them and, of equal importance, you can direct where supplies are to be offloaded. Having a lorry-load of bricks in the most convenient position will save you carrying them by hand to where they are needed or, if labour is going to be subcontracted, having to pay extra for the time it takes someone else to do it.

Having decided to make the building plot your temporary home, you will need to consider the best type of accommodation for the size of your family and budget. This will probably involve buying a mobile home or static caravan, which are available in abundance on the second-hand market. It also makes good economic sense because a good quality caravan is an asset that can be sold once the building work is completed. When looking for this type of accommodation, consider the following:

■ Although much will depend on the number and age of those in your family unit, always aim for maximum comfort and space. Caravans are primarily designed as holiday homes, but you and your family will be living in it for a considerable period of time and you will need to accommodate more possessions than just a suitcase full of clothes.

■ Storage will be an issue and although you may be able to distribute some possessions temporarily amongst family and friends who have spare space, you are likely to need commercial storage for most goods. Do your research in advance of buying the mobile home. Assess the amount of storage you will need and, once a supplier is identified, check that their containers are secure and dry and that the contents will be insured against damage.

■ A trip to the nearest seaside resort can pay dividends when searching for second-hand caravans to buy. Holiday parks require that static caravans above a certain age are withdrawn from use by the general public. These are removed from site by the owners or are sold *in situ*. Holiday parks are therefore good hunting grounds for the self-builder looking for alternative accommodation.

■ Dealers can always be found within a few miles of holiday parks and they usually have a wide range of trade-in static caravans. Check advertisements in local newspapers or seek advice from a holiday park.

■ Buying your caravan is one thing, but getting it back to the building plot is quite another: it may not be roadworthy or be of a type unsuitable for normal towing. Large mobile homes will need to be transported by a low-loader, and there are specialist firms that offer this service. Contact details can be found in *Yellow Pages* under 'Road haulage'.

■ Positioning the caravan on your site is an important decision and best planned beforehand. The entrance area is preferred from a security point-of-view but make sure it doesn't interfere with access for deliveries. It should also be close to a water supply, mains drainage and electricity. You will also need a telephone line installing, as this will be cheaper than using a mobile phone for day-to-day matters. You will probably also require a landline for connection to the Internet. If these services do not currently exist on your site, you should arrange for their provision in advance of buying the caravan, otherwise the normal routines of family life could become intolerable.

■ Bear in mind that you will probably need planning permission to install a caravan on your site. This is unlikely to be refused, but care must be taken to ensure it does not present an eyesore to adjoining neighbours or conflict with the style and appearance of a housing estate. It is much more difficult to get permission when the intention is to place a caravan outside the boundaries of a site, as this may interfere with a highway or infringe on other people's rights.

■ Fuel for heating and cooking is often provided by bottled gas and, as you will consume at least a bottle a week, you will need to make arrangements with a reliable supplier nearby. Ask around and get estimates from different suppliers to secure the best deal.

Though it may be a daunting prospect at first, living on site can become a great family unifying experience, as it is impossible to escape from the sense of adventure. Long hot summer months will provide the family with opportunities to discover healthy outdoor living and, through winter, patience and tolerance will become newly acquired virtues. In all, it will be a wonderful experience with many rewards.

FAMILY CONSIDERATIONS

The self-build project will invariably disrupt family life for the period of construction. The natural tendency will be to move and settle into your new area as soon as possible, regardless of whether this is in rented accommodation nearby or on the site itself. Good planning and preparation will help to reduce anxiety and prevent disharmony. This is a time when you need to stick together as a family and offer each other support.

It is going to be a shared adventure and all members of the family have a part to play in its success. For example, young children could be given the responsibility of recording the entire project as it progresses. Armed with a camera and scrapbook, they will find it a continuous source of fun, and you will cherish the chronicle of fond memories in future years. Regardless of their level of skill, partners *must* be included in the self-build scheme. Find a task they will enjoy that is within their ability. Make sure they are involved in major decisions throughout and seek advice from them when required. Always remember, you are not doing this on your own – there are other family members who will want to embrace the project and play an active part in creating the new home. By working together, you will improve productivity and intensify the level of satisfaction gained at completion.

SUMMARY

■ Consider the practicalities of keeping your existing home while building the new dwelling, giving due regard to profitability and the impact on family life.

■ If the best course of action is to move nearer to the building plot, examine the two main alternatives: rented accommodation nearby or living on site. Quantify each according to the advantages they present.

■ Assess your needs prior to moving and devise strategies to deal with important issues, for example the storage of personal possessions and furniture.

■ Plan ahead when buying a static caravan. Decide where it will be located on the site and make arrangements for services such as electricity, water and drainage. Be certain to obtain planning permission prior to installing a mobile home on your plot.

■ Make sure that all family members feel involved in the scheme from the outset. Allocate specific tasks through discussion and according to ability.

USEFUL INTERNET WEBSITES

www.caravan-sitefinder.co.uk
Provides contact details for holiday parks throughout the UK and links to hundreds of second-hand caravans and mobile homes for sale.

www.storing.com
A useful facility on this site allows you to enter the number and range of possessions you need to store, then, by using the online calculator, it tells you the approximate cubic space of storage required. An immediate online estimate of the cost involved is also available.

www.themovechannel.com
A superb resource covering all aspects of moving home. Of particular value, their online guide to renting is excellent and offers the would-be tenant a wealth of information. The site also provides various links to rented property throughout the UK.

Chapter 4
Finding Suitable Land

This chapter covers:

- estate agents

- advertising

- personal enquiry

- the Internet

- land auctions

- land agents

- buying property with sufficient land

- remodelling an existing property

- derelict property

It is likely you already have in mind the ideal location for your new home. If not, then consider it now by narrowing the field to a specific region of the country. Next, decide what you and your family would prefer:

- urban living – in or close to a city;

- semi-rural – in a town or close to one;

- rural – a countryside location.

This is the same process you would ordinarily undertake if you were simply moving home from one place to another, but finding a suitable and affordable building plot is not as straightforward, so try to keep your options wide. The 'prized' site is out there waiting for you to identify it and there are a variety of methods you can employ in your search and discovery mission.

Estate agents

Estate agents don't just sell ready-built houses. They often have building land in their portfolio too and, even if they don't have any available when you contact them, they may know about something suitable in the area. Agents also have valuable contacts and most will be prepared to help point you in the right direction.

Successful local builders keep what is known as a personal 'land bank', which they expand by adding to whilst trading. This maintains a continuous supply of plots ready for constructing new houses on and allows the builder to move on to successive sites as each development is completed. Some release a plot of land back onto the market, usually because it is surplus to their needs, and they often do so by using a local estate agent. These sites can vary considerably in size and quality. Some will be single plots, whilst others may be larger expanses of land, sub-divided into units, and may come with or without access roads or installed services. Make sure you receive full details from agents you contact and, if a plot of land is too big for your needs, ask whether the builder would consider selling a small portion of it.

Estate agents may also have land available from private clients with secured planning permission attached to it. These are valuable plots and often sell very quickly. It is important to remember that you will be up against local builders who will know the locality far better than you and will have close and regular contact with agents, so once a suitable plot is identified, swift action may be required to prevent disappointment.

Land is becoming an increasingly scarce commodity and the use of estate agents to identify something suitable should not be your only resource; it is only one of a number of potential sources you should fully investigate. Remember too that the price of plots sold through an agent is often inflated because an accurate value is harder to assess. An agent may not have tested the market before and therefore will have little to compare it against, preferring to err on the high side rather than devalue it. As a result, you may have to negotiate hard to acquire it at an appropriate price.

Advertising

Visit newsagents in the region to obtain copies of any local papers. Inspect them closely for advertisements of land for sale. Most evening newspapers have a specific 'property' night, so ask for advice before buying. Finding advertisements can be a bit hit-and-miss and you may need to obtain several editions over a prolonged period before you find anything worthwhile. Occasionally, private sellers place adverts for a direct sale, and builders also use this method to dispose of small surplus plots. You may also be lucky enough to find a local authority selling off small infill sites, though these are usually subject to a restrictive tendering process, and buying them can therefore be somewhat difficult and protracted for the self-builder.

It is also worth considering placing an advert yourself in these papers under the 'building land wanted' section of the small ads. By specifying that you are interested in land with or without planning permission, you will open up the possibilities of acquiring a site owners have not thus far considered selling or who have not wanted to pay the expenses involved in applying for planning consent. You will also be ahead of competition, because the land may not have been advertised elsewhere and, therefore, professional buyers are unlikely to be aware of its existence. This puts you in a strong negotiating position and, provided a deal can be made and permission to build on the land is confirmed quickly, you could pick up a bargain.

PERSONAL ENQUIRY

Estate agents are efficient at finding land for you and advertisements can sometimes provide information about new plots, but neither come close to the benefits of exploring with your own feet. If your ideal location is in another part of the country, book a weekend break in a centrally positioned hotel and pack stout walking boots, a good map, pen and notebook and an A-Z guide. Quite apart from potentially finding suitable land, this exercise will allow you to become much more familiar with the area and aspects of it which may previously have been unknown.

A personal search can be great fun and by trekking out-of-the-way routes, lanes and highways, idyllic places can be discovered that might otherwise have remained concealed. Some of these may be straightforward, such as an owner who erects a 'land for sale' sign on his garden and who hasn't the time or resources to sell it through more traditional methods. However, others will require a more sensitive approach. You may, for example, find superb land but no 'for sale' sign, indicating that the owner hasn't even considered the possibility of selling it. The old adage of 'nothing ventured, nothing gained' applies – all you can do is ask. But this should be done carefully and without offending the owner. A general enquiry can be made, asking whether they know of anyone in the area with spare land suitable for a self-build project. If they don't offer information then the conversation can be advanced with, 'Actually, any land similar in size and position to yours would suit me'.

THE INTERNET

The World Wide Web is rapidly becoming the most efficient and effective way to find plots of suitable building land but, because not all vendors are able or willing to exploit it, the Internet should not be considered the *only* source for your investigation. Use it in combination with other methods to increase the opportunities of locating admirable sites. Bear in mind when using the Internet that:

■ Facts and details are not always up to date. You can spend several hours online before finding a suitable plot and only after contacting the seller discover it was sold months ago.

■ Although many websites are freely accessible to potential buyers, some charge a fee. Read the 'Terms & Conditions' carefully when executing a search.

■ You can easily find yourself swamped with data owing to the volume of land advertised. It is often better to restrict yourself to a handful of websites that you can visit repeatedly over several weeks. This will help you to focus on a particular area and the type of plot sought.

■ Once you see something you like, act fast, as there may be several hundred or even several thousand other self-builders keen to get their hands on it. But, never commit yourself to something without first visiting the location in person to satisfy any questions you may have.

If you don't have a well-connected computer, there are libraries and cafés where you can access the Internet (sometimes at a modest charge). Check *Yellow Pages* for details of establishments in your area. Once online try visiting the following:

www.buildstore.co.uk

www.lovedays.fsbusiness.co.uk

www.newpropertiesforsale.co.uk

www.perfectplot.co.uk

www.dreweatt-neate.co.uk

www.propertyspy.com

www.selfbuildcentre.com

uklanddirectory.org.uk

LAND AUCTIONS

Newspapers are often the best source for information about forthcoming land auctions taking place in your area. Land sold by auction often comes as a result of mortgage foreclosure or bankruptcy and is therefore usually new to the market and available for immediate purchase. Buying at auction is not for the fainthearted. It is easy to get carried away and enter bids over and above what the land is actually worth. Novice buyers should initially attend auctions as an observer to become familiar with the process, before contemplating taking an active role in one.

LAND AGENTS

Land agents operate in the same manner as estate agents but deal purely with building plots and sites with or without planning permission. The agents who solely trade in land are limited in number and many act primarily as estate agents or property developers. The contact details of local agents can be found in *Yellow Pages*.

BUYING PROPERTY WITH SUFFICIENT LAND

An alternative to buying land alone is to buy a property with sufficient building space within its garden boundaries, on which you could construct a second property. Some owners may already have recognised the potential of their estate and have a plot identified and ready for sale, together with suitable planning permission. Others may insist on the entire estate being purchased first which would involve you selling part of it immediately or, if sufficient capital is available, after the self-build project has been completed. The ideal would obviously be to buy and live in the house whilst building your own home on the adjacent land, but this decision invariably depends on your own personal finances.

The real reward lies in identifying the inherent possibilities of land located within the boundary of an existing dwelling, particularly if the owner is unaware of his asset and its development potential. Hiding your intentions will probably allow you to buy at a keen price, but keeping the secret may be difficult because you will need to confirm whether the local authority will give planning consent. In addition, you must consider:

■ whether or not a shared or new access can be created so that both properties can function independently;

■ whether there would be sufficient distance between the properties;

■ whether each would retain a viable garden area;

■ whether there would be enough space to build an additional garage;

■ whether the exterior design concept of your self-build would be sympathetic and compatible with the appearance of the existing property, particularly if they are going to be in close proximity to one another.

REMODELLING AN EXISTING PROPERTY

An *unsuitable* property found in an ideal location opens up a whole new set of possibilities for the self-builder. Whilst the residential nature of the site is pre-determined, it is the other physical aspects of the accommodation that may be unacceptable, for example the condition and style of its fabric or shell structure. Here is an opportunity to return to the first principles of construction by looking at site orientation, access and views. Simply redesignating the main rooms, adding an extension or altering an elevation can be enough to transform a bland dwelling into something exceptional.

If the interior is okay – what about the exterior? Is it possible to strip the outer shell away, modify it or replace it? Remember that many of the 1960's flat-roof boxes have had a total face-lift in recent years, and it is amazing what can be done with relatively little capital. Dated old homes can become stylish modern dwellings with careful planning and a little flair. Ugly ducklings turned into swans! Substantial changes of this nature will of course require planning permission and be subject to building regulations approval, so make sure you undertake thorough research and investigate all the practicalities before proceeding.

The opportunities are endless and such transformations are not confined to those buildings currently existing exclusively in the residential market. There are enormous possibilities for all kinds of structures, including water towers, barns, mills, churches, windmills, schoolhouses, chapels, outbuildings and railway stations. Enthusiasts have even successfully turned derelict follies, World War II gun-turrets and fire-engine sheds into desirable homes. Converting these examples into residential homes may seem a challenge, but it is one that is both stimulating and exciting for many self-builders and brings a whole new dimension to the project. By retaining the distinctive or historical features during conversion, you can add depth and character and create a unique dwelling to live in yourself or sell for profit.

DERELICT PROPERTY

There are two main opportunities when considering a derelict property. The first is to use the most desirable features of a barn or other building and redevelop it into a house, which we have discussed above. The second and more important alternative for the self-builder is to acquire a derelict property purely to secure the land on which it sits. Before proceeding, buyers must always consider the implications as well as the potential of purchasing this type of land. Specifically, they should ensure that all relevant planning and local authority approvals are received and assess the additional costs involved in demolition.

The decision to demolish a building should not be taken lightly. It is a complex procedure with considerable health and safety implications and rarely something the self-builder is able to undertake himself. It is, however, important that he takes control of the demolition and supervises the entire process, otherwise he may lose valuable salvage material which he could otherwise keep and incorporate into his new home or sell to offset demolition fees. The quantity and variety of useful materials are endless and might include doors, handles, fire-surrounds, carvings, mouldings, light-fittings, spindles, timber panels, stained-glass, sinks, baths, taps, roof-slates and bricks. In fact, anything that is of historic or distinctive interest and which can be integrated sympathetically into the newly designed dwelling will add to its character and increase its market value. Any excess can be sold separately as there is always high demand for good quality architectural materials from home-improvers, renovators and developers.

Whilst salvage is an advantage, there are disadvantages. For example, it may not be possible to start building your new home on the same foundations, even if the scale and outline plan are identical. The concrete may have weakened over time or may be damaged by the demolition. It is critical at this stage to take professional advice and assess thoroughly what additional costs might be involved.

Buying a derelict property can release land that is not currently scheduled for residential use and may enable the self-builder to obtain more than he might initially need. It should be considered as a viable opportunity but one with potential complications. If the structure is in an urban setting with neighbouring properties closely positioned, there are likely to be additional environmental considerations such as potential damage to the foundations of existing buildings, cellars and other underground storage areas and tanks, and the build-up of tipped waste material. All these have cost implications, which you will need to assess thoroughly and accurately before submitting an offer for the site.

SUMMARY

- Explore local estate agents and check newspapers for details of land that may be available in your ideal location.

- Walk through and around the area to identify hidden opportunities.

- If you find something suitable that is not advertised for sale, have the courage to ask an owner about its availability. The worst they can do is decline your offer.

- Utilise the Internet as it is a valuable source of land for sale.

- Examine the alternatives to traditional land buying and particularly the potential of a derelict property, but be aware of the likely complications involved.

USEFUL INTERNET WEBSITES

www.selfbuildcentre.com
Lists UK contact details for land auctions.

www.safety.odpm.gov.uk/bregs/brpub/br-booklet/whole.htm
Read information about building regulations before altering or demolishing a dwelling, direct from the government's own website.

www.periodproperty.co.uk
An excellent site for renovators of derelict property with a historical interest. Contains informative articles and local contact lists for everything from salvage experts to estate agents.

Chapter 5

Assessing the Site

This chapter covers:

- is the land contaminated?

- what is the 'use' class?

- is there suitable access?

- how do you assess a site location?

- are services available?

- what future developments might there be?

Never judge a book by its cover! The seemingly perfect plot can have hidden characteristics that may frustrate or even prevent you from building on it. Assessing the site involves much more than looking at elements within your range of view: you *must* explore what lies beneath the surface. You will also need to investigate the history of the site, check the 'use' class and establish what constraints (if any) might be imposed upon you by the local authority. All these tasks need to be performed prior to purchase and with considerable speed and efficiency, otherwise someone else may enter the arena and snatch the plot right from under your nose.

This chapter deals with standard pre-purchase research issues and, although much of the work can be undertaken by you, there are some aspects best dealt with by the professionals. This will be an added but essential expense, with the amount being dependent on the number and level of services required and the size, qualities and considerations presented by the plot. Asking the right questions and investigating thoroughly at this stage will either increase your enthusiasm for building on the land or confirm your worst nightmares! Either way, it *must* be performed *before* negotiations begin, to prevent the alarming consequences of buying into a site that ultimately cannot be used in the way you had planned. It is time to swap rose-coloured spectacles for a microscope and inspect the land for the hidden treasure it holds or, conversely, the buried secrets of a chequered past.

IS THE LAND CONTAMINATED?

If you are planning to build on a 'virgin' site where you are certain there has been no development of any kind, then there should be little risk of any land contamination. However, an increasing number of plots are 're-use' sites with a prior history. This may range from a fairly innocuous activity, such as having had the ground levels altered with 'fill' consisting of soil and rubble from elsewhere, to the contours of the land having been changed; but may equally be something more disconcerting such as the disposal of chemical waste or other noxious or toxic materials on or in the ground.

The land could also be what is termed a 'cleared site'. This means it has had a number and variety of operations conducted upon it over many years. You may never be able to identify all the uses, as records have a tendency to become lost and, if the operation was an illegal one, a record is unlikely ever to have been made. It is therefore important you check for any residual contamination resulting from such operations. This can only be done by procuring a professional report. A contamination report will be a valuable negotiating tool if you proceed to purchase the land and, in any event, it will almost certainly be a requirement when approvals are sought from the local authority. For details of private companies you can employ, look in *Yellow Pages* under 'Site investigations'.

WHAT IS THE 'USE' CLASS?

During the legal process of buying a plot, your solicitor will conduct the necessary searches, but there are some essential tasks you must perform yourself, and one is to visit your local authority planning department to identify its 'use' class. All local authorities have a planning department and most are open during normal office hours for you to visit and make preliminary enquiries about the site. An investigation may provide indications about previous uses, if any. Ask to view earlier ordnance and town plans and seek advice from departmental staff, who are usually very helpful.

It is also here that you can discover the current designation of the land. If it is residential it may be referred to as 'pink' land. If it is not designated as residential, the planning officer may be able to offer guidance by indicating whether it might be considered as such in the future. Most local authorities have a 'development plan' which clearly sets out what land is designated for, and this should be scrutinised for any evidence or proposals regarding your particular plot.

If the site requires a 'change of use', you will probably need to involve professional advisors such as a local architect or planning consultant. They can save you a small fortune by advising on the likelihood of achieving a change in the plot's 'use' class and prevent you from getting progressively dedicated to something with no potential.

Although they will offer good advice, they will not offer a one hundred per cent certainty of acquiring a change in the 'use' class and, in the end, it will be up to you to decide whether it is worth proceeding to buy the land, given the level of risk involved.

The classic example of a change of use in self-building has been the barn conversion. For 30 years and more, farmers have needed to exploit their land in every possible way to diversify and develop alternative sources of income. Some recognised the advantages of supplying bed and breakfast accommodation and, latterly, self-catering units. This paved the way for investors, who saw the potential lying dormant in empty, unused barns. It has successfully demonstrated over the length and breadth of the country that the argument for putting a redundant building and land to a new use is sustainable. The movement grew to such a scale that even when a local authority had not wished to support a developer's application, national guidelines enabled government inspectors to overturn such decisions on appeal.

The barn conversion is the perfect example of good common sense and proves, beyond any doubt, that even the most derelict structure can be given a new lease of life. As the population grows, so too does the demand for housing, and this has caused both central and local government to look more favourably at many self-build proposals. Designations regarding 'use' class were once largely inflexible but, given the increasing demand for new accommodation, local authorities are now much more amenable, providing the application is feasible and meets local requirements.

IS THERE SUITABLE ACCESS?

Planning law provides the opportunity for approval to be given to develop land into residential use *without* suitable access onto the land being agreed. It is therefore essential to check whether the plot is 'land-locked' before proceeding any further. At the same time, you should check whether or not an access has been approved for the site by the local authority.

If access has been approved, find out whether it is intended to cross land owned by someone else. Purchasing the land will be complicated where any shared access or legal rights of way are going to be required to convert the plot into viable residential use. There will also be additional legal and building expenses involved, and these will need to be considered carefully and offset against the current valuation of the plot of land.

Once you are fully content that access onto the site is certain and secure, you should investigate:

- the distance of the access drive from the nearest appropriate highway;
- the condition of the access road surface.

The surface and dimensions of the road will need to be (or made to be) suitable for a whole convoy of trucks, vans and delivery lorries. Initially, there will be excavation work and this will involve JCBs, earth-moving vehicles and possibly articulated low-loaders delivering a mobile home or site-cabin onto the plot. A succession of commercial vehicles bringing everything from concrete, blockwork, sand and cement, to roof timbers, floorboards and internal fixtures and fittings, will need room to manoeuvre and unload close to the location where you will want to use these materials. The road must have the width-capacity to accommodate this traffic and the surface should be fairly robust, otherwise there will be inevitable complications. If the access road is not currently wide enough, is there scope for making it wider? Do trees need pruning to allow large vehicles to gain access? Do potholes need filling? Remember that any work required will have a cost implication and, if the road and land either side of it are owned by someone else, legal permission will almost certainly be needed to conduct any alterations.

Regardless of the form the access takes during the construction phase, security is a prime concern, and this becomes much more important if you do not intend living on the site. Temporary fencing and a lockable gate are ideal and usually adequate, but individual sites present their own unique security problems and each should be assessed according to their individual needs.

How do you assess a site location?

The primary considerations in assessing a site location are generally subjective:

■ Does it fulfil your personal aspirations?

■ Does it provide the essential ingredients that will allow you and your family to feel comfortable?

■ Does it feel instinctively right?

■ Does it provide enough space for adaptations and expansion in the years ahead, particularly if you are planning to have a larger family?

Assessing 'best value' for a particular plot of land is difficult, as much will depend on your needs, the funds you have available and the plans you have made for the future. Quality and quantity need to be considered and compared against the asking price for each plot. The higher priced building plots are likely to be located in higher valued neighbourhoods, and this fact alone will underwrite and influence the property's completion value. However, a larger plot in a pleasant but out of the way location may cost less to buy and therefore enable a more substantial property to be built upon it. This, in turn, will allow you to create a property with more rooms, better living space and an extensive garden. Finding the right balance between quantity, quality and cost is essential at this early stage, as it will determine how you proceed and the kind of property eventually built. One of the greatest rewards of a self-build scheme is the opportunity it gives to control the living spaces you require. The more space you have, the more creative you are able to be and the easier it is to produce something unique and satisfying.

Location may be viewed quite differently if the project is a short-term proposal and merely a stepping-stone to a more adventurous self-build scheme. In this case, the purpose is to maximise value by building a property appropriate to the site and its surrounding locality, ensuring that the plot can be easily landscaped and presented quickly to the market. In this situation, the old developer's adage applies: 'Minimise costs and maximise profits'!

The geographic position is a major consideration, regardless of the site. It is fundamental for a self-builder to make himself aware of the physical nature of the plot and how it may affect him and his family in the future. The most significant questions include:

- Is it more than 500 feet above sea level? This is known as the theoretical 'snow-line'; buying a plot at this altitude means there is an increased likelihood of severe winter conditions. This may, of course, not be obvious if viewing is undertaken during the mild weather of other seasons.

- Is the plot on a local flood plain? The ground may be dry when you visit it, but what happens during long periods of wet weather? Has a nearby stream burst its banks in the past or does water typically flow from a field onto the plot of land being considered? Neighbours are often a useful source of information, particularly if they have lived in their home for a number of years. Consulting the local authority can also produce valuable historical data and they will usually give advice about the suitability of a particular plot.

- Does the site occupy an unobstructed south-facing position so that the maximum amount of natural light and heat can be enjoyed? If tall trees obstruct light, can these be felled or are they a protected variety? If you are viewing the plot during winter, bear in mind the effect nearby trees will have during spring and summer when they will be in full leaf.

There are also additional matters to contemplate, including the type and size of other properties close to the site. If the plot is substantial and you intend constructing a home to fill the expanse of land, will it be incongruous with other housing in the neighbourhood? The size and design should be sympathetic with those nearby, otherwise it may never realise its true market value. You should also take a wider perspective and look beyond the plot's boundary to assess the amenities and facilities available. Do they meet the needs of your family? Important matters might include the quality of local schools, leisure facilities, shopping, health centres and, of course, access to the motorway network and to public transport. Consider the fact that commuting *time* is much more important than commuting 'distance'. This factor can greatly increase the number of potential areas you might look at when trying to identify where a suitable plot will be found. Where a motorway junction is nearby, it could take much longer to get to it, if the linking road is one frequently congested with traffic. Conversely, a junction some miles away could be advantageous, if there are quiet roads leading to it.

ARE SERVICES AVAILABLE?

A site that has been identified through an estate agent is likely to have the availability of mains services listed in its sales particulars. The agent will normally have established and recorded the fact that they exist. If these details are missing from the agent's brochure, you will need to ask about them and authenticate any information given. Services to check include mains drainage, mains water, mains electricity and mains gas, together with underground communications such as telephone and cable TV.

However, if you have 'self-selected' the site, you will need to investigate and identify for yourself which services are readily available. It is usual for them to be brought in from the nearest road but, in some cases, you may be required to connect up to your neighbours' services or cross their land in order to access them. In either case, there will be added costs and potential legal expenses that should be assessed and deducted from the price of the land before purchase is considered. In addition, where services for the drainage of foul or surface water do not already exist, you must check and establish that any planning permission allows for it. Not all planning permissions guarantee a right to create drainage from a site.

It is fairly economical to lay cables and small pipes for mains water and electricity over a considerable distance, but the same is not true for gas pipes and mains drainage, which may simply be out of the question. Preliminary investigations about the availability of mains water and drainage can be conducted by visiting the mains drainage department of the local authority. They maintain records of the size, depth and location of pipes, and will inform you about those nearest to the land you are considering. For mains electricity and gas, write to the local provider and include a site plan on which they can indicate the proximity and size or capacity of the service. Likewise, contact British Telecommunications or alternative telephone service providers operating in the area, as well as cable television companies, to identify where such services are in relation to the plot.

It has to be borne in mind that, in some of the more isolated locations, alternative measures will have to be taken, as mains services will not be available. For example, septic tanks may be required for foul drainage, soakaways for surface water drainage and spring water filtration for household water needs. Although mains electricity is widely available, in some areas of the country mains gas is not so common. This could affect your design plans to some extent as, for example, it would be pointless preparing a construction based on gas central heating if this type of energy is not going to be available. There are, of course, many alternative power sources including bottled gas, solar power, wind power and water turbines, and these are all worthy of consideration at this early stage.

The advantage of self-building your own home is that you can determine the best solution to any specific problem and do not necessarily have to rely on the cheapest conventional alternative (as a builder would do). It is entirely up to you how you resolve the problem. Traditional methods are likely to be the least expensive in the short term, whilst environmentally friendly alternatives may cost more to install, but save you money in the long term.

WHAT FUTURE DEVELOPMENTS MIGHT THERE BE?

When you instruct your solicitor to draw up the contract to purchase the land, he will carry out the necessary legal searches, which will include the possibility of any future developments directly affecting your plot. It is advisable to make yourself aware of such possibilities at a much earlier stage, if only to avoid wasting your valuable time and effort pursuing a site that may prove impractical. For example, there may be a road-widening scheme planned or a new by-pass being considered or the development of land nearby involving the construction of an industrial estate or some other undesirable structure.

The planning department of the local authority will be aware of proposed developments. It is also worth asking them to what 'use' the surrounding land has been designated and whether there are plans to change, add to or create highways within the vicinity of the plot under consideration. The local highways department will have maps and details showing approved and proposed road schemes and, by talking to officers of the local authority, you may gain access to information about other proposals yet to reach the public domain.

This research is essential to safeguarding your future. The local authority is not the only available source of information. By talking to neighbours, local shopkeepers and publicans, you may acquire details about plans under long-term discussion but which have yet to be formally recorded. Forearmed is forewarned! Gather as much information as you possibly can and never rely on one source alone.

SUMMARY

- Check for land contamination by procuring a professional report.
- Consult the local authority to identify the 'use' class and designation of the land being considered.

■ Has suitable access to the plot been approved? If not, can one be created and will it be adequate for the delivery of goods and equipment required during construction? Be aware of the practical, legal and financial problems associated with a 'land locked' site.

■ Assess carefully whether the plot is contained within an area that provides you and your family with all the amenities and facilities required. Consider the implications of its geographic location and guard against buying land with a history of flooding.

■ If mains services do not already exist on the site, assess the cost and practicalities of installing them and any alternatives that may be suitable.

■ Research the area thoroughly to identify any proposed future local developments, which may adversely affect your self-build scheme.

USEFUL INTERNET WEBSITES

www.environment-agency.gov.uk
Visit the official government site for information about the area in which you intend building your new home. Enter a post-code or click into multi-level maps to identify pollution concerns, floodplains and flooding indicators, sewerage and landfill sites.

www.self-build.co.uk
A good resource for self-builders from 'Build It'. Includes a free service where visitors are able to ask a question of the experts (answers received within five days).

www.upmystreet.co.uk
A mammoth range of information, contacts and statistics pertinent to post-code regions is available through this free resource. Don't even consider proceeding with a purchase without checking its neighbourhood particulars made available through 'upmystreet'.

Chapter 6
Buying the Site

This chapter covers:

- assessing the value

- determining the correct order of work

- estimating hidden costs

- employing a solicitor

- raising the finance

- proceeding with the legal work

- protecting yourself and your site

By this stage in your self-build endeavour, you will have identified a plot of land suitable for your plans, checked that the ground conditions are appropriate for building on and gathered extensive research material about the site and surrounding location. Having spoken with the local planning department, you will also have confirmed that constructing a residential unit on the plot is feasible, and be aware of any preparatory groundwork and the type of foundations required.

Other than paying for professional inspections and reports, you have not yet committed substantial funds to the plot. But it is at this point that things start to change because, once you buy the land, you become much more obligated to starting and completing the project. This is therefore the final opportunity you have to withdraw from this particular location and venture. Only if you are 100 per cent confident that this plot is *the* desirable site for your dream home should you cautiously proceed towards purchasing it (but not too cautiously, otherwise another interested party may submit a bid and, quite literally, snatch the ground from beneath you).

ASSESSING THE VALUE

For many, the value of land is hard to quantify and it would therefore be financially quite reckless to proceed by blindly trusting a vendor's assessment alone. It may be that the asking price is inflated way beyond what the plot is really worth. So, judging whether your plot of land is worth the asking price is a difficult but essential exercise. It is important for two reasons:

1. It will have a considerable impact on the market value of your completed dwelling and it is therefore a deciding factor in the eventual success or failure of your *investment* -v- *profit* strategy.

2. Paying an amount above market value is the same as throwing money down the drain when it could be put to a much better purpose, for example by enhancing the construction with superior quality building materials.

But how can you quantify something so varied as a piece of land, which unlike residential property, can be used for many different purposes? There are two recognised methods and neither should be employed in isolation because, by conducting each exercise and combining the results, you will achieve a more reliable valuation. It is, in fact, the very nature of assured 'land use' which so often determines its worth. For example, typically, a plot without planning permission will be valued at considerably less than a similar plot that has already received planning permission. In some cases, the difference can be 500 per cent to 1000 per cent. The value of the land without planning permission is lower because the use to which it can be put is uncertain and therefore the risk to the buyer wanting to build on it is much higher.

In addition, because building land is becoming increasingly scarce, more developers and self-builders find themselves scrambling after a decreasing number of available plots. The rules of supply and demand have now come into play and are pushing prices up. In 2002, *The Times* reported that London building plots had risen by almost 24 per cent, with similar increases in the east of England. On average, prices throughout England and Wales had gone up by 12 per cent, a figure well above the annual rate of inflation. Property has always been seen as a sound and reasonably stable investment and now, quite suddenly, people are starting to recognise that land could offer the same promise. As a result, plots are being bought and retained for sale at a later date by those who once would have invested in stocks and shares. This influential element inflates the value of land and has caused 'prime building sites' to escalate rapidly and unpredictably in some areas of the country.

The erratic movement in estimated values has caused many landowners to become over optimistic about plots they have available. As a result, they are hiking the offer prices above what they are actually worth, in an effort to make lavish profits from novice and naïve buyers. This is the reason why you should give close and careful attention to assessing the true value of your intended purchase. Get it right and you will keep on a straight and narrow profit-track and remain within the boundaries of your initial budget; get it wrong and you are likely to find that costs spiral out of control and hopes of profiting from the self-build project will diminish. Remember that buying the site under consideration is not just a means to an end: it is a real and tangible asset, which if all else fails, you will need to sell to recoup your original outlay. Selling the land at a loss because the price was inflated when you bought it will not appease your lender, who will continue to demand full payment (including interest) on any loan acquired.

Method 1: 'comparables'

The use of 'comparables' is the traditional method of assessing the value of residential property. It can be applied to land in a similar way but, because there are many fewer plots on the market than there are dwellings, the results are more an estimation and less exacting. It is nonetheless a useful rule-of-thumb for the novice buyer and can be employed as a rough guide. A more precise valuation can be calculated later, using the second method outlined below.

In using comparables, as with any survey, accuracy is determined by the *similarity* and *volume* of individual plots in the data collected. Quite simply, plots with outline planning permission of an equivalent size, location and composition, can be readily compared; and the more there are to compare, the more precise the resulting 'mean-figure' calculation is likely to be. If your search for plots was exhaustive (following the advice given in Chapter 4), you may already have enough facts and figures on file to proceed. If not, you will need to obtain them by approaching agents, brokers, scouring through newspapers and magazines and/or by using the Internet. In the following example, we used the website at **www.buildstore.co.uk** to gather data (BuildStore Ltd claim to have the largest and most accurate database of plots currently on offer in the UK and provide a reliable and efficient subscription service to self-builders wanting to buy land in any area):

Fictitious plot of land 'under consideration':

(a) Size	=	0.25 acre
(b) Location	=	Nelson, Lancashire
(c) For sale at	=	£50,000
(d) Equivalent price per acre	=	£200,000

Actual comparable data:

(A total of 129 plots was examined, of which 74 did not have outline planning permission, 23 had insufficient plot size details and another 16 were offered with shared ownership or had existing buildings attached – these were therefore deemed not comparable.)

(e) Number of plots	=	16 with outline planning permission
(f) Average size	=	0.34 acre (ranging from 0.05 to 2.00 acres)
(g) Location	=	throughout Lancashire
(h) Average price per acre	=	£396,000

In our example, the quarter-acre plot would appear to be a reasonable buy and almost 50 per cent below the average price of similar land in the region. The main problem in using this method is that, unlike property valuation data obtained from reliable sources such as the Land Registry, the details obtained are of land yet to be sold rather than the true market prices achieved at the point of sale. It may be prudent therefore to reduce the resulting 'price per acre' figure by a 'negotiating percentage' of between 5 per cent and 10 per cent. The second concern is that the data collected takes no account of the aspect of the land and quality of the location, or potential costs involved in preparing the ground or creating suitable access. A wise buyer will, therefore, proceed to the second valuation method before committing himself to a purchase.

Method 2: 'development potential'

The secret to identifying the true value of any plot of land is found by examining its development potential. What is its most profitable application? In reality, there is no 'average' price for land in the UK because there are simply too many variables to consider. Does it have planning permission? If so, what can be built on it? How much will the building(s) cost to construct? What degree of preparatory groundwork is involved? How much will the building(s) sell for upon completion?

An indication of these variables was found in our survey of land undertaken in Method 1: two equally sized plots in the same region with radically different market values. Plot 1 with 0.35 acre offered at £18,750. Plot 2 with 0.35 acre at £150,000. The difference between the two plots was the first had no planning permission and the potential to develop it as building land was unlikely; the second already had outline planning consent for a four-bedroomed detached house, which once built, could be sold for in excess of £300,000. Imagine if the same plot could gain planning consent for a block of ten apartments with a market value upon completion of £125,000 each. Such land is a goldmine to developers and, because of its potential for creating vast profit, its base-value is elevated accordingly.

The point is that the land you are interested in might be capable of being developed far beyond what you personally intend using it for. Although you may only wish to build one home, it could have the potential for several dwellings to be built on it. This would increase the profitable capability the land has for a developer, and the offer price may well reflect this fact. The question you must ask yourself is this: 'At completion of my self-build project what is more important, an immediately realised high level of profit or the satisfaction of a family home with extensive gardens which can be enjoyed for many years to come?'

If your intention is mainly to maximise profit, it is *essential* you conduct the following exercise as fully and carefully as possible, so that the true market value of the land under consideration is revealed. Once this is known, you can determine whether the plot is one worth buying at the price at which it is being offered. There are two aspects to the calculation:

■ the costs involved in constructing your property;

■ the market value of the property upon completion.

You can only ever hope to estimate these figures, but the more accurately they are determined, the more reliable your land valuation will be. Evaluating construction costs may seem a daunting task but bear in mind that undertaking the exercise now will pay dividends in the future. Not only will you confirm, or conversely be able to challenge, the financial merits offered by the building plot under consideration, you will also be creating an outline budget to guide you through construction and you will have the necessary figures required for any loan application. The exercise will, in effect, provide you with an insight into the practical and financial implications of turning your dream into reality.

Your own self-build project may have expenditure elements in addition to those listed in Figure 1 and some listed may not be appropriate to your situation. Be as thorough as you can in identifying each expense according to the quality of materials and installations you hope to use, the type of design specification and the amount of sub-contracted work likely to be involved. Although a builder will be able to assist you in part of this task, much of it involves making a catalogue of telephone calls and spending some time undertaking research on the Internet or alternatively 'on foot'.

There are several guides that offer reasonable estimates for construction. One of the most useful can be found at Travis Perkins, the builder's merchants. Visit their website at: **www.buildthedream.co.uk** where plans can be submitted and a full detailed schedule of materials produced, together with summary estimates, all for a fee which is refundable, providing a minimum amount of supplies are bought from them. As a general rule, most self-build guides suggest that construction costs are approximately £50 per square foot of total floor space. But this estimation method is too imprecise and falls more in the realm of guesswork – a recipe for disaster if you underestimate the funds required to complete the dwelling! The variants affecting building costs include the quality of materials you expect to use and the way in which you intend managing the project.

For example, if you are going to undertake most of the labour-intensive tasks yourself but employ a few tradesmen for the essentials, the cost can be as little as £30 per square foot using mid-quality materials; whereas if you wish to have the entire venture project-managed by someone else and incorporate high quality materials, it could cost upwards of £70-£80 per square foot. You will need to apply the relevant guide-price according to your own self-build vision. *Tip:* try visiting **www.self-buildit.co.uk** and apply their self-build calculator to your project.

Figure 1   Expense elements

Expense element	Average	My build
Professional reports regarding ground conditions, land contamination, stability, foundation requirements, etc.	£500 to £1,500	
Outline planning application (per 0.1 hectare)	£220	
Detailed planning application (per dwelling)	£220	
Building regulation approval (plans, inspection & notice)	£350	
Architect (production of drawings and plans only – not acting as project manager)	£1,000 to £5,000	
Demolition of any existing derelict building and any associated site preparation and debris removal	£5,000 to £15,000	
Professional and legal costs (solicitor, interior design, quantity surveyor, structural engineer, etc.)	£1,000 to £5,000	
Creating suitable access onto the building site	£2,000 to £10,000	
Supply and connection onto the site of services for mains gas, electricity, drainage, water, sewerage, telephone	£1,000 to £5,000	
Construction of the dwelling with _____ sq ft of floor space (amend according to the quality of materials and the degree of personal involvement in the work)	£50 per sq ft	
Labour, sub-contractor(s) and tradesmen costs	£10,000 to £25,000	
Loan interest payable over the term (average is based on £100,000 borrowed with repayments over 25 years and with a static interest rate of 5.95 per cent). NOTE: total interest falls dramatically with shorter loan terms, appropriate if the dwelling is to be sold at completion	£92,000	
Mortgage application and other loan associated fees (average is based on a £100,000 advance)	£300 to £800	
Site security (hire of fencing and lighting plus indemnity insurance for public liability)	£1,500 to £2,500	
Hire of tools and equipment during construction	£250 to £5,000	
Landscaping (hard and soft)	£5,000 to £15,000	
TOTAL OF ESTIMATED COSTS INVOLVED =		

There are two additions that should be made to the expenses total:

- ▪ (a) a 15 per cent contingency for inaccurate estimations or unexpected complications arising during construction (advised by many self-builders and their mortgage providers);

- ▪ (b) a 25 per cent developer's profit (the average most builders anticipate receiving and a minimum requirement when conducting the calculation that follows).

The next stage of the process in Method 2 Land Valuation is to assess what the market value of your self-built property would be if it were to be sold today. You would be right to assume this is a difficult task, considering the fact that the property does not yet exist! However, you have a reasonable idea of the type of dwelling you want to construct and the location where you would like to build it. These two elements are enough to facilitate a rough assessment. Visit all local estate agents and collect offer-price data of contemporary properties that are similar in design, size and location. Significant factors include the number of bedrooms, size of gardens, garage or car-parking space, number of bathrooms and type of construction. From these details you should be able to gauge the comparative current market value of your own dwelling.

If you are already in receipt of design plans or architect's drawings or even just an artist's impression, take them to local estate agents and ask for a valuation opinion. Most will share their expert local knowledge with you and offer sound (free) advice, particularly if they think you might employ them as your selling-agents once the property is completed.

The formula for assessing the residual plot value to a developer is:

Current market value of the self-build dwelling
minus
Expense elements total

The figure remaining is the true value of the plot of land. This completes the procedure and is a good and proper basis for the valuation of any building land in the UK. Armed with this information, you can decide whether the plot is suitable for your needs at the price offered – or you may conclude there is some hard negotiating to be done before you proceed.

DETERMINING THE CORRECT ORDER OF WORK

The process we have chosen to follow for the purpose of this book is:

- ▪ Identify a suitable plot of development land with outline planning permission (OPP) and buy it after checking the ground conditions, access and foundation requirements.

- Draw up detailed plans for a dwelling of suitable size and design to fit the plot and OPP, giving due regard to budget restraints and thorough cost analysis.

- Apply for full planning permission.

- Prepare the site and begin construction.

This order of work is by no means appropriate for every situation. However, it *does* tend to produce the best outcome for most self-builders and improves the potential to make a good profit from the venture. There may be considerable time periods between each task or all may be undertaken in quick succession. Indeed, some may occur simultaneously.

The ideal situation would be to have an architect draw up plans of your dream home and then find a stunning location for it, obtain planning permission after buying the land (as land sold without permission is cheaper) and then construct the dwelling. Sadly, this order is virtually impossible to achieve without the most severe complications, and we would discourage anyone from attempting it. The potential for disaster is high and the cost implications are alarming. The most likely scenario is a fall at the first hurdle: an inability to find a plot of land suitable for your expensive architect-drawn plans. This means the dream home never gets built or additional expenses are incurred because new plans need drawing to fit an alternative site. The worst-case scenario is buying land that cannot be developed after having paid an architect to create detailed plans.

Although there is no absolute right or wrong way of proceeding, it is often advisable to follow a well-trodden path, thereby learning from the mistakes of people who have gone before. By finding a suitable building plot then compromising your house design aspirations accordingly, you will be taking a less complicated route and promoting a more fortuitous outcome.

ESTIMATING HIDDEN COSTS

If the plot you intend to buy is uneven and overgrown, saturated with water or the subsoil is of an uncertain composition, you will need to have a site survey undertaken before an architect can begin drawing your plans. The potential for further costs are momentous, given that a simple survey could raise additional questions that, in turn, could lead to an inordinate variety of other tests being demanded. Bear in mind that the first estimate of £500 could rise to £3,000 or more if planning consent requires an archaeological survey. A straightforward soil investigation alone usually means acquiring the services of an engineer to design and advise the appropriate type of foundation. This can increase your first estimate by 100 per cent and more.

Hidden costs are by their nature *'hidden'* – it is difficult to plan for them since you have no idea when or even whether they will arise. In addition, by budgeting for their potential occurrence you will alter your cost-analysis and price yourself out of what might otherwise be a worthwhile venture (where the cause of hidden costs fails to materialise). It is for this reason that you need to add a reasonable level of contingency to your budget, but not one so pessimistic that it provides for a myriad of disasters striking you and your project. As we mentioned earlier, a financial padding of 15 per cent allows for the unexpected to occur whilst still keeping you on a steady profit-driven course.

EMPLOYING A SOLICITOR

The legal process for buying land is generally a great deal less involved than buying property, so most experienced solicitors will be competent in dealing with your purchase. Provided you explain the full purpose behind acquiring the plot, your solicitor will be able to offer you good sound advice. Always take heed of any concerns expressed and accede to any recommended investigations. When deciding which solicitor to employ, consider the following:

■ The best are not always the cheapest and, if speed and efficiency are important, you may have to pay a little more to beat other self-builders competing for the plot.

■ Your solicitor can only provide answers if you ask the questions. Use their expertise and knowledge to become fully acquainted with the land and any implied liabilities, particularly those governing boundaries, footpaths, access, easements and the rights of neighbouring landowners.

■ Confirm that all routes for gaining information about ground conditions are fully explored, including any appropriate searches, for example for existing or prior mining that could affect the stability of the land.

■ Where possible, employ a solicitor used and recommended by another self-builder.

■ Use a solicitor within your own local area. There will be occasions when talking to them direct or visiting their office at short notice will benefit you.

■ Your solicitor is unlikely to attend the site in person so they will have to rely on you and existing plans to visualise the scope, shape and condition of the land. Photographs will greatly assist them, so make these available at the earliest opportunity. If you have Internet access, find out whether an aerial photo of the plot exists by visiting **www2.getmapping.com**

■ Once your solicitor is in possession of legal documents relating to the site, check that what is described actually exists. For example, is the shape consistent with the plan, and do measurements correspond with actual boundaries?

■ Ask your solicitor to find out whether VAT is to be charged by the vendor. It is important that you inform the landowner, *prior to purchase*, that you intend building a residential dwelling on it. If you do so, VAT should not be charged. If you fail to inform the vendor of your intentions, you may be charged VAT and, once paid, it cannot be reclaimed.

■ Proceed to purchase *only* once you and your solicitor are *entirely* satisfied that everything is in order and confirmation is received that the land can be developed for residential use (see Chapter 9).

RAISING THE FINANCE

We have, so far, looked at financing your project from an idealistic point of view. That is, arranging sufficient resources to buy the land you like and constructing a property that best fits the site. However, in reality, the biggest limiting factor in creating your dream home is likely to be the funds you are *able* to acquire. This reverse-route to budgeting could have dramatic consequences and must be examined carefully, otherwise your aspirations will remain just pipedreams without ever succeeding to fruition.

The good news is that self-build loans are quite different to traditional mortgages, and many lenders now recognise the increased property value and immediate profit to be gained at completion. This means that the plan to buy land and build is in itself considered an asset worthy of encouragement and investment. The bad news is that the interest paid on a loan is probably going to be one of the biggest expenses attacking your end-profit and, if things do not go according to plan, the amount you finally pay may eat up all the net gains. In short, the financial advantages of self-building can be wrecked by too much borrowing and too little planning.

Living in an existing home whilst the new one is built may offer comfort and convenience, but how will it affect your budget and final profit margin? Although the existing home can be used as security to raise finance, it is likely you will need to borrow more to buy the land and meet construction costs. This in turn involves paying more interest on the loan and probably from an earlier date. Conversely, selling the existing home may provide enough capital to buy land and prepare it for building on; there may even be enough to begin the first stage of construction. This means the total loan amount would be reduced along with the level of interest and, importantly, repayments would begin much later into the project. There would, however, be more discomfort and further expenses for on-site accommodation.

Making the right decisions now, according to personal and financial circumstances and the nature of the self-build project, will impact on the success of your venture. What is appropriate for you may not be suitable for someone else and, although you should listen to the experiences of other self-builders, it is not always wise to adopt the same financial plan. Instead, examine all of your options and progress them to a theoretical conclusion, as this will help you identify a strategy that best fits your own situation. But, regardless of the financial plan, bear in mind that the primary objective should be to pay as little loan-interest as possible, because this will improve proportionately the profit you make at completion. To keep interest payments low, you should:

■ have a carefully drafted expense plan so you only borrow according to need;

■ aim to acquire the most flexible type of loan with the lowest percentage of interest and with payments spanning over the shortest practical period;

■ plan to buy the land out of personal funds, if possible, so that only the construction is subject to financial backing (delaying loan repayments and reducing the overall amount borrowed);

■ examine the benefits of *staged-payment* self-build loans, which only involve you borrowing money as required for each phase of construction, but where the total amount of advance has been agreed.

It was once very difficult for people who wanted to build their own home to obtain financial support from traditional lenders, but with some 20,000 self-build projects starting each year, accounting for one in eight of all new homes, lenders are supplying a variety of products to meet the rising demand. There is now an array of banks and building societies offering a range of loans, and of these the Norwich & Peterborough, Britannia, Skipton, Lloyds TSB, The Nationwide, and Bradford & Bingley (in association with BuildStore Ltd), are amongst the most pro-active.

If you intend raising funds through a lender, bear in mind the following:

■ Most lenders require a structural guarantee in the form of an insurance policy for the completed dwelling. Costs vary according to the provider, the size of property, range of cover and number of inspections conducted during construction. Further details about structural indemnity policies can be obtained from the National House Building Council (NHBC) 'Solo' scheme (01494 735363), Zurich Municipal 'Custom Build' scheme (01252 387592), FE Wright 'Project Builder' package (0207 7165050), and online at **www.self-builder.com**

■ There are no self-build loans currently available for 100 per cent of the entire project cost. Typically, they range from 50 per cent to 80 per cent of land value, which means you will require some degree of accessible capital to begin with, and up to a maximum of 95 per cent of the completed property value.

■ You will only be able to borrow up to your level of repayment risk, assessed according to the lender's own criteria. Ordinarily, this means three times your annual income plus one times that of your partner.

- Many lenders make it mandatory for borrowers to have adequate site insurance to protect against damage caused to the building during construction and theft of materials.

- The success of your loan application will not be entirely dependent on your financial circumstances or your ability to repay the sum borrowed. It will also depend on the quality and credibility of your presentation. Lenders will want to know that you have properly planned the project, made a thorough cost analysis and have available an itemised budget requirement. They will also consider your enthusiasm, experience, confidence in completing the building within an acceptable timescale and your reasons for undertaking the venture in the first place.

- Lenders usually require sight of adequate plans, produced by suitably qualified professionals, prior to a loan being considered or advanced. They will use these to assess the value of your plot of land and the end-value of your self-build scheme. Typically, they charge a 'valuation fee' for this service of £150 to £300.

If you are uncertain of which mortgage/loan company to approach or which variety of loans to apply for, a good starting point is to acquire a copy of the monthly magazine *MoneyFacts* from 66–70 Thorpe Road, Norwich, Norfolk, NR1 1BJ (01603 476476). This publishes explanations of the different types of mortgage and information about the rates available. They also have a website at **www.moneyfacts.co.uk** There is no quick way of identifying the best self-build lender because there are simply too many variables to consider. What may be appropriate for one person and their particular project will not necessarily be suitable for another. The way forward is to contact a favoured few lenders and ask for written details of the products they have available, then consider the advantages and disadvantages of each before submitting an application.

The following table represents the most comprehensive list of self-build mortgage lenders you are likely to find *anywhere* (accurate at time of survey). It may be of interest to note that the bigger the lender, the more difficult it was to communicate with them (let alone obtain details about the products they have available or negotiate a loan). This may be considered a disadvantage and one that encourages you to approach a smaller lender who is likely to take a more personal interest in your application. However, we found that smaller lenders tend to offer more restrictive loans, for example making it mandatory for an architect or NHBC registered builder to act as project-manager. There are 'swings and roundabouts' to every loan and self-build is no exception. We advise you apply to a lender whose product best meets your individual requirements and specific situation.

Figure 2 Table of self-build mortgage lenders

Name & Address Details	Product Name	Website Address	Staged Loan Release	Land Purchase Option
Barclays Direct Mortgages. Barclays Head Office. 54 Lombard St., London. EC3P 3AH. (Tel: 0845 677 0002)	Self-Build Mortgage	www.personal. barclays.co.uk	Yes	Yes
Belmont International Ltd. Becket House, Vestry Rd., Otford, Sevenoaks, Kent. TN14 5EL. (Tel: 0800 018 6220)	Time-Line	www.self-builder.com	Yes	Yes
Bradford & Bingley. PO Box 88, Croft Rd., Crossflats, Bingley, West Yorkshire. BD16 2UA. (Tel: 0800 718191)	Guided by a Charcol advisor	www.bbg.co.uk	Yes	Yes
Britannia Building Society. Britannia House, Leek, Staffordshire Moorlands. ST13 5RG. (Tel: 0800 013 1140)	Accelerator	www.britannia.co.uk	Yes	Yes
BuildStore Ltd. Lomond House, Beveridge Sq., Livingston. EH54 6QF. (Tel: 0800 018 5740)	Accelerator	www.buildstore.co.uk	Yes	Yes
Cheshire Building Society. Castle St., Macclesfield, Cheshire. SK11 6AF. (Tel: 01625 613612)	Self-Build Mortgage – Standard variable rate	www.thecheshire.co.uk	Yes	No (60 per cent of land value released after purchase)
Claycross Building Society. Freepost, Clay Cross, Chesterfield, Derbyshire. S45 9BR. (Tel: 0800 834497)	Heritage Mortgage Scheme	www.claycrossbs.co.uk	Yes	Yes
Cumberland Building Society. Cumberland House, Castle St., Carlisle. CA3 8RX. (Tel: 01228 541341)	Self-Build Mortgage	www.cumberland.co.uk	Yes	Yes
Darlington Building Society. Sentinel House, Lingfield Way, Darlington. DL1 4PR. (Tel: 01325 366366)	Only for County Durham, Tees Valley & N. Yorks	www.darlington.co.uk	Yes	Yes
Dudley Building Society. Dudley House, Stone St., Dudley. DY1 1NP. (Tel: 01384 231414)	Self-Build Mortgage	www.dudleybuilding society.co.uk	Yes	Yes
Earl Shilton Building Society. 22 The Hollow, Earl Shilton, Leicester. LE9 7NB. (Tel: 01455 844422)	Owner/Occupiers only	www.esbs.co.uk	Yes	Yes
Ecology Building Society. 18 Station Rd., Cross Hills, Keighley, West Yorkshire. BD20 7EH. (Tel: 0845 674 5566)	Ecology Mortgage	www.ecology.co.uk	Yes	Yes

Figure 2 Table of self-build mortgage lenders *continued*

Name & Address Details	Product Name	Website Address	Staged Loan Release	Land Purchase Option
Hanley Economic Building Society. Granville House, Festival Park, Hanley, Stoke on Trent. ST1 5TB. (Tel: 01782 255000)	Self-Build Mortgage	www.thehanley.co.uk	Yes	Yes
Harpenden Building Society. Aberdeen House, 14–16 Station Rd., Harpenden, Hertfordshire. AL5 4SE. (Tel: 01582 765411)	Self-Build Mortgage	www.harpendenbs.co.uk	Yes	Yes
Hinckley & Rugby Building Society. Upper Bond St., Hinckley, Leicestershire. LE10 1DG. (Tel: 0800 774499)	Self-Build Mortgage	www.hrbs.co.uk	Yes	No
Kent Reliance Building Society. Reliance House, Sun Pier, Chatham, Kent. ME4 4ET. (Tel: 0800 783 4248)	Self-Build Mortgage	www.krbs.co.uk	Yes	Yes
Leek United Building Society. 50 St Edward St., Leek, Staffordshire. ST13 5DH. (Tel: 0800 093 0004)	Self-Build Mortgage	www.leekunited.co.uk	Yes	Yes
Lloyds TSB Scotland. Henry Duncan House, 120 George St., Edinburgh. EH2 4LH. (Tel: 0131 225 4555)	Advanced Flexible Self-Build Mortgage	www.lloydstsb.co.uk	Yes	Yes
Loughborough Building Society. 6 High St., Loughborough. LE11 2QB. (Tel: 01509 610707)	Based on buy-to-let mortgage, released in stages	www.theloughborough.co.uk	Yes	Yes
Mansfield Building Society. Regent House, Regent St., Mansfield, Notts. NG18 1SS. (Tel: 01623 676300)	Self-Build Mortgage	www.mansfieldbs.co.uk	Yes	No
Nationwide Building Society. Nationwide House, Pipers Way, Swindon. SN38 1NW. (Tel: 0800 302010)	Self-Build Mortgage	www.nationwide.co.uk	Yes	Yes
Norwich & Peterborough Building Society. Peterborough Bus Park, Lynch Wood, Peterborough. PE2 6WZ. (Tel: 0845 300 6727)	Self-Build Mortgage	www.npbs.co.uk	Yes	Yes
Principality Building Society. P O Box 89, Principality Buildings, Queen St., Cardiff. CF10 1UA. (Tel: 0800 454478)	Self-Build Mortgage	www.principality.co.uk	Yes	Yes

Figure 2   Table of self-build mortgage lenders *continued*

Name & Address Details	Product Name	Website Address	Staged Loan Release	Land Purchase Option
Royal Bank of Scotland. 36 St Andrew Square, Edinburgh. EH2 2YB. (Tel: 0131 523 6308)	Self-Build Mortgage	www.rbs.co.uk	Yes	Yes
Scarborough Building Society. Prospect House, P O Box 6, Scarborough, North Yorkshire. YO11 3WZ. (Tel: 08705 133149)	Self-Build Mortgage	www.scarboroughbs. co.uk	Yes	Yes
Scottish Building Society. 23 Manor Place, Edinburgh. EH3 7XE. (Tel: 0131 220 1111)	Self-Build Package	www.scottishbs.co.uk	Yes	Yes
Shepshed Building Society. Bullring, Shepshed, Leicestershire. LE12 9QD. (Tel: 01509 822000)	Self-Build Loan	www.theshepshed.co.uk	Yes	Yes
Skipton Building Society. The Bailey, Skipton, North Yorkshire. BD23 1DN. (Tel: 01756 705030)	Accelerator	www.skipton.co.uk	Yes	Yes
Standard Life Bank Ltd. Standard Life House, 30 Lothian Rd., Edinburgh. EH1 2DH. (Tel: 0845 8458450)	Arranged on an individual basis	www.standardlifebank. com	Yes	No
Swansea Building Society. 11 Cradock St., Swansea. SA1 3EW. (Tel: 01792 483701)	Arranged on an individual basis	www.swansea-bs.co.uk	Yes	Yes
Tipton & Coseley Building Society. 70 Owen St., Tipton, West Midlands. DY4 8HG. (Tel: 0121 557 2551)	Self-Build Mortgage	www.tipton-coseley.co.uk	Yes	Yes
Universal Building Society. Universal House, Kings Manor, Newcastle upon Tyne. NE1 6PA. (Tel: 0800 028 8383)	Self-Build Mortgage	www.theuniversal.co.uk	Yes	Yes
Yorkshire Building Society. Yorkshire House, Yorkshire Drive, Bradford. BD5 8LJ. (Tel: 0854 1200 100)	Instalment Advance	www.ybs.co.uk	Yes	Yes

New lenders are constantly entering the market, offering variations of the staged-mortgage product. Every loan is slightly different and it is essential you spend some time and thought examining the merits of each one, with due consideration being given to your own self-build project and how the specific features of a loan may affect it. The elements to consider include:

■ What is the maximum loan-to-value (LTV)?

■ Who assesses the valuation of land and property (existing home, if applicable, and the new dwelling) and how much will this cost?

■ Are staged payments made in advance or in arrears of each stage? If in arrears, you will need to find funds for land purchase, materials and labour before starting each phase.

■ Is outline or detailed planning permission required as a condition of the advance?

■ Will you be charged for multiple inspections and valuation surveys prior to funds being released? Lenders often undertake formal inspections at the end of each stage.

■ What guarantees do they require from you that the construction will occur according to plan and within an agreed timescale? Penalties may occur if you go beyond an agreed timescale or go over budget.

■ How flexible is the lender going to be if you need or desire to alter the design of your self-build during construction?

■ Will they demand you take out a warranty or other form of structural insurance?

■ What is their policy on building regulation approval?

■ Are there any early termination/completion/redemption fees?

■ Are you allowed to 'manage' your own construction? Some lenders will insist on an architect or other professional 'project managing' the entire build.

■ What construction conditions are attached to the loan? Many lenders make restrictions on the type of build and materials that can be used.

The following example is typical of a *seven stage* self-build mortgage. Other mortgages may offer a variable number of staged releases. This particular product is available from the Norwich & Peterborough Building Society, whom we thank for providing us with permission to reprint the details in this book.

Raising the finance to build your home is likely to be one of the most daunting aspects of the entire project and once you succeed beyond this stage, there is no turning back. The money will be in your bank account and you will be paying interest on it, so you must employ the funds as soon as possible. Make it work for you – not against you – go build your dream!

Typical example of a self-build mortgage

A borrower, applying for a repayment mortgage of £110,000, over 25 years, for the construction of a self-build property valued at £150,000 when completed. Mortgage released in seven stages.

Stage		Release	Gross monthly payments rising in effect from each release date, paid over 300 months
1	85% Plot value (£59,000 advance remaining)	£51,000	£319
2	15% Foundation to damp proof course level (including slab)	£8,850	£375
3	15% First floor joist level	£8,850	£430
4	15% Wall plate level	£8,850	£486
5	20% Roofed in	£11,800	£559
6	15% Plastered out	£8,850	£615
7	20% Completion	£11,800	£689

The APR for the whole loan would be 5.9% variable (correct at time of writing)

The total amount repayable to the Society by monthly payments over 300 months would be £206,854. This includes:

Initial amount borrowed	**£110,000**
Solicitor's charge	**£150**
Sealing fee	**£70**
Mortgage application fee	**£225**

The APR, monthly repayments and total amount repayable in this typical example have been calculated with the assumption that the interest rate remains at 5.69% for the duration of the mortgage term. The rate is, however, variable (which means that it may go up or down from time to time). In practice, the interest rate will change on a number of occasions during the mortgage term. The APR and repayments would then be different from those quoted in the typical example. The premiums, charges and fees may also change during the mortgage term. NOTE: Re-inspection fees will also be charged before each stage release.

(Authors' note: this is not a recommendation of the product though we feel it is a fair representation of those available.)

PROCEEDING WITH THE LEGAL WORK

In reality, the legal process of buying the land and the raising of finance are likely to flow simultaneously. There are matters concerning each task that will affect the other and, in an ideal world, you will obtain your mortgage advance and complete the plot purchase in quick succession. If a delay occurs in buying the land, it is essential you contact your lender and inform them, to prevent the possibility of unwarranted fees accruing; equally, your solicitor should be informed if the mortgage advance has to be postponed (for example, if site investigations and survey reports are outstanding).

Once everything is in place and provided you are content to proceed, urge your solicitor to arrange completion. You now have the land *and* the money to start building on it.

PROTECTING YOURSELF AND YOUR SITE

We cannot stress enough the importance of protecting what you now own against vandalism and theft and the financial catastrophe of storm damage, flooding and fire. You also need to shield yourself, your family, those you employ and visitors to the site (including intruders), against claims for personal injury, death and any loss of property arising from your self-build project. Make no mistake – once you own the plot of land, *you* become liable for almost everything that happens on it!

There are obvious physical access and security concerns that are easily resolved by installing suitable fencing. This can be constructed and erected personally or hired for the duration of the build. Depending on the degree of risk and the size and scale of the project, you might also consider installing security lighting, an alarm system or even employing a night watchman. If you intend living on site, you should consider the fact that your own personal possessions will also be at risk. Attention should therefore be given to the installation of additional locks on caravan doors and windows.

With regard to insurance, you are likely to require policies covering:

- employers' liability (a legal requirement if you employ subcontractors);
- public liability;
- contract works;
- plant, machinery and tools (personally owned or hired);
- your own on-site living accommodation;
- services connection (in case of damage to main drains, etc.);
- legal expenses (in the event you are sued for damages);
- buildings (during and after construction).

There are many good policies available through established insurance companies but it is wise to shop around, as the conditions, cost of premiums, excesses, periods of cover and inclusive elements vary significantly. Policies available and worthy of consideration include:

AXA Selfbuilders Insurance. Tel: 01909 591652.
Website: **www.selfbuild.armor.co.uk**

Belmont's Self-Builder Site Insurance Package. Tel: 0800 018 7660.
Website: **www.self-builder.com**

Buildstore's BuildCare (underwritten by Allianz Cornhill). Tel: 0870 872 0908.
Website: **www.buildstore.co.uk**

Country Mutual Self Build Insurance Scheme. Tel: 0118 978 7000.
Website: **www.tredray.co.uk**

Sterling Hamilton Wright's Project Builder Insurance. Tel: 020 7716 5050.
Website: **www.project-builder-insurance.com**

The earlier you can arrange your insurance policy after buying the land, the better. It will not only provide you with legal compliance, enabling work to commence, but peace of mind too!

SUMMARY

- Make sure the plot you are buying is worth the price being asked for it – conduct a proper development valuation assessment.

- Calculate construction expenses thoroughly and guard against underestimating. Be as meticulous as possible and repeat the process again in more detail once architect's plans are drawn.

- Instruct your solicitor at an early stage and explain your proposals thoroughly so they can offer you sound advice from an informed position. Ensure they undertake the appropriate searches and investigations and never contemplate buying a plot without first acquiring sufficient knowledge about it.

- Obtain full details of various self-build mortgage schemes before applying for any particular one. Ask about all the fees and charges associated with the loan and include these in your project cost analysis, together with the interest you expect to pay.

- When you buy the land, arrange for adequate site insurance and install security measures to protect yourself, your family, other site visitors and the new dwelling under construction.

USEFUL INTERNET WEBSITES

www.ricsfirms.com/spec.htm

A public access section of the Royal Institute of Chartered Surveyors where you can locate professionals from amongst 100+ specialised skill categories: everything from quantity surveyors to listed building experts are here.

www.adviceonline.co.uk

A good starting point where you can learn more about mortgages and receive free recommendations from independent financial advisors. There is also free access to guides and calculators.

www.barricade.co.uk

A firm offering a variety of security fencing to buy or hire for your plot of land. They cover all areas and deliver nationally.

Chapter 7
Taxation

This chapter covers:

■ records and receipts

■ value added tax (VAT)

■ council tax

■ capital gains tax (CGT)

■ stamp duty

■ tax advisors

There is every likelihood you began reading this chapter with a deep and melancholy sigh. Taxation is a subject that often evokes trepidation and foreboding but it is, unfortunately, just one of the inevitable consequences of owning and investing in property. Being aware of the implications at the outset can help you to prepare for what is an inescapable liability and enable you to budget for it. As with all matters involving duty payable to the government, it is imperative you become acquainted with the rules and regulations *before* you start your project. Then, by understanding what is involved, you can alter your plans accordingly and limit the effect that taxation will have in the long term.

For the self-builder, paying tax is thankfully not all doom and gloom. There is at least one distinct advantage, which is seldom reported in the press or promoted by government. It is a well-kept secret that professional developers have long exploited and sometimes at the expense of their novice counterparts. *At completion of the project, self-builders are able to reclaim most of the VAT paid on materials purchased for construction.* This can be a significant saving and one all too easily forfeited by making a late or defective claim. It is for this reason that we intend dealing with it in full at this early stage, along with other taxation issues that may affect you and the new dwelling.

RECORDS AND RECEIPTS

The earlier you get into the habit of keeping adequate records and retaining receipts the better. You may ask, 'But which receipts should I keep?' The answer is simple: *all of them!* No matter how insignificant they may seem, every paid invoice has the potential of improving the return on your investment and contains valuable information about what, when and who you bought materials or services from. It should become a part of your normal routine to sit down at the end of each day and write notes about:

- what you have done and who you have contacted;

- what you have ordered or paid for;

- how materials or services have been purchased (cash, cheque details, etc.);

- the supplier and their contact details;

- how the items or services will be used.

By keeping these records attached to the receipts in an organised and date-order manner, you will find it so much easier to identify them, when required, later into the project.

VALUE ADDED TAX (VAT)

VAT is charged as an additional percentage on most building materials (currently 17.5 per cent). Receipts should clearly identify the VAT element, but some may not, for example if they have been handwritten or the goods paid for with cash. In such cases, ask for a VAT receipt and check that:

- VAT has been paid on the goods;

- the supplier's VAT registration number is visible;

- the quantity and description of materials is given;

- the price for each item is on the receipt;

- your name and address is shown if the receipt value is more than £100;

- the receipt details are legible (ask for a replacement receipt if the ink is faded).

Receipts used for a VAT claim must be the originals; photocopies will not be accepted.

Forms needed for VAT refund

Obtain *Notice 719 – VAT refunds for do-it-yourself builders and converters* from HM Customs and Excise (HMCE). This explains the procedure in much more detail than we are able to do here and is an essential precursor to completing the claim forms. The notice and forms (VAT 431 parts 1, 2A, 2B, 3 and 4) are included in a *Self-Build Claim Pack* available from HMCE's National Advice Service. Telephone 0845 010 9000 or print the notice and forms direct from the website at **www.hmce.gov.uk/forms**

Can all self-builders make a claim?

No. The works must be carried out in the UK (including the Isle of Man, but not the Channel Islands), and the building must not be intended for business purpose use. Examples of people who cannot use the VAT refund scheme include speculative developers, landlords, bed and breakfast operators, residential care home operators, and membership clubs and associations. However, if you generally work from home and use one of the rooms as an office, you can still make a claim.

You do not have to conduct all (or any) of the work yourself to be eligible for a claim. If you employ a builder, you can still claim for the materials you provide him with to incorporate into the dwelling. You can also claim for 'fitting out' a shell bought from a developer, but you cannot claim for extra work you might do to a 'completed building' bought from a developer (for example, by adding a garage or conservatory).

There are restrictions where an existing building is to be demolished or converted into residential use, or where an existing residential building is to be extended or altered. See *Notice 719* for a full description of those who qualify.

Using a builder to supply goods and services?

Most builders' merchants and retailers charge VAT at the standard-rate on the materials they sell. However, if you employ a builder to supply goods, it depends on his VAT rating whether or not a) you will be charged VAT and b) whether, in turn, you will be able to claim for them. If the builder is zero-rated or reduced-rated for his work, then so too will the 'building materials' that he supplies. If you are charged VAT by your builder in error or at an incorrect rate, you will not be able to reclaim it. In general, if you employ a builder in the construction of a new dwelling, his services should be zero-rated.

What goods can I claim VAT back on?

Any 'building materials' defined by HM Customs and Excise that meet *all* of the following criteria:

■ They are incorporated in the building (or its site). This means they are fixed and form part of the structure (or site) and removal would involve using tools or result in damage to the fabric of the building (or its site) or damage to the goods themselves.

■ They are incorporated in the course of the construction or conversion of the building, for example works such as drainage, main paths, driveways, retaining walls, boundary walls and fences.

■ Builders of the type of building being constructed, incorporate them 'ordinarily'. For example, a tap is considered ordinarily incorporated, even if it is gold plated. Interestingly, other items considered 'ordinary' for the purpose of claiming VAT back include:

air conditioning	fixed bathroom towel-rails and soap dishes
burglar alarms	light fittings (internal and external)
fitted kitchen cupboards	heating systems
curtain poles	decorating materials
internal swimming pools	plumbing installations (including showers)
TV aerials	solid fuel cookers and oil-fired boilers
ventilation	power sockets
windows	doors
smoke alarms	solar panels

turf, plants and trees (but they must be detailed on a planning authority approved scheme and conform to planning conditions)

fitted wardrobes (restricted and conditional – see Notice 719)

[even this comprehensive list is *not* exhaustive].

■ They are not finished or prefabricated items of furniture (except kitchen furniture) or materials for the construction of fitted furniture.

■ They are not electrical or gas appliances. There are exceptions to this rule, including where the appliance is designed to heat space or water (including cookers with a duel purpose).

Building materials bought in any European Union (EU) member state qualify for a VAT refund. You can also claim the VAT back on importing materials into the EU, provided you can supply adequate evidence of the importation, and that VAT has been paid.

What goods can I not claim VAT back on?

Essentially, anything that does not form part of the structure of the dwelling or items outside of the site of the building cannot be claimed. This includes:

- fitted furniture (except kitchen furniture);

- most electrical and gas appliances, including washing-machines, refrigerators, waste-disposal units, door bells;

- carpets, including underlay and carpet tiles but excluding fixed flooring such as vinyl, ceramic tiles, parquet flooring and other wooden systems;

- garden ornaments, ponds, sheds and greenhouses;

- tools and equipment, including soil-moving plant and machinery;

- consumables not incorporated into the dwelling, for example sandpaper and white spirit;

- the land itself (see Chapter 6).

Can I claim VAT back on services received?

No. If you receive services from a builder, he should not charge you VAT (see above). You cannot claim VAT back on other professional and supervisory service fees, for example from architects, surveyors, designers, planners, managers and consultants. Neither can you claim for hiring or buying plant, tools and equipment (including scaffolding, skips and ladders).

When should I make my claim?

Ideally, when *all* the building work for your dwelling is completed (see Chapter 22). Bear in mind that *you are only allowed to submit one claim* so, if you decide to leave the construction of a driveway or paths or the landscaping of your garden until some later date, you will not be able to claim VAT back on the materials needed for these purposes. The construction is said to be complete when the dwelling is finished according to the original plans and, in cases of doubt, when the local planning authority issues a certificate of completion.

From the completion date, you have three months during which to submit a claim. If you anticipate a delay, it is essential you contact HM Customs and Excise to explain the reason because, if circumstances advocate leniency, they may provide you with extra time. Payment of the refund is usually made within 30 working days after submission of the completed forms and documentation, provided there are no additional enquiries made by HM Customs and Excise.

COUNCIL TAX

Council tax is a local tax set by local councils to help pay for local services. It is made up of two equal parts: the *personal* element and the *property* element. The personal element (50 per cent of the council tax) is based on the assumption that two people are occupying the property so, if you are the only qualifying person occupying it, you can apply for a single person discount. This is 50 per cent of the personal element, which is equal to 25 per cent of the whole bill.

It is important to be aware that, although the self-builder cannot evade paying council tax, his liability *can* be delayed or the amount reduced in certain circumstances. The concessions that are available to him are currently under scrutiny by the government and, if proposals become policy, the various discounts and exemptions presently permitted may be revoked. One such proposal is to remove the reduction entitlement to second-home owners, and provide local authorities with discretion to apply it or not in the region for which they are responsible. It may therefore be prudent in the future for self-builders to examine more closely which local authorities offer council tax allowances, before deciding on the location to build.

In addition, every local authority imposes different council tax charges. These are assessed according to the needs of the local population, the efficiency of the authority and the cost of services provided. You can find out what different local authorities are charging by visiting **www.local.dtlr.gov.uk** on the Internet (follow the 'council tax' link). Bear in mind that the amount of council tax may not just be of concern to you but also to any future buyers of your self-build home.

The question 'When will my new dwelling become liable for the council tax charge?' is a difficult one to answer. In theory, a chargeable dwelling will not exist until the building is capable of occupation, but that may occur before final completion. For example:

■ A dwelling that is constructed with all the basic facilities in place but lacks decoration, a stair balustrade or some internal doors, is likely to be deemed 'capable of occupation' by a listing officer. He will therefore take action to enter it in a council tax band on the valuation list, even though it may not yet be occupied.

■ A dwelling that is lacking basic facilities such as foul water drainage or is open to the elements or cannot be secured against intruders because external doors and windows have yet to be installed, will be considered unfit for occupation and will not therefore be council tax banded.

The most likely scenario is that liability will begin as soon as a 'completion notice' is issued for the property. The notice will specify a date when the building is deemed to be complete and, on receipt of a request from the billing authority to enter a band on the list, the valuation-listing officer must comply. The effective date for commencement of the liability will therefore be the date specified in the completion notice.

It is worth pointing out that a completion notice *can* be issued by the billing authority even though a formal inspection has not been requested, for example due to the construction taking longer than what the authority considers reasonable. There is a right of appeal if the self-builder believes the property remains unfit for occupation after a compulsory notice has been issued.

The variety of discounts and exemptions that are available depend largely on the living arrangements of the self-builder:

■ Caravans and mobile homes are not exempt from council tax so living in on-site accommodation will not help you to avoid the payment. However, if you are living in the family home as your main residence and using the caravan only whilst working at the site, you can apply for it to be 'empty rated' (generally a six-month exemption is allowed even if the caravan is furnished) – the grant of this allowance will depend on how the local authority classifies your occupation. Provided the construction work is not prolonged, the local authority may exempt the caravan by classifying it as 'temporary accommodation'.

■ Council tax on the newly completed dwelling can be minimised by keeping it unoccupied *and* unfurnished. It will be exempt for six months and liable to a 50 per cent 'empty' charge thereafter. This is helpful if your intention is to sell it rather than live in it yourself. Bear in mind that these concessions are not automatic – you must apply for them.

■ Students in full-time or a qualifying course of education are in the best position of all because they are completely exempt from council tax liability. So, if you have the time and energy to study *and* self-build, do it now!

Capital gains tax (CGT)

CGT is a tax on capital gains. For self-builders, this means the increase in value realised when the newly constructed dwelling is disposed of. It is at the point of disposal, that is when you no longer own the asset, that CGT payment normally becomes due. In some cases, the payment can be deferred – so whilst the tax cannot be evaded, it can sometimes be delayed. The most important concession is that *CGT is not usually payable on an individual's own home*. However, it *does* apply to second homes and therefore any self-builder who retains the family dwelling, whilst building a second one that he later intends to sell, needs to be aware of how CGT will affect him. Remember that, if you opt to live in the new dwelling, your old home could become a chargeable asset under certain circumstances.

The Inland Revenue provide self-builders with a concession not to occupy the new dwelling for up to 12 months whilst it is being built, or to remain in the family home whilst trying to sell it. After that, if you decide to occupy the new dwelling, you can make a principal residence election in respect of the new home. This provides exemption from CGT on the old home for a period up to 36 months. Once the concession periods have expired, you will become liable for CGT on any gains made from selling either the family home or the newly built dwelling, depending upon which you consider to be, and have nominated as, your private residence.

The rules are complex and the amount payable depends on many factors, including personal status, financial circumstances, others involved in ownership of the property, whether the property has non-business asset qualification, the period of ownership and, not least, the generosity of the Chancellor during any particular tax year. In an effort to minimise CGT liability, self-builders should consider the merits of obtaining professional tax advice before starting their project, during the construction phase, and at completion.

STAMP DUTY

Stamp duty is payable on certain documents. It is a charge levied in the UK for the transfer of ownership and the liability for payment falls on the buyer. Most self-builders are affected because they need to purchase a building plot and it is at this stage that good negotiating skills can save them a small fortune. For example, a plot advertised at £60,100 in February 2003 would attract a liability for stamp duty of £601. By negotiating to pay £60,000 (just £100 less), the self-builder would save himself the entire stamp-duty charge. The reason for this is that the threshold for stamp-duty is currently £60,001 and, beyond this, it is calculated at an increasing percentage for the entire sum (not just the amount beyond the threshold). So, any land purchase up to £60,000 is exempt; from £60,001 to £250,000 it is one per cent; £250,001 to £500,000 it is three per cent; and four per cent for more than £500,000 (accurate at time of writing).

Self-builders with a keen eye for development can escape stamp-duty liability by purchasing land (beyond £60,000 and up to £150,000) in certain designated 'disadvantaged areas' identified under the Valuation of Stamp Duties Regulations 2001. Visit the Inland Revenue's own website for full details: **www.inlandrevenue.gov.uk** or contact the Stamp Taxes Helpline on 0845 603 0135.

TAX ADVISORS

A competent tax advisor should be able to save you much more than the fee charged for their services. Their knowledge and expertise should guide you into making the best arrangements for the acquisition and disposal of assets. The timing of your self-build can also be of significance and they will suggest the best starting and most advantageous completion and/or disposal dates to legally minimise your exposure to taxation. When employing an advisor, it is important you provide them with full details of your employment particulars, financial resources and personal or jointly-owned assets, because they need to be able to see the big picture and not just the self-build part, so they can provide you with dependable good advice.

If you consult an advisor for help, make sure they are suitably qualified and a member of a recognised and regulated professional body. One such body is the Chartered Institute of Taxation, which can be contacted at 12 Upper Belgrave Street, London, SW1X 8BB or by telephoning 020 7253 9381. Use them to identify a local advisor or to check that the designatory initials CTA, FTII and ATII are genuine. The Institute also has a website at: **www.tax.org.uk**

SUMMARY

■ Keep receipts in a safe place and record the full details of all purchases for future reference.

■ Obtain the necessary forms required for your VAT refund and complete as you progress through construction.

■ Consider the physical and financial practicalities of completing all relevant work before submitting your VAT claim. Remember that you can only claim once so, if work remains outstanding after submitting the forms, you will not be able to claim the VAT back on any additional materials you buy.

■ Be aware that council tax is payable on most dwellings once they become habitable, but simple arrangements can remove, reduce or delay this liability when self-building.

■ The liability to capital gains tax can be avoided or reduced providing you observe the time-sensitive limits imposed by the Inland Revenue and apply for 'principal private residence' status appropriately.

■ Although stamp duty applies to land plot purchases, it can be avoided by buying land below the threshold or in designated disadvantaged areas.

■ The merits of consulting a professional and suitably qualified tax advisor, prior to starting your self-build project, should not be underestimated.

USEFUL INTERNET WEBSITES

www.moneyworld.co.uk

Visit the site's tax centre for up-to-date news about taxation and for a host of tax-solving tips, tools and guides.

www.digita.com

Use any of the tax central calculators to assess liability, including the amount of stamp duty you will need to pay on land purchase.

www.inlandrevenue.gov.uk/local/index.htm

Gives full contact and location details of your nearest tax and valuation offices.

Chapter 8
The House Design

This chapter covers:

■ the dream house or the first of many?

■ designing into the site

■ orientation of the site

■ external appearance

■ rooms and layout

■ integral or stand-alone garages?

■ future adaptations and extensions

■ architects and interior designers

■ alternatives: 'build in a day!'

For someone embarking on your first self-build project you should, by now, have decided on the purpose behind buying your plot of land. It may be the ideal site on which you intend building your dream home, or, the first of a number of speculative ventures through which you intend climbing the housing investment ladder. Regardless of your original intention, things can change as you progress along the road to completion, and if this happens to you, be comforted in knowing you certainly won't be the first to alter course mid-build. The majority of self-builders invest heart and soul in their creation and, once completed, some find it very difficult to part with.

Changing course is not a problem, except that the design may have been compromised by earlier plans. This can reduce the enjoyment of an ideal home or diminish the profit of one built for sale. Take time out now to contemplate your intentions. Think things through logically, until you have established with 100 per cent certainty exactly what it is you want from the new dwelling. Once your aspirations are confirmed, the route ahead will seem clearer and the process of designing into the site much less complicated.

THE DREAM HOUSE OR THE FIRST OF MANY?

For the 'first of many', it is economical to design and build so that the minimum required legal standards are satisfied. Although elements that will appeal to most home buyers should be included in the design, you will need to keep a more watchful eye on the marketability of the finished dwelling, whilst reducing construction costs to an absolute minimum. Combining these objectives successfully can be a difficult conjuring trick, but it is essential if you are to realise enough profit to help fund your next project. An aspiring developer needs to be detached from any personal feelings they may have for the dwelling. By looking upon the construction coldly (and only as a means of increasing profit), they are able to avoid the mistake made by many novice investors, who indulge excessively in personal design whims. The golden rule is: *don't design for yourself if your intention is to build for others!*

In most cases, this is likely to be the self-builder's one venture into creating a home for themselves and their family and, as such, time and consideration should be given to assessing how they would really like to live and enjoy their home. This is likely to be the most pleasing and enjoyable part of the entire venture. It involves using all of your creative skills, widening your horizons to such an extent, that aspirations and desires become actual blueprints for the house of your dreams. You will need to consider your family's daily, weekly, seasonal and annual routines and invite ideas from all involved to devise a mutually satisfying scheme.

The design of the house will involve careful analysis of the site. You must:

- exploit the plot of land to its full potential;

- explore the possibilities of the dwelling's external appearance, giving due regard to the locality and other neighbouring properties;

- plan the internal layout based on living requirements now and in the future;

- decide the position, prominence and scope of a driveway for vehicle access, parking space and garaging.

The process can begin in many different ways:

- you may wish to emulate an existing property you have seen elsewhere;

- you may have a basic design concept that needs expanding;

- you may have visited a show home and would like to adapt its design;

- you may have a photograph or sketch from a book or journal that has inspired you to consider self-build.

As the design process begins, it will soon become evident when architectural assistance is required to achieve your goal. The services offered by professionals in this field range from simple plan drawing to total design, and every level in between. A complete service might include:

- an initial consultation where the architect can assess your innermost desires for the new home, the scale of funds available for your project and your general likes and dislikes regarding style;

- the development of your own design ideas into basic plans and schematics;

- the suggestion of using new and innovative materials and products you may not previously have known even exist;

- the production and submission of plans for local authority and building regulation approval;

- the supervision of construction and certification at each required stage to enable the release of funds from your bank or building society;

- arranging for and overseeing the issue of a completion certificate when all construction has finished.

The extent of involvement required by your professional advisor will depend entirely on personal circumstances and the level of your own practical skills, experience and knowledge of the building process. It may also be determined by a mandatory condition attached to any loan advance. The employment of architects and drawing technicians is discussed in more detail later in this chapter.

It may interest you to know that the self-built home of one of the co-authors of this book was developed from a single image: Gandalf's hat from *The Lord of the Rings*. The concept was progressed from sketches to plans and finally produced a unique sundial-roomed building with a magnificent central atrium (see Chapter 9, Figs. 8 and 9). His home is evidence of the fact that designing your own dwelling has only two limits: the degree of funds available and the bounds of your own imagination!

DESIGNING INTO THE SITE

Assessing the full potential of your site will involve some outdoor contemplation, so choose a dry and sunny day where possible. Stand at a suitable position on or close to the roadway outside the plot and consider:

- Is the access route level or does it slope up or down?

- Is there a natural level area where the house can be sited?

- Is there natural shelter from the elements to one side of the plot?

- Are there any other buildings close to the boundary?

These factors will influence where you position the house. Excavations are costly and anything that can reduce major-earth moving work should be considered an advantage. A first priority will be to explore how the natural and existing features of the site can best be employed. Bear in mind that by disturbing or removing mature trees and shrubs you could endanger the foundations of other nearby properties and this situation should be avoided wherever possible.

Visualise positioning a house-sized block on the plot of land. Ignore for now the number of storeys, shape or form. This part of the exercise is purely to determine land levels and the amount of work that may be required to create a flat plain for the house to sit upon. Considerable expense can be avoided by limiting the volume of excavated material to be removed from the site (and the costs associated with tipping it). In addition, the use of natural levels can reduce the necessity for retaining structures that would otherwise certainly be required to stabilise the land around the dwelling. There can also be legal implications if changes in the level have an impact on an adjoining owner. Complications are the last thing you need as a self-builder, as they invariably cause delays which will cost you both time and money, so avoid, wherever possible, having to enter into secondary legal agreements in which permission to dig below a neighbour's foundations or existing ground and garden levels becomes necessary.

Now turn your attention to the family's vehicles and where they will be parked in relation to the 'block'. How will they get to the dwelling? Is a drive required and, if so, could it follow the contour of the land or will some levelling be needed? Remember to consider 'all weather' conditions and the daily needs of your family; for example, in icy weather a gentle gradient will allow the delivery of shopping direct to your front door whereas a deep slope may prevent vehicle access.

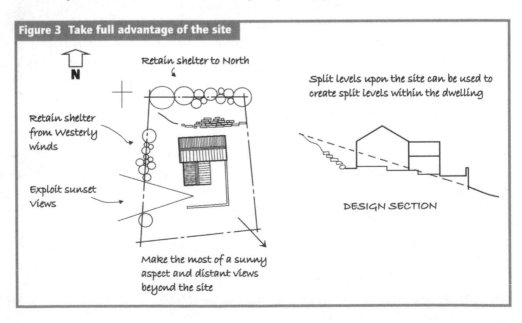

Figure 3 Take full advantage of the site

N

Retain shelter to North

Retain shelter from Westerly winds

Exploit sunset views

Make the most of a sunny aspect and distant views beyond the site

Split levels upon the site can be used to create split levels within the dwelling

DESIGN SECTION

In this broad overview of the potential of your site, it is worth remembering that the plot and 'block' will be subject to further contemplations and considerations. It may be that some ground material will have to be removed to create a pleasing contour for the garden area or for other proposed buildings such as a garage or greenhouse. Time spent now considering the site and its general layout could save hours of wheelbarrow work later on and particularly at the stage of designing and landscaping your garden. Once you have the position of the 'block' and any driveway roughly confirmed, commit it to paper by making a sketch of the plot boundary and the basic elements within it. Include any notes about how you arrived at the decision and what influenced you. The sketch and notes will be useful as a reference and will remind you about what has been decided and why, as you proceed through the next stage.

ORIENTATION ON THE SITE

Visualise the 'block' once again and now move position so that you are standing within it on the plot. Look beyond the boundaries and into the distance to assess the views. Use stepladders to gain some height, then repeat the process, bearing in mind that most of the rooms in your dwelling are likely to be above ground level. Think about the principal living areas and what you would like to see from them, as this will help you to decide the orientation of your 'block' and where the main rooms will be ideally located. If the site is very restricted and distant views are obstructed, consider the alternative of choosing the most secluded and private corner of the plot where you can eventually create a peaceful and serene view of your own.

For your next observation task you will need a sunny day. Stand in the space of the 'block' and look outward from it. Identify the journey of the sun through the day, pinpointing the position of sunrise and sunset. The aim here is to ensure you take full advantage of natural daylight and warmth when planning the position of your new home. Ideally, the morning sun should greet rooms such as bedrooms, the breakfast room and kitchen; whilst living rooms, formal dining rooms and other reception areas will benefit from afternoon and evening sunshine. If the intention is for a dining area or conservatory to link up with an exterior patio or garden, be certain to include this in your plans. There is nothing more advantageous than being able to enjoy the last few hours of sunshine in your garden or dine with a magnificent view of the sun setting.

It is worth remembering that, historically, people in the pre-industrial revolution period sited their homes to take full advantage of natural heat (produced by the sun). They also created garden areas that could be enjoyed at the end of the working day all through the summer months, and made certain that important rooms benefited from natural daylight. As the density of populations grew and people moved increasingly to live in towns and cities, the choice over house design and orientation has become more restricted. Consequently, they are now valued more intensely than at any other time. A good view and sunny garden are now worth a small fortune and add to the attraction and value of all residential property for sale!

Having considered the general orientation of the house, you should now stand inside the 'block' again and think about how the house and garden areas will function. For example:

■ **Control and security**. Do the location and neighbourhood demand good front-aspect observation? If you need to keep an eye on who is coming up the path to your front door, the more frequently used rooms will need to be at the front of your house. Alternatively, you may choose to install an electronic surveillance system such as closed-circuit television, which would allow other reception areas to take priority at the front.

■ **Main entrance and parking**. How important is the main entrance to you? How will visitors be greeted? The answer to these questions may encourage you to create an imposing approach to the dwelling with a sweeping driveway and enough space for several vehicles to park.

■ **Deliveries and collections**. Where will electric, gas and water meters be sited? If the intention is to place them at the rear of the property, how will inspectors gain access to read them? And what about the location of dustbins and the receipt of mail, milk and newspapers?

■ **Natural elements**. If an old stone wall on the site is particularly attractive, try to absorb it into your scheme. The same is true for mature trees and shrubs, large rocks or boulders and many other natural features, which can add instant character to the finished dwelling. An early decision needs to be taken whether to keep them or lose them, because the position of these elements may dictate the orientation and position of the property.

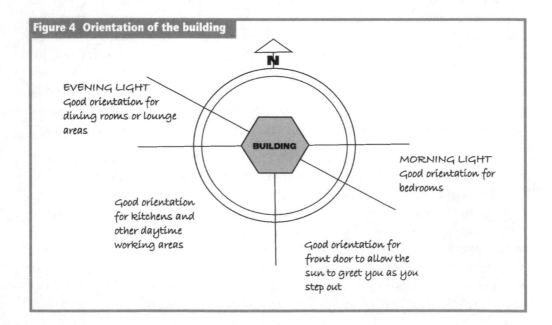

Figure 4 Orientation of the building

EVENING LIGHT
Good orientation for dining rooms or lounge areas

MORNING LIGHT
Good orientation for bedrooms

Good orientation for kitchens and other daytime working areas

Good orientation for front door to allow the sun to greet you as you step out

BUILDING

■ **Size and shape**. The size and shape of your plot of land is likely to impose limits on what can be done with it. For example, a long narrow plot with a small frontage will influence the direction that major rooms will face and may well be the deciding factor in whether to build a single or two-storey property.

EXTERNAL APPEARANCE

The external appearance of your self-build project will be affected by planning control to a greater or lesser degree. If your plot stands within a conservation area or within the curtilage of a listed building, the controls are likely to be strict and inflexible. The characteristics and building references will already be determined according to an existing property or those in the neighbourhood. The design of your dwelling, and the materials you can use to build it, will be specified in rules and regulations affecting the site and, of course, this may well be the reason why you chose the location in the first place.

Alternatively, where planning controls are more relaxed, greater flexibility is possible and you will only be limited by your own and your designer's imagination. But where do you look for inspiration? Architectural and home-style magazines are useful and there are many widely available from good newsagents. The public library will also stock reference material on the subject and it is also worth visiting high-street bookshops to search for ideas. Whenever you are out and about, look at residential dwellings with a more inquisitive eye. The design of certain buildings may strike you as more attractive than others and, as the saying goes, imitation is the sincerest form of flattery. No one will criticise you for following someone else's design lead.

An idea does not have to encompass the entire building. There may be an entrance porch you have seen that is particularly captivating, or the formation of a wall or roof shape that could be incorporated into your own design. The same is true for internal aspects such as the colours, textures and materials used for floor tiles and doors; the style of glazing used in windows; the contour of a stairway; and even simple detail such as a cupboard handle or light-fitting. The diversity of inspirational ideas can originate from visits to historical homes and gardens, art galleries and museums, holidays abroad, and even from memories of childhood. There is a wealth of stimulation contained in the world around us but, for most, these pass by without a second thought. The self-builder should consider the buildings he visits as a rich source of conceptual ideas he can admire, adapt and adopt.

There are an extraordinary variety of building materials you can explore. The choice of materials will greatly influence the external appearance of your new home and, whether traditional or contemporary, it is the way in which they are likely to weather and age that should be considered a priority. The life expectancy of many lightweight materials is limited, and poor quality goods may suffer from the detrimental effects of rain, wind, pollutants, sunlight and frost. It is worth remembering that the external appearance of your home over time will be inextricably linked to the calibre of materials you use. There is no escaping the fact that quality counts!

Do not feel you have to be limited by the range available through your local builders' merchant. Take inspiration from architectural and design magazines that usually list the contact details of materials featured and, if an architect and/or designer is already on board, he will be happy to suggest alternatives and even obtain samples for your consideration. The Internet is another infinite source of design concepts and materials and, with the entire world at your fingertips, the only danger is that you will become flooded with an abundance of new ideas. These are just a few sites worth visiting:

www.archrecord.construction.com	A compelling mix of design concepts, ideas and trends from the US magazine, *Architectural Record*.
www.collectivedesigns.com	America has been self-building for decades and this site has a huge range of plans and designs which, if liked, can be ordered online (may not comply with UK regulations). A very inspirational site.
www.greatbuildings.com	An impressive gateway to architecture around the world, with over a thousand photographs and details of outstanding contemporary and historic buildings.
www.housebuilderxl.co.uk/plans	One of only a few UK sites offering a good range of online plans and design schemes at affordable prices.
www.ibstock.co.uk	Ibstock is one of the country's leading suppliers of bricks, and this site offers the self-builder photographic access to 1000s of designs, colours, textures and shapes.

The Internet is useful for software too. '3D Architect' is a company who produce several exceptional programs, all of which offer superb and inspirational design facilities to the self-builder. One such product allows you to create a two-dimensional plan and then watch as it is reconstructed into a three-dimensional model on your computer screen. There are endless tools, fill patterns, shapes and materials you can explore to produce your finished design (see Figure 5). Once you have become familiar with the program, you can create as many designs as you like, and then gradually narrow down the features, materials, styles and elements, until you have your dream home identified. For more information telephone the company on 01420 520023 or visit their website at: **www.3darchitect.co.uk**

The shape and form of the external aspect of your self-build home may be determined by the function and scope of rooms within it. Conversely, internal planning may be secondary to a distinctive exterior design. If design is not prohibited by location, consider as wide a variety as possible before settling on any one in particular. Every decade of the last century has produced its own unique style of residential property, and each has its merits and handicaps. Those that are attractive to you could form the basic framework out of which a new design could be cultivated. On the other hand, if you want to combine different features and fashions, aim for subtle interpretations to achieve a successful blend. Fusing together two extremes is difficult but not

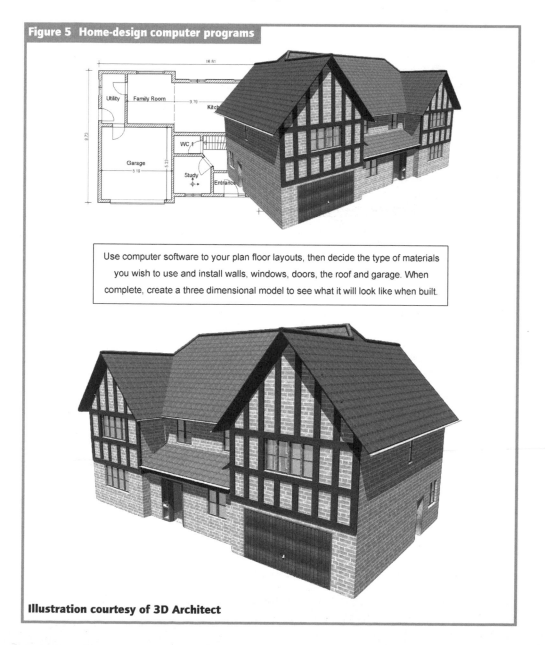

Figure 5 Home-design computer programs

Use computer software to your plan floor layouts, then decide the type of materials you wish to use and install walls, windows, doors, the roof and garage. When complete, create a three dimensional model to see what it will look like when built.

Illustration courtesy of 3D Architect

impossible: fad and convention can make good partners when paired carefully. Good examples of this are now visible in our major cities where modern steel and glass have been used to refurbish historic or traditional buildings.

The outline of the external shape and form is referred to as 'the massing'. When considering this aspect you should look at:

- **Roof design styles**. For example, several small roof areas can add interest to the overall roofline whereas either one large roof or no roof visible at all can look elegant and appealing.

- **The levels**. For example, the way in which single-storey and two-storey levels connect can change a box-shaped dwelling into a much more interesting home.

- **Outdoor space**. For example, the inclusion of courtyards, an internal garden area or walls that help extend the building form can improve the exterior space and help to improve privacy.

- **Single-storey designs**. The long, low and graceful lines of a single-storey dwelling can take a self-build scheme in a completely different direction.

Once the basic shape of the dwelling has been decided, the major external features start to present themselves, and the architectural design begins flowing in a progressive and almost natural manner. The first and most prominent of these features is the actual door and principal entrance to your property. Consider whether the main intention is for this is to be a solid barrier protecting the private areas beyond, or a visual link from inside the home to the exterior with expanses of glass. It is possible to combine the need for security and privacy yet still produce a bright, welcoming and elegant entrance area by using appropriate materials and a little design flair.

Remember that the entrance will be the first thing you and your guests see when approaching the dwelling. It should be strikingly impressive and a focal point for all who visit your home. However, it is easy for mistakes to be made at this crucial stage and you must be careful not to go-over-the-top with your design. For example, the owners of some traditional 1930s stock semi-detached properties have constructed entrance areas of Roman proportions with marble pillars and stone columns, totally out of keeping with the neighbourhood and properties adjoining. There is a fine line between grandeur and absurdity, so be wary of creating something colossal which will be inappropriate for the area.

By defining the massing and the entrance point, you will have considered two of the most important features of your house, and this will enable all other external character references to be developed. These include:

- the window design, size, shape and positioning;

- the patterns and shape of the outer shell, such as brick colour and design, string-courses (a projecting line of mouldings along the face of the building), quoins (external angles and corner stones), corbels (supporting stone or timber projections from walls) and smooth cladding;

- the use of visual timber details;

- outbuildings such as garages and storerooms, workshops and annexes and whether these are to be linked with the main building;

- the inclusion of chimneys and roof-lights and the form they will take;

- the garden and pathways and how hard landscaping will be formed, for example with paving, cobbles, pebbles, timber decking, shingle or brick.

These are the aspects and features that will determine the external appearance. They will influence (and be influenced by) the internal layout.

ROOMS AND LAYOUT

This is the moment you sit down with a blank piece of paper and consider what rooms you would really like. Do you want a games room or a music room, a red room or a green room, a Japanese room or a Mediterranean room? The list is endless and entirely decided by the personalities and interests of you and your family.

If you enjoy cooking and entertaining, a huge kitchen may be a priority and here you can create your own separate storage room or pantry and build-in all the facilities desired. Artists might want to have their own tranquil studio with views over the garden or, if you work from home, how about an office with enough power points and shelving to meet your needs. Instead of an en-suite in the master bedroom, you could have one for every bedroom and a fully tiled and waterproofed walk-in shower-room, instead of a cubicle. You could also create room-sized wardrobes and separate dressing rooms with enough hanging and storage space for you and your family, now and in the future. Did you ever fancy having your own gym, or a sauna and steam-room or a soundproofed den for the children? Now you can have them because, when you are building your own home, the possibilities are infinite.

We have already looked at the major living areas (kitchen, dining and reception rooms) from an exterior position, including their orientation to the site and the views they might enjoy. It is now important to consider the relationship they should have with each other and the distance from the point of entrance. It may be advantageous, for example, to have the dining room near to the kitchen so that hot food can be transported easily. Are the rooms to be on one level or split levels? This may depend on the fall of the site. Are reception areas to be open plan, with a single decorative style, or closed rooms with distinctly different styles? Are the rooms to be physically linked in some way? For example, a second doorway could allow you to walk direct from the dining room to the main living room without entering a common hallway. You might also consider the flexibility of walls and rooms. It is possible to have sliding screens and panels and movable (non-supporting) walls, so the interior can change according to need and mood. This kind of design requires a great deal of careful thought and planning but, once achieved, it makes the internal space extraordinarily versatile and creates an exciting and ever-changing home. We all move our furniture around from time to time to create a different look – imagine being able to move the walls as well!

Whilst contemplating the position of rooms in relation to one another, it is worth visualising how the layout will affect guests. If you plan having a large entrance hall as a major feature, it may be desirable to have guests return to this reference point before entering other rooms. Alternatively, the hallway may be your main link to more private areas of the house, such as a home-office or the bedrooms, so you will need to devise a plan which would keep guests restricted to the main living areas instead. Bear in mind that you are not confined to the traditional designs adopted by builders and can create corridors, hallways and access routes according to desire and preference.

The number one complaint amongst those who buy new homes from established developers is the lack of adequate storage space, which makes this element a major consideration for self-builders. Think about the rooms and what you will be using them for. Then assess what you will need to store in them. For example:

- In the kitchen, will you require a pantry, a utility room, and an ironing or food preparation area? Where will all your gadgets, pots and pans, crockery, dry stores and tinned foods be kept? What about glassware, large casserole dishes, summer entertaining goods, your 'best' dinnerware and tablecloths? And, if you enjoy a variety of good wines, this is your opportunity to create suitable storage for as many bottles as you would like to keep, or even to create a full wine cellar maintained at the appropriate temperature.

- In the main living room, where do you intend storing your compact disc collection, videos, DVDs, books and magazines?

- In the dining room, you might want to have suitable out-of-sight storage for a multitude of different table decorations, candles, napkin holders, condiments and serving dishes.

- In the breakfast room, you could plan to store an assortment of toys for the children, have a place to keep keys secure and display a comprehensive cookbook library. You could even have a concealed built-in safe for treasured documents, jewellery, credit cards and chequebooks.

Minimalists and enthusiasts of open-plan living will find they need far more storage space than others to prevent rooms becoming cluttered and untidy. A room that is constantly 'on view' should have sufficient hidden space for all non-ornamental items.

Unless you are proposing to construct a single-storey dwelling, you probably intend the bedrooms to be on an upper floor. This is the traditional building method and the place where we have been indoctrinated into thinking they ought to be – but there is nothing that says it *has* to be this way. The design is entirely up to you and, if you wish, you can create bedrooms on the ground floor, on different levels or even in a basement. By changing the location of bedrooms, you can gain space for other rooms to occupy the upper floor, for example a living room that would then enjoy panoramic views beyond the plot's boundary, or a large main bathroom with split-levels, double-basins, podium bath and Jacuzzi.

INTEGRAL OR STAND-ALONE GARAGES?

The location of the garage can affect the layout of the dwelling and the design of the pedestrian access routes and driveway. For example, if your intention is to have a garage at the rear of your property, which would provide better security for your vehicle, you will need to consider how you can drive to it and how the garage will intersect with the main dwelling. Other matters of concern include fire-protection for the house and connecting doors into it from the garage (useful in bad weather and for personal security). Alternatively, a garage at the front of the property could be used to create a barrier of buildings that could help prevent intruder access to the rear.

We all store a multitude of tools, equipment and half-empty tins of paint in our garages, and here is the opportunity to plan proper storage of these items. If you have sufficient land, you might want to build a separate workshop or secure shed where garden maintenance equipment, sunloungers, bicycles, general building tools and all those tins can be kept in an organised and tidy fashion. In fact, if the garage is planned to be a stand-alone structure, it may be prudent to build this before construction starts on the main dwelling because you will then have a safe and secure place to keep equipment and to work whilst operations proceed on the house.

Consider also the fact that building above the garage could create a useful annexe for guests, a private space for your teenage children to relax and play music (as loud as they want without disturbing anyone else), a study, home office or artist's studio. Access to it could be gained from the main dwelling or by steps on the outside, as required. As with the garage and other outbuildings, plan to install electricity, water and drainage so these additional spaces become multi-functional and are easily converted for other purposes, if a need arises in the future.

FUTURE ADAPTATIONS AND EXTENSIONS

At the design stage, it is wise to think about your immediate requirements *and* how things might change over the next few years. Extending your family may involve a demand for more bedrooms, particularly as children grow into young adults, but when they leave the parental home, the space needed for sleeping accommodation may be less. Careful planning can prevent these rooms becoming redundant. For example, connecting doors between two bedrooms could allow the conversion of one into a dressing room, walk-in wardrobe or even a private sitting room if elderly parents need to be accommodated in the future.

As funds improve, appropriately located dining rooms may enable the addition of a conservatory, and living rooms could be opened onto gardens and patio areas. Bedrooms could be extended to create guest wings, and guest wings extended to create leisure facilities.

Built-in flexibility is the key to maintaining a home fit for the future. Although adapting your new home may not necessarily be considered a priority at this stage, planning for it is essential if the design is to withstand the inevitable change in circumstances and requirements that will occur over time.

ARCHITECTS AND INTERIOR DESIGNERS

Architects are a diverse group of professionals and it is essential you identify the right one to help you, if you are to be successful in creating *the* dream home. Personal recommendation is always useful, but only if you are certain the architect is *tuned in* to your own personal and preferred style. When you approach an individual architect or an architectural practice, ask for an initial consultation to assess:

■ what their area of speciality is: residential, commercial, contemporary or traditional;

■ their experience of self-build schemes;

■ whether they have the required skills and expertise to satisfy your design plan and to produce an innovative and unique scheme;

■ the cost of their services, according to both their own and your expectations of the time and involvement required;

■ whether you are able to develop a good working relationship with them, so that your desires and aspirations are appreciated and interpreted accurately;

■ their ability to produce plans for submission to the local authority planning and building control departments and supervise the construction through to completion, if required;

■ whether they are members of a professional body, such as the Royal Institute of British Architects (RIBA).

The contact details of local architects can be found in *Yellow Pages* or through professional organisations. RIBA offer a client advice service with access to a database of architect practices, including details of the type of work they undertake. Contact them on 0207 307 3700 or in person at 66 Portland Place, London W1N 4AD.

There is a cheaper alternative to using an architect, but only if you have progressed your design to the point where you know *exactly* how you want your new home to look (and providing any mortgage lender hasn't made the employment of an architect a mandatory requirement). Architectural technologists, once known as technicians, tend to draw plans in detail according to a set of instructions and have less artistic flair than architects. They construct drawings from a 'scientific' perspective, which means they are able to produce plans once given a pre-defined guide to work to, but they are less able to offer advice on imaginative solutions to problems or be innovative in design. For more information, contact the British Institute of Architectural Technologists at 397 City Road, London EC1V 1NE or telephone them on 0207 278 2206.

If you intend consulting an interior designer, you should follow the same enquiry procedure as outlined above for employing an architect. It is essential you check that they are suitably qualified and experienced and are able to provide you with the kind of inspirational designs you seek. Although there is no nationally recognised formal training, there are college and university courses including a BA Honours degree and a diploma in interior design. Always enquire what form of certificated training they have had and ask to see samples of their previous work. Professional interior designers should be up-to-date with modern technology, systems and materials, and have access to a wide variety of hard and soft furnishing suppliers. A good designer will be enthusiastic about your plans and sufficiently motivated to produce visually exciting colour, fabric and layout schemes. If you employ an interior designer, make sure they are aware of the architect involved at the earliest possible stage, and visa-versa, because the work of each will impact on the other. It is imperative they communicate with each other, and with you, to enable production of the most effective and dynamic design plans.

The British Interior Design Association (BIDA) exists to promote and support the profession. It encourages excellence in design through education, training and continued professional development. Its members keep up to date with the latest statutory regulations and carry professional indemnity insurance for the protection of their clients. BIDA can be contacted at 1-4 Chelsea Harbour Design Centre, Chelsea Harbour, London SW10 0XE or by telephone on 020 7349 0800. Their website at **www.bida.org** has contact details of members operating throughout the country.

Most architects and interior designers are creative and intuitive people, but they are not usually psychic! It is important you communicate your desires at the outset, explaining what it is you need from them and what you expect them to do for you. Also inform them about yourself, your preferred design style and living arrangements, so they can produce layouts and plans that match your personality and standards. If you feel your professional advisor is heading off in the wrong direction, tell them, so that they don't waste time (and your money) creating something unsuitable.

ALTERNATIVES: 'BUILD IN A DAY'!

As the self-build movement grows and expands, so too does the volume and variety of services being offered. There are now companies available up and down the country that will happily relieve you of the burden of self-build by supplying a complete design and build package. The service comes at a considerable cost and there is usually some compromise that has to be made regarding construction, but this can be an answer for those who have time and/or skill-related obstacles that would otherwise prevent the project from proceeding.

Some offer to take your ideas and convert them into plans, then arrange and manage the entire construction on your behalf (known as a 'turnkey' project). Others have a range of 'off-the-shelf' timber-frame homes that they can deliver on a low-loader to the plot for you to assemble, being much like a flat-pack item of furniture, though rather larger and more complex than your average wardrobe! There are combinations of turnkey and timber-frame packages to suit every situation and virtually all budgets.

The following list represents a small selection of companies offering these services (others may be available locally through architects and/or builders):

Design & Build	**Timber Frame Packages**
Abbott Project Services Ltd	Border Design Centre
Tel : 01293 822835	Tel : 01578 740218
www.abbottps.co.uk	**www.borderdesign.co.uk**
Benfield ATT	Christian Torsten
Tel : 01291 437050	Tel : 01939 233416
www.adtimtec.co.uk	**www.christiantorsten.co.uk**
Custom Homes	House Builder XL Ltd
Tel : 01787 377388	Tel : 01530 415600
www.customhomes.co.uk	**www.housebuilderxl.co.uk**
Design & Materials Ltd	Keywood Homes
Tel : 01909 540123	Tel : 020 7724 6578
www.designandmaterials.ltd.uk	**www.keywoodhomes.com**

Fleetman Construction
Tel : 01522 778455
www.fleetman-construction.co.uk

K F Hume
Tel : 01256 881344
www.kfhume.freeserve.co.uk

Lifestyle Construction Ltd
Tel : 01949 869183
www.lifestyleconstruction.co.uk

Neatwood Homes
Tel : 01981 240860
www.neatwoodhomes.co.uk

Newhaus Systems
Tel : 01745 585952
www.newhaussystems.co.uk

Potton Self-Build
Tel : 01480 401401
www.potton.co.uk

Sierra Designs
Tel : 01977 513249
www.sierradesigns.co.uk

Scotframe
Tel : 01435 868898
www.scotframe.co.uk

Springfield Properties
Tel : 01343 552550
www.springfieldproperties.co.uk

Woodco
01847 821418
www.woodco.clara.net

SUMMARY

- Commit yourself to building either a dream home for yourself or one to sell at a profit and don't alter this course unless absolutely necessary.

- Identify the most advantageous position for your new home on the plot, giving due regard to the direction of the sun, the lay of the land and any neighbouring properties.

- Consider the internal aspects according to the type of property being built, the views available, security and access.

- Try to be unconventional when planning internal rooms and their position in the dwelling, as this will encourage you to find unusual solutions to any problems.

- Identify the best location for a garage and space to accommodate additional vehicles on the site.

- Don't just plan according to your needs today – think about how your family circumstances and resulting living requirements might change over time.

- Employ an architect when required and make sure they are the right person for your self-build project. Ask to see examples of their work and confirm they have the ability to transfer your design aspirations into construction plans.

- If you decide you don't want to get physically involved in the construction of your new home, consider the alternatives, including a turnkey project or timber-frame 'off-the-shelf' design and build package.

USEFUL INTERNET WEBSITES

www.marcus-beale.co.uk

A site for architects and their clients with an excellent guide on the work you should expect your architect to undertake, once appointed (follow the 'small works' page links).

www.rias.org.uk

The Royal Incorporation of Architects in Scotland website provides access to a huge database of professionals working in this part of the UK.

www.kpmdesignonline.com

This site is said to be the UK's largest online source of interior design information, including details of 1,800 interior designers and architects.

Chapter 9

Planning Permission

This chapter covers:

- planning permission

- outline permission to detailed design

- changing existing planning approval

- the considerations

- the choice of materials

- detailed design to approval

- approval conditions

- the appeal procedure

The grant of planning permission is governed by primary legislation contained in The Town and Country Planning Act 1990 and The Planning and Compensation Act 1991, and by several Statutory Instruments including The Town and Country Planning (General Permitted Development) Order 1995 and The Town and Country Planning (Use Classes) Order 1987. There is a hierarchy of legislation and regulations dealing with associated issues such as conservation, mobility and disability, green belt land, listed buildings, general housing and tourism. This area of law is complex and planning consent for your self-build project is therefore best dealt with by your architect.

The repercussions of failing to acquire proper permission can be disastrous. The authorities have the power to impose severe fines, enforce corrective action and, at worst, they can compel perpetrators to return the entire development to its original state. Neighbours and other third parties affected might also have a cause for taking action against you. Those who transgress the planning system can lose everything – their savings, their business and even their own home – simply by failing to acquire the appropriate permission before starting construction.

Many self-builders operate through slightly blinkered vision, believing that the local authority planning officer's main role is simply to frustrate them at every step of the way. But, in reality, the legal requirement to receive consent for building something new is essentially one intended to protect the environment in which we *all* live.

Whilst we may view the decisions being made as directly affecting only ourselves and what we want to do, the planning officer sees it from a much wider perspective. They need to satisfy themself that the proposed dwelling does not adversely affect the surrounding environment and the other people who live in it, that construction methods and materials are in keeping with current legislation *and* that the completed building will be sympathetic in appearance to others nearby.

PLANNING PERMISSION

Virtually all proposals to build new residential dwellings require planning permission. The likelihood is that you are buying a plot of land *with* outline planning permission (OPP) attached to it. If not, then it will either have no planning permission at all or detailed planning permission (DPP).

Land sold with an existing OPP means it has already been established, in principle, that a new building can be constructed. However, the type and size of dwelling, the method of construction and materials used, have yet to be approved. As the saying goes, 'everything is in the detail', and the site of the property, its design and layout, orientation, access and landscaping, are all contained in what is known as a 'reserved matters' application. This follows after an OPP has been received. The OPP and the approved 'reserved matters' application together form the equivalent of a detailed planning permission. Once an OPP has been granted, the buyer of the plot has three years during which they must submit the 'reserved matters' application, otherwise the entire process begins again or, alternatively, they could just proceed with a DPP application.

If the plot has both OPP and 'reserved matters' consent, it is essential you check the wording of the approval and any conditions attached which may restrict the design, extent of development and construction of the new dwelling. Particularly important are:

- the legal implications when the rights of neighbouring land and/or property owners are involved;

- any rights of way that may exist;

- the rights and physical ability to connect to services outside the plot, which may be on a nearby public highway or three fields away, thereby requiring the negotiation of easements (a right or privilege to cross the land) with adjoining owners;

- the design limitations, which may reduce your interest in the scheme and prevent you from building 'the dream home'.

An OPP does not have to be in your own name (unless you are the one making the application), because approval refers to the site and not to the individual seeking it.

If you *are* the person making the application, your initial enquiries will be concerned with five rudimentary elements, from which you will be required to seek approval based on one or more of the following:

1. Siting
2. Access
3. Design
4. External appearance
5. Landscaping

It should be understood that approval could exist without certain important issues being resolved. Some local authorities will request additional information, for example they may enquire how the site is to be drained, or seek confirmation that easements are in place for connection to mains drainage. There is no statutory obligation for an authority to follow this rather heavy-handed early course of enquiry, though many do simply to prevent minor problems developing into bigger and more protracted arguments later.

There is good reason for arranging a pre-application meeting with a planning officer of the local authority where the land is situated. Most officers welcome such arrangements being made and will offer constructive informal advice to assist you in submitting a successful application. Always telephone for an appointment beforehand and attend with whatever documents and details you have already in your possession. If the officer is amenable, it is best to arrange an on-site meeting, where you can explain your proposals more fully and with reference to what actually exists. The officer will help you by pointing out site-specific elements that concern them and any which are likely to affect the planning application. These will include:

- the access route proposed onto the site and its impact on neighbouring properties, highway safety and the environment generally;

- the natural features of the land and surrounding area, for example, ground levels, hedgerows and trees – the alteration or removal of which might be detrimental to the landscape or subject to other legislation;

- the relationship with existing buildings on and off the site and how the position of windows, orientation on the site and structure size and height, may affect them and their owners;

- obstructions to any development, for example overhead cables, telegraph poles, electricity pylons and water courses running over or under the plot.

The planning officer is likely to be aware of any previously unsuccessful applications relating to the site and will give advice about how you can alter your plans to reverse an earlier decision. Once you have spoken with them, you should have a clear indication about the likely outcome of making a formal planning application. But, whether the officer's comments are positive or negative, they are *not* definitive. It will be the council's planning committee that makes the decision and, although they may take note of an officer's comments, they do not always rely on them during the final analysis.

An OPP, in its simplest form, should be considered as a red line around a piece of land with a representative block showing the position of the intended dwelling. A plainly drawn site-plan, together with a one-line description of the development proposal, is all that is required. All other aspects can be appraised at the detailed design stage. Be aware that intricate particulars are not helpful or required for the OPP application so, when describing the kind of development being proposed, explain it in simple terms. For example, 'the erection of a dwelling with garage' is usually quite sufficient. The forms required are available from your local authority planning department together with guidance notes to help you complete them.

One final point, if your plot is close to and/or likely to affect a listed building, you will not be able to make an OPP application because the planning department will need to have full details before they can consider the implications. If your plot falls within the curtilage of a listed building, it is highly likely the design of your new build dwelling will come under very close scrutiny and be subject to the most stringent development controls. These will affect the materials you can use, the style of dwelling and the attention to detail. These mandatory restrictions will increase the construction costs considerably and a reappraisal of the scheme will be necessary to assess and justify continuing with it.

OUTLINE PERMISSION TO DETAILED DESIGN

A building-plot *with* OPP approval is all very well, if you are the one selling the land, because the value rises accordingly, but as a buyer you will need to assess how relevant it is to your own self-build project. It may be appropriate to tackle any concerns over easements through your architect and solicitor, while you gauge the value of the land and its full potential. By the time you decide whether or not to purchase the land, you will have already checked the outstanding 'reserved matters' and be aware of just how restrictive these issues might become. These investigations may confirm that the land is suitable for your intentions or, conversely, that the design plan you had will need altering, if you are to continue any further with this particular plot.

At the point of land purchase or immediately afterwards, and following discussions with your architect and solicitor, you will have examined all of the physical and practical aspects of the site and be ready to develop it to its maximum potential. Once the external aspects of your house design are on paper, you will be able to submit a formal DPP to the local planning department (see Figure 10 for a typical example of a completed planning application form).

An application for detailed planning permission (also sometimes referred to as 'full planning permission') involves providing the local authority with all the particulars of your proposed dwelling. Drawings produced must show the intended structure's location and orientation on the site, parking spaces and driveway, access position, floor plans, elevation plans and/or graphic illustrations of how the dwelling will look from the front, back and each side. When applying for full permission, you must give due regard to the 'site-specific' elements that the planning committee will consider before reaching their decision. It is essential that you examine each element and address any issues or concerns before submitting your application:

■ **Access**. The highway authorities will be consulted by the council on matters relating to your self-build project and access arrangements. The major issues are vehicle parking and turning space on and off the site, traffic flow and safety. The local authority will be able to inform you about the highway standards pertinent to your plot and location. You must ask for these details – it is unlikely they will be supplied voluntarily. Once in receipt, read them carefully and examine your proposals to assess what impact they will have. It is essential you meet the standards or address any issues by providing documentary evidence and alternative proposals, to prevent a refusal of your application.

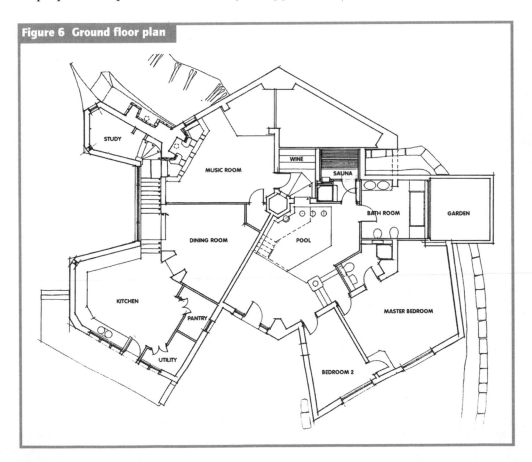

Figure 6 Ground floor plan

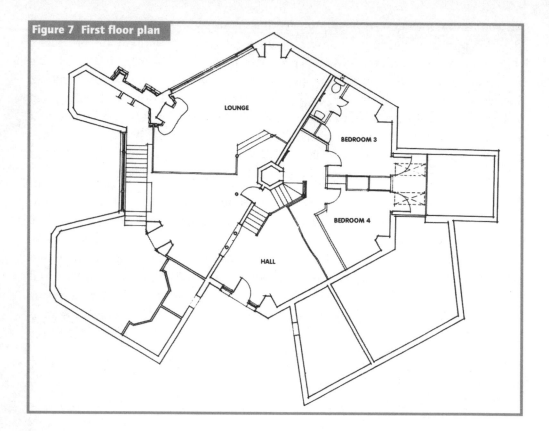

Figure 7 First floor plan

LOUNGE

BEDROOM 3

BEDROOM 4

HALL

■ **The lie of the land**. Sloping sites present a real challenge to architects, because retaining walls and split-level designs must be aesthetically acceptable to neighbouring property owners and others affected by them. Access can also be a problem, particularly if a driveway causes a vehicle to be parked above the level of a nearby highway. Cross-section drawings are useful additions to any planning application involving a sloped site, and these should show the levels and any proposed changes.

■ **Size and shape**. It is crucial that you obtain an accurate scale plan of the site, particularly if the shape is complicated and the plot small. It may be easy enough to construct one for a square or oblong-shaped piece of land with parallel lengths and widths, but you may need a land surveyor to assist you with more complex shapes. The plan can then be used to assess how the fundamental structures of the dwelling (house and garages) and other important elements (drive, access, paths and garden areas) fit onto the site. It should be noted that many applications fail because of 'over building', that is, trying to fit a large house or too many elements on a small plot. Plan according to the land available and you will improve your chance of succeeding.

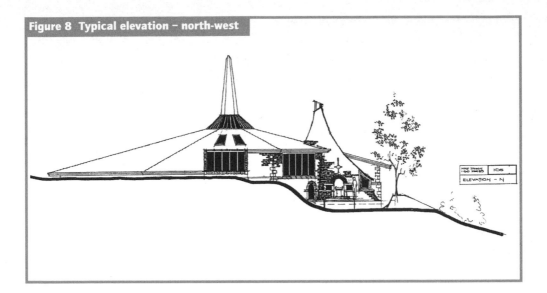

Figure 8 Typical elevation – north-west

- **Orientation**. Whilst your priority might be to secure the best views, maximum sunlight and suitable access for your new home, the position of the proposed structure may cause problems to neighbouring property owners. Objections could arise, if neighbours feel they will lose some natural light or privacy.

- **Ground conditions**. It is not so much the ground condition itself that concerns a local authority, but the extent of any design constraints on the dwelling caused by it. The exception is a plot with contaminated land, because it has health and safety implications and the authority will want evidence of how you intend dealing with it.

Figure 9 Typical elevation – south-west

■ **Trees**. Councils are concerned over the loss of mature trees, now and in the future. So they will not only look at the impact of any proposed site clearance prior to construction, they will also consider the repercussions of any trees you may want to fell in the future. The council's concerns will include how tree felling will affect the soil structure and landscape, and the resulting loss of privacy or weather protection to adjoining properties. The conservation of protected trees is quite another matter and one we will discuss in more depth later in this chapter.

■ **Services**. Although you may have identified mains services existing close to the plot and believe connection to them will be straightforward, there are restrictions on the proximity of building work to pipes, cables, sewers and mains gas. The danger is that construction work might damage these installations, and you should find out, in advance, what degree of exclusion zone exists. This can vary according to the size of plot and scale of construction. Approach the planning officer for advice on this subject and also each individual service authority.

■ **Legal complications**. These will usually come to light through your solicitor when they examine the deeds for the land and any covenants that may exist. There are, of course, other matters and some we have already outlined include easements, public footpaths and limitations imposed by the 'use' class. It should be remembered that even though planning permission might be received despite a contrary legal issue, this does not give you the right to build your property because, in doing so, you will still be breaking a prior agreement or legal obligation. It is always advisable to attempt a settlement of any outstanding legal issues before making an application and certainly before buying the land, as this removes obstacles that could ultimately frustrate the construction process or even prevent it starting.

■ **Current use**. Councils will consider the existing use of the land and decide whether your proposal is likely to improve or aggravate it. If a derelict building occupies the plot, then clearly demolishing it and building a new residence would be seen as largely favourable. However, if the site has always been open land, then building on it might affect the landscape and potentially infringe on a facility enjoyed by local people. Consider carefully what impact your project will have and devise plans which will appease any anticipated protests.

When submitting application plans, it is important they include an accurate reference to the boundaries of your plot. Your solicitor and architect will assist you to mark up the legal boundary on a site plan and, once identified, it should be thoroughly checked on site. Over a period of time, neighbouring landowners and other users may have planted hedges or built walls that trespass onto the plot, or a prior owner of the plot may have trespassed on your neighbour's land without any objections being raised. Incorrectly positioned existing boundary hedges, fences and walls are likely to confuse the proper identification of a boundary and, depending on the length of time they have been in place and any earlier agreements made, it may prove difficult, if not impossible, to remove them.

Figure 10 Typical example of a completed planning application form

PART ONE

Planning Application Form

Please read the guidance notes which
will help you to complete this form.
4 copies of the form and 4 sets of
plans should be submitted.

1 Name and Address of Applicant and Agent

Name and Address of Applicant

Name   JOHN SMITH

Address   603 LAPWING ROAD

MANCHESTER

Postcode M92 8ZB Daytime Tel. No.

Name and Address of Agent (if any)

Name   G. BROWN ASSOCIATES

Address   96, MARKET PLACE,

MANCHESTER.

Postcode M26JT Daytime Tel. No. 0 1161 8945

Person to contact   PARTNER

2 Proposed Development

A Location or Address of Proposed Development

LAND ADJOINING MARKET FOLD,
SEVERN LANE, MANCHESTER

B Description of Proposed Development (specify the number of units in the case of housing development)

ERECTION OF TWO STOREY DWELLING
AND GARAGE

C Size of Site (edge in red on submitted site plan)   O.15 hectares

D Is the proposal for a temporary period? Answer YES or NO No   If yes, for how long

E Do you own or control any adjoining land? (edge in blue on submitted plan)   Answer YES or NO No

3 Type of Application

Please tick **one** box

A This is an **outline** application   ☐ If so go to Question 4

B This is a **reserved** matters application   ☐ If so go to Question 4

Outline Application No.

Date of Outline Permission

C This is a **full** application for:-

(i) Building or engineering operations only ☑

(ii) Change of use **without** any building or engineering operations at present ☐

(iii) Change of use **and** building or engineering operations ☐

(iv) Mining operations or waste disposal ☐ Complete additional form

(v) This is an application for **renewal of a temporary permission** ☐

Application No. of existing permission

(vi) This is an application for **removal or variation of a condition** of a previous planning permission ☐

Condition No.   Application No.

Now go to Question 5

4 Outline Applications and Reserved Matters Application

If you have ticked **A** or **B** in Question 3, please tick the relevant boxes.

Do you wish to seek approval for any of the following matters as part of this application? Answer YES or NO ☐

If yes, please tick the relevant box(es).

Siting ☐   Design ☐   External Appearance (including materials) ☐   Means of Access ☐   Landscaping ☐

Figure 10 Typical example of a completed planning application form *continued*

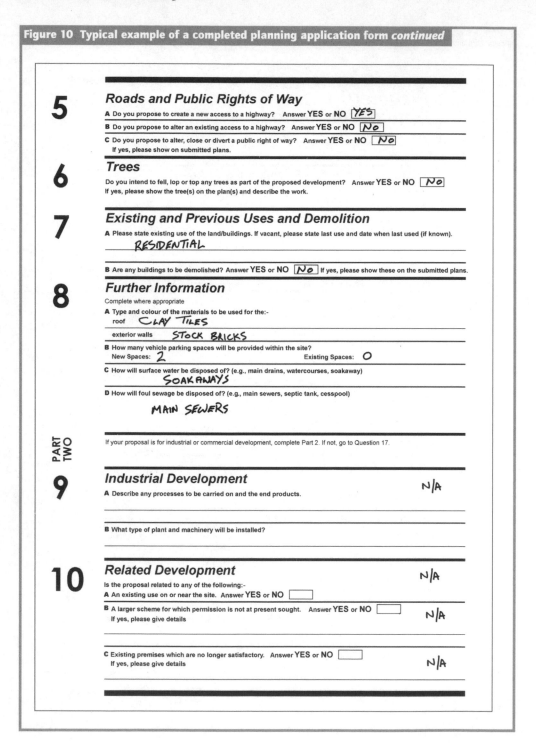

5   Roads and Public Rights of Way

A Do you propose to create a new access to a highway?   Answer YES or NO YES

B Do you propose to alter an existing access to a highway?   Answer YES or NO No

C Do you propose to alter, close or divert a public right of way?   Answer YES or NO No
If yes, please show on submitted plans.

6   Trees

Do you intend to fell, lop or top any trees as part of the proposed development?   Answer YES or NO No
If yes, please show the tree(s) on the plan(s) and describe the work.

7   Existing and Previous Uses and Demolition

A Please state existing use of the land/buildings. If vacant, please state last use and date when last used (if known).
RESIDENTIAL

B Are any buildings to be demolished? Answer YES or NO No If yes, please show these on the submitted plans.

8   Further Information

Complete where appropriate

A Type and colour of the materials to be used for the:-
roof CLAY TILES

exterior walls STOCK BRICKS

B How many vehicle parking spaces will be provided within the site?
New Spaces: 2   Existing Spaces: O

C How will surface water be disposed of? (e.g., main drains, watercourses, soakaway)
SOAKAWAYS

D How will foul sewage be disposed of? (e.g., main sewers, septic tank, cesspool)
MAIN SEWERS

PART TWO

If your proposal is for industrial or commercial development, complete Part 2. If not, go to Question 17.

9   Industrial Development   N/A

A Describe any processes to be carried on and the end products.

B What type of plant and machinery will be installed?

10   Related Development   N/A

Is the proposal related to any of the following:-
A An existing use on or near the site. Answer YES or NO

B A larger scheme for which permission is not at present sought.   Answer YES or NO   N/A
If yes, please give details

C Existing premises which are no longer satisfactory. Answer YES or NO
If yes, please give details   N/A

Figure 10 Typical example of a completed planning application form *continued*

11 Floorspace   N/A

Please specify the total amount of floorspace involved in the proposal.
If more than one use is involved, please specify the extent of each use.

12 Employment   N/A

A How many new staff will be employed on the site as a result of the proposal?

B How many existing staff are employed on the site?

C How many of the new staff will be transferred from other premises?

  Please give the address of the other premises

13 Hours of Working   N/A

Please specify the proposed hours of working/opening.   Thursday

Monday   Friday

Tuesday   Saturday

Wednesday   Sunday

14 Servicing   N/A

What provision will be made for loading and unloading and the turning of vehicles within the site?

The location of such provision should be shown on the plans.

15 Vehicular Traffic Flow   N/A

How many vehicles will visit the site during a normal working day? (excluding employees vehicles)

a) Heavy Goods Vehicles: b) Other Vehicles:

16 Hazardous Substances

Will the proposal involve the use or storage of any substances of the type and quantity mentioned in Note 16?

Answer YES or NO [   ]

If yes, state the substances and quantities   N/A

17 Interest in the Site

State the nature of the applicant's interest in the site (eg: are you the owner, lessee, prospective purchaser etc.)

OWNER

18 Please Complete

I/We submit this application and attach the necessary plans.

AND I/We attach a completed ownership certificate

AND I/We enclose a fee of £   [220~00]

Signed   J.Smith

On Behalf of   Date   1st Aug. 2003

Disputes with neighbours over the position of boundaries are not uncommon and they often rise to the surface when a new owner buys land and wants to use it in a different way from that of their predecessor. The best course of action is to mark the site plan with a red line showing where you and your solicitor *believe* the boundary ought to be. This should be used for the planning application and any disputes can then be settled later.

CHANGING EXISTING PLANNING APPROVAL

The owner of the land might have had an earlier intention to develop it and could have submitted a DPP application themself. There may even be an approval in place. In either case, it is likely you will want to re-submit your own detailed proposal based on your personal requirements and aspirations, because these will inevitably differ from the prior application.

Of equal importance is any prior application that has been refused. Armed with details of the refusal, you can set about amending your application to meet the requirements of the planning authority. In addition, there will be a record of comments made by neighbours, the highway authority, drainage authority and the parish council, which should assist you in producing a more viable application.

It is important that you recognise the environmental changes that may have taken place from the time of an earlier planning application refusal to the present day. Objections made by neighbours may no longer occur because the ones objecting have since moved out of the area. Once stringent design controls may now be more relaxed. A new highway might have been built or a road layout changed to address an earlier safety hazard. These and other examples could mean that an application will succeed, not because of changes to the scheme, but simply because of everyday changes to the environment and attitudes that occur with the passage of time.

THE CONSIDERATIONS

The primary interest of the council will be whether your planning application meets the policies contained in its 'local plan'. There are policy documents called 'structure plans', devised by county and regional councils, which lay down the standards, instructions and restrictions for the development of the county. The policies embrace issues such as town expansion, new highways, protection of the countryside and the building of new dwellings. District councils use the structure plan as a reference when creating their own local plan.

The local plan is essentially a written document stating the district council's development policies. It is accompanied by a 'proposals map', which details the area governed by the local plan and identifies where specific policies apply. For example, it will show clearly the areas where new housing can be built, as well as where new housing is prohibited. The local plan's main purpose is to identify and distinguish areas of countryside, towns and villages, and protect each against invasive or insensitive development.

Taking the above into consideration, it may seem easy enough for planning committees to examine the structure plan and the local plan when deciding whether or not a new dwelling in a particular location will be allowed. If only things were that simple! Unfortunately, policies frequently contradict each other and, even when they don't, they can be open to different interpretations. This means that nothing can ever be said to be 100 per cent certain and, although all applications to the planning authority must observe local plan policies, each scheme will also be considered on its own merits.

There are very specific policies pertaining to conservation areas, areas of outstanding natural beauty (national scenic areas in Scotland) and green belt land. The local plan will show which areas are covered by these policies (if any) and particular care will be needed in the design and presentation of your scheme, if affected. In addition, any land that is considered to be of archaeological merit will be subject to supplementary rules and regulations limiting development or setting out construction procedures. These policies are not exclusive or exhaustive. Local councils may also identify and designate zones of particular interest, referring to them as 'areas of high landscape value', and these will have yet more policies applied to them.

We mentioned earlier that a tree preservation order (TPO) could protect some trees on your site. This in itself does not prevent you from felling or pruning them if the scheme demands it, but such action can only be undertaken *after* planning approval has been received *and* assuming the local authority were informed about the tree felling or pruning when the planning application was made. The position of protected trees will be known by the local authority tree officer, whom you should consult at the earliest opportunity. TPOs can be applied to any species or size of tree. The unauthorised removal, pruning or damage caused to a protected tree is an offence and liable to a severe fine of up to £20,000.

THE CHOICE OF MATERIALS

For a planning application to be successful, the choice of materials used and the design of the dwelling should be sympathetic with the surrounding area. This is particularly relevant in sensitive locations such as a conservation area, where local architectural styles and the use of local materials is often a compulsory prerequisite to any new construction.

There are numerous examples in our towns and cities of brash and incongruous buildings standing out like a sore thumb amongst their neighbours! These are situations where architects, builders, planners and the local authority all got it wrong. But then there are other examples of extraordinary modern structures that seem somehow to fit harmoniously amidst traditional historic buildings. The elements that make one design look right and another look wrong are fiercely debated amongst planning officers up and down the country and, in reality, there can never be a simple set of rules guaranteed to unify a structure with its environment. There are just too many variables.

Steel and glass are the favoured materials of our age, and constructions using these materials have erupted in some of our most ancient towns and cities over the last few years. Despite grumbles from a minority of traditionalists, these contemporary buildings appear as sculptures on the skyline, standing proud but also nestling comfortably amongst their Victorian counterparts. This blend of 'the modern' and 'the old' works because of the simplicity of materials (frequently walls of pure glass being the only visible part) and meticulous attention to design. There is no reason why you cannot emulate this mix of style on a smaller scale, but be aware that it will be a risk, and fainthearted committee members could thwart the scheme at the planning application stage. That said, sometimes the brave do succeed and consequently enjoy the reward of living in a unique home.

DETAILED DESIGN TO APPROVAL

Once you or your architect have submitted the planning application, it is useful to monitor its progress as closely as possible. The council will issue an acknowledgement, confirming (hopefully) that the application has been correctly submitted and that the consideration process has begun. The letter will include a planning reference number and usually an indication of the date a decision can be expected (normally within eight weeks). Whenever you communicate with the council, you will need to quote the reference number given, so keep the acknowledgement handy.

After two or three weeks, and assuming nothing has been heard in the meantime, contact the council to assess progress. Enquire about any formal objections and ask when the case officer will be visiting the site. At least three days before the committee sits to consider your application, a report containing the planning officer's recommendations will be produced for public inspection. This is an appropriate time to submit supplementary evidence, which will back up your case, and reply to any concerns expressed.

Some local authorities provide applicants with an opportunity to speak at the committee meeting. If this is allowed, ask about speaking-time limits and go prepared with the results of any new research you have undertaken or other documented evidence, which may be helpful. Always attend the committee meeting in person and, if practical, take your architect with you.

The committee may pass the application and grant planning permission for you to build your home (subject to building control consent and other conditions) or they may refuse it outright. In the case of a refusal, it is important you take notes about what has been said, so that you can address these issues before making a new application. Alternatively, the committee may defer a decision. A deferral is usually made when the committee wish to receive additional reports or make further enquiries or request changes to the scheme that will make it more acceptable. Consider a deferral as a second chance to get your scheme approved. Use this time profitably to strengthen your case or to remedy concerns expressed by the committee.

APPROVAL CONDITIONS

The planning permission will always have conditions attached to it. One of these will be the timescale for starting work and this varies according to each local authority, but generally the period is five years. Work must begin within the timescale, otherwise a new application will be required. There are certain standard conditions, such as a requirement for materials used in the construction to be approved by the council, and there are also usually more site and design specific conditions, which will depend entirely on your individual scheme. You must observe the conditions and keep to them or you will be in breach of planning consent.

THE APPEAL PROCEDURE

If your application is refused, there is an appeal procedure. All appeals are made to the Secretary of State (England & Wales). This may sound rather discouraging at first but, in fact, appeals are heard by inspectors from the Planning Inspectorate on behalf of the Secretary of State. An appeal must be submitted on a prescribed form within six months of the council's decision. There are variations of the procedure for Scotland and Northern Ireland. In Scotland, appeals are decided by the Inquiry Reporters Unit and, in Northern Ireland, by the Planning Appeals Commission.

Most appeals are dealt with by written representations, but the success rate is low, and advice should be taken from your architect about whether it is worthwhile proceeding or not. In most cases, it will be beneficial to submit a new application with amended plans which take into account the comments of the planning committee. If you do decide to appeal, you will need to deal fully with the explicit criticisms and concerns expressed by the committee. Appeal forms and a set of guidance notes can be obtained from the Planning Inspectorate, Temple Quay House, 2 The Square, Temple Quay, Bristol BS1 6PN; in Scotland from the Scottish Office Enquiry Reporters Unit, 2 Greenside Lane, Edinburgh EH1 3AG; and in Northern Ireland from the Planning Appeals Commission, Park House, 87-91 Great Victoria Street, Belfast BT2 7AG.

Summary

- If the plot has an existing outline planning permission, find out how long it has left to run and whether this will provide you and your architect with enough time to prepare documents for the 'reserved matters'.

- If the plot has 'reserved matters' in place or has full planning permission, examine the details thoroughly to confirm they are appropriate for your self-build scheme. Alternatively, submit your own planning application describing your original scheme.

- Arrange an informal meeting on-site with the local planning officer. The advice and information they can offer you to prepare your application ARE invaluable.

- Always get professional assistance if your scheme is likely to be affected by a nearby listed building or where the plot lies within a conservation area, on green belt or is designated as an area of outstanding natural beauty.

- Consult the council's local plan and devise a scheme that conforms to the policies contained within it.

- Once you submit your planning application, follow its progress and be prepared to respond quickly and competently to any concerns expressed formally or informally.

Useful Internet Websites

www.planning-applications.co.uk
A superb site that provides independent professional advice and guidance on town planning and related issues, with links to information on the Scottish and Northern Ireland planning systems.

www.ukplanning.com
The UK's leading planning portal that puts you in direct contact with planning services throughout Scotland, England and Wales, offering straightforward concise information and advice.

www.tagish.co.uk
Claims to maintain the most up-to-date list of links to local government websites including county, metropolitan, unitary, borough and district authorities. Also contains a list of town and parish council sites. From here you can visit your local planning department, get forms, seek advice and view local policies.

Chapter 10
Building Regulations

This chapter covers:

- practicalities before starting to build

- statutory obligations

- structural considerations

- drainage

- natural and mechanical ventilation

- heating and insulation

- fire protection

- going beyond the minimum standards

The Building Regulations contain the minimum requirements designed to protect the health, safety and welfare of all people involved with buildings. This includes members of the public, occupiers, neighbours, visitors, disabled people, and maintenance and construction personnel. The Regulations also enforce standards aimed at conserving fuel and energy, and deal with such additional matters as fire safety, access, protection from impact, toxic substances and glazing safety. They affect all buildings in England and Wales (Scotland and Northern Ireland have their own set of Regulations) and are created by the Secretary of State, under powers provided by the Building Act 1994.

The Great Fire of London (1666) prompted the Government of the time to issue by-laws to prevent the spread of fire between buildings in London. Later acts of parliament expanded their scope to deal with sanitation and public health. In 1965, these local building by-laws were replaced by national Building Regulations, which exist to this day. The current format (Simple Regulations plus Approved Documents giving technical guidance) of the Building Regulations was created in 1985. They are divided into 'parts' and each 'part' deals with a specific technical aspect of construction or design. The Building Regulations were fully updated and reissued in both 1992 and 2000, with further major amendments in 2002. Whilst writing this book, an additional six revisions were announced.

They are one of the most complex set of rules ever devised and complying with them is a formidable task. Just understanding them is difficult enough! The problem is that they are open to different interpretation and do not remain static. The Building Regulations are a fluid set of documents that are constantly added to, amended, revised and updated, according to when new research is undertaken, new methods devised and new materials produced. Even those directly involved in enforcement of the Regulations, such as local authority building control officers, and those acting on behalf of clients, such as architects and surveyors, find keeping up to date is often demanding and arduous – so self-builders acting on their own really do not stand much of a chance!

This is one area of professional advice where the value of your architect can be truly recognised. Once given an insight into your proposals, ideas and the variety of materials intended for construction, he can suggest a means of achieving compliance with Building Regulations. This may involve some degree of compromise, or alternatively he may discourage progressing the scheme any further because it is unrealistic and impractical. Early advice is essential to prevent proceeding with, and spending funds on, what may prove ultimately to be a futile project. These initial discussions with your professional advisor are the equivalent of 'laying theoretical foundations' for your self-build venture – only by exploring what is possible within the confines of the Regulations can you safely proceed to plan and build.

PRACTICALITIES BEFORE STARTING TO BUILD

Having obtained planning consent, it is crucial that you chart the process through in job sequence order and resolve all construction issues, prior to presenting them for Building Regulations approval. This will provide a set of information details that confirm your plans comply with the minimum standards as laid out in the statutory documents. Once these are submitted to the local authority, formal approval should be received.

However, this procedure will not provide you with a full set of construction drawings. For you to carry out the work yourself or for your builder to begin the work, you will need to request detailed drawings from your architect. The information required will need to include specification and preparatory detail for:

- the setting-out for foundations;
- the setting-out for walls (internal and external shell);
- the setting-out for all openings (windows, doors, etc.);
- the type and composition of concrete mix to be used;
- the type and composition of mortar mixes;
- all other materials to be used (timbers, compounds, bricks, etc.).

Any structural requirements, such as unusual foundations, beams, flooring and roof elements, will be identified at this stage, and your architect will advise on the employment of a structural engineer, who may be required to provide the necessary dimensions and calculations. Your architect will also arrange for the details to be submitted to your local authority for approval.

Once approval is received, make several copies of the drawings so you can identify clearly the aspects of work you intend doing yourself and those you propose subletting to a contractor. The drawings will be needed by outside agencies so they can assess the scale of work involved and compile accurate estimates and quotations. This process will also help you to manage the construction time frame and assess the cash-flow situation as work progresses.

STATUTORY OBLIGATIONS

The local authority is charged with the responsibility of first inspecting the proposal on paper and then establishing whether the intended dwelling complies with all current regulations. To consider and eventually issue an approval, they need to inspect your plans and for this they will charge a 'plans inspection fee'. You will receive a formal decision after the checking process is complete. A copy of the approval notice will be of considerable value when you approach financial institutions, solicitors, surveyors, other professionals and advice agencies.

The second function of the local authority building control section is to conduct site inspections to ensure the actual construction complies with the regulations. A couple of days before starting work, contact the building control officer to make arrangements for their first visit, and explain your proposals so the number and timing of future inspections can be planned. Traditionally, inspections are conducted at:

- commencement of the build;
- excavation of foundations;
- pouring of concrete foundations;
- damp-proof level;
- drainage testing;
- completion of the dwelling.

After the first site visit, you will become liable for payment of the inspection fees to cover all subsequent visits. The final inspection will be to check the building conforms to the approved drawings and, if it does, the building inspector will 'sign it off' and grant the issue of a 'Completion Certificate'. This is a very important document and should be safely stored for future reference. The certificate is essential if your intention is to sell the property, because your conveyance solicitor will require it. A copy may also be required by your lender to release any outstanding funds.

STRUCTURAL CONSIDERATIONS

A full set of construction details from your architect will enable you to set out and construct with confidence, knowing that every building element is accounted for and all aspects are equipped with guidance instructions and drawings.

It is worth noting that the Building Regulation requirements are only *minimum* standards and these *can* be improved upon. For example, floor joists, stud partitions and roof timbers will all flex slightly, even though the timbers are within recommended sizes. While they will be far from flimsy, they will almost certainly benefit from a more robust approach to the materials used for construction. Increasing the size of joists will make for a much more stable and solidly built house. Similarly, lintels over doorway and window openings can be made from metal, which are lightweight and easy to lift into place. But if solid fixings are required, for example for curtain poles and rails, then a heavier concrete lintel will prove much more practical.

The whole structure will benefit from being solidly built. Increasing the amount of bracing between floor joists and the number of noggins in stud partitions will eradicate movement within each element, and also help resist differential movement between elements. If it is both practical and financially viable, aim to build your home with materials that go beyond the limited quality of your approved specification. It really is worth doing. The advantages to living in a more substantial home will be realised immediately and for very many years to come.

DRAINAGE

As the construction details are being prepared, it is very important to assess all environmental health issues relevant to a domestic dwelling, and drainage is a factor of considerable significance in this process. A foul drainage waste disposal system must be designed to provide adequate falls throughout the pipework and ensure proper ventilation back up through it. Ease of access for maintenance is another matter that must be carefully considered and planned.

The lay of the land is just one of many influencing factors which will determine the method and means of installation. If underground drainage pipes are positioned at too steep a pitch in hilly regions, this can result in a separation of solids and fluids leading to occasional blockages. Conversely, in low-lying regions, a more critical design approach must be taken as falls can sometimes be as small as 1 in 60 or even less.

Calculations for the anticipated volume of waste materials the household will generate are tabulated to determine the fall and diameter of pipework required. This vital information will be made available to you and marked on the construction drawings. However, it will be your responsibility to interpret this data and lay drainage in accordance with the instructions and specifications given. To this end, you will need to become familiar with one of the several methods available for assessing and measuring ground levels.

The easiest of these is to hire professional electronic survey equipment from your local hire shop and follow the instructions given with it. But for those who prefer to 'get stuck in', the Ancient Egyptians provided a time-proved method that has survived to this day and continues to be used by builders up and down the country. It involves the application of a long length of conduit or tubing and a graded funnel at each end to measure and transfer a level over a considerable distance. Originally, this system allowed the Ancient Egyptians to measure up or down relative to the first level and, with careful planning, they successfully established high performance conduits over vast stretches. Modern variations of this method have evolved in the form of long lengths of hose with graded measuring tubes at each end, and these are available from most good builders' merchants.

There is a definite point in the stages of your self-build when the excavation for and installation of drainage should be undertaken. The connections from the exterior to inside the structure are often made very early so that masonry bridges below ground are created and made available at the appropriate junctures. This can be planned when forming the lower wall sections by installing bridged holes to accept the drainage pipework.

In commercial buildings, the underground pipework tends to be composed of hefty glazed clayware, but most domestic situations rely on plastic systems. These are produced in a wide range of sizes and are accompanied by connectors and small manhole units which, depending on how they are put together, provide endless network possibilities. Unlike their clay counterparts, plastic drainage pipes are impact resistant yet lightweight and very easy to handle. In fact, they are at their most vulnerable to becoming damaged whilst above ground resting on the building site awaiting installation. If the pipes are not stored in a safe place and tied down, they can easily be caught by a gust of wind and blown in the way of a manoeuvring delivery truck or excavator.

The building inspector will be happy to advise the most suitable time for excavating trenches and laying pipes, which is best done when the risk of crushing by heavy vehicles and deliveries has passed. The inspector will also want to witness a formal and predetermined testing of the system to ensure everything works according to the plan and within specification demands.

NATURAL AND MECHANICAL VENTILATION

Care must be taken to provide adequate ventilation to all habitable rooms in the dwelling. This involves the installation of opening windows and more subtly controlled 'trickle' venting for the removal of condensation and the replacement of stale air.

Fitting extractors in certain rooms usually provides mechanical ventilation and is a requirement determined by the Building Regulations. Minimum standards again apply in this situation and extractors must be designed to operate within specific parameters. Mechanical extraction and ventilation generally pertain to areas that generate large volumes of moisture and odour, such as kitchens and bathrooms.

The minimum volume of air to be extracted will be stipulated in terms of litres of air per second. However, this can result in a noisy intrusion into the room, which despite *sounding* efficient may not actually *be* efficient. Typically, extractors supplied as part of, and fitting neatly into a kitchen design, and some smaller devices available for bathroom ceilings, do not always perform as well as one would like, and create considerable noise, particularly if they are not regularly cleaned of dust and grime. A better method is to install a larger fan along the duct and away from the extract grill. This will reduce the background noise while increasing efficiency.

HEATING AND INSULATION

Heating systems have evolved considerably over recent years and there is now an appliance available to suit every conceivable situation. The conventional gas boiler with piped water and radiators remains one of the most efficient and cost effective, but the wise self-builder will at least explore the variations and consider whether the traditional approach best suits his particular dwelling and living arrangements.

Hard surfaces such as stone or ceramic can benefit from underfloor heating, which will warm these cold materials and improve the level of comfort afforded during cold mid-winter periods. Underfloor piped hot-water systems are easily included within a traditional system along with, for example, decorative radiators or heated towel-rails. Alternative energy sources, though criticised for being expensive in the short term, are available in various forms for those who are more environmentally aware and 'keen to be green' in their self-build. It is rare for these sources to fully provide for the entire needs of the household but, as a supplementary heat source, they can be cost-effective and well worth installing. It is of course important for the two systems to harmonise and work as a single unit or separately, as required, and this may involve taking specialist advice from manufacturers or independent experts prior to installation.

The provision and quality of insulation for the building is governed by a basic standard dictated by the Building Regulations. Once again, you can increase the basic standard and, because the materials used for this purpose are relatively cheap, this will prove to be one of the most cost-effective things you can do. The money saved over any particular heating season is inescapably linked to the level of insulation provided. Consider the fact that heat generally rises and you will appreciate the first area for attention should be the roof space, whilst secondary insulation can also be added to cavity walls and floor voids.

FIRE PROTECTION

The Building Regulations concern themselves with the built-in design elements allowing occupiers to escape from fire. They are *not* based on how easy it may or may not be for the fire service to rescue occupiers. The regulations specify among other things that:

■ windows in each habitable room must have at least one opening pane to allow occupiers a means of escape;

■ mains-operated and interlinked smoke alarms should be fitted to each level thus providing an early warning of fire.

The Regulations are also concerned with:

■ the internal space and how it will be divided up;

■ how and at what speed fire and smoke could spread through the structure (particularly if there are open staircases and kitchens, mezzanines, galleries and voids through floor levels);

■ the fire resistant quality of materials proposed;

■ the intended use of rooms and how each room is linked to others in the building (for example, whether they are exited through another room or onto a landing or hallway).

In general, it is wise to ensure that all internal doors and frames offer a minimum of half an hour smoke and fire protection. This becomes even more critical if the design includes an integral garage, as it will need to be adequately lined to protect the rest of the house. Any direct through doorway into the house from the garage must have a minimum of a half-hour protection rating (currently accurate but subject to change).

GOING BEYOND THE MINIMUM STANDARDS

We are sure we have mentioned this enough times in previous paragraphs and chapters for you to get the idea – provide your building with muscle and it will remain attractive for years to come, will withstand battering from the elements and will be a comfortable residence for you and your family. However, much depends on the nature of your build and the period of time, if any, that you intend living in the finished dwelling.

Speculators do not usually have a need or desire to go beyond the minimum standards imposed by the Building Regulations. For them, reducing the cost of construction is more important than improving quality, unless the target sales audience considers this feature an asset. In the end, the degree of construction quality beyond the minimum standard is entirely a personal and economic matter that depends on your own particular circumstances and desires.

SUMMARY

- Take advice from your architect when designing your building so as to keep within the imposed directives of the Building Regulations.

- Ask your architect to supply additional detailed construction drawings for each building element.

- Consider the options open to you to go beyond the minimum standards, if you want to build a home of quality and stability.

- Be aware of the legal implications when planning the design of the structure, drainage, heating systems, ventilation and fire protection.

USEFUL INTERNET WEBSITES

www.safety.odpm.gov.uk/bregs/building.htm
The website of the Office of the Deputy Prime Minister with information pertaining to the Building Regulations. This site also offers a downloadable and comprehensive explanatory booklet covering all the major issues involved.

www.hunter-jones.freeserve.co.uk
A very useful and informative site that explains the regulations in easy-to-read terms.

www.tso.co.uk/bookshop
Visit the Stationery Office website if you want to buy copies of the full up-to-date regulations and statutory instruments.

Part Two
Let's Get Started

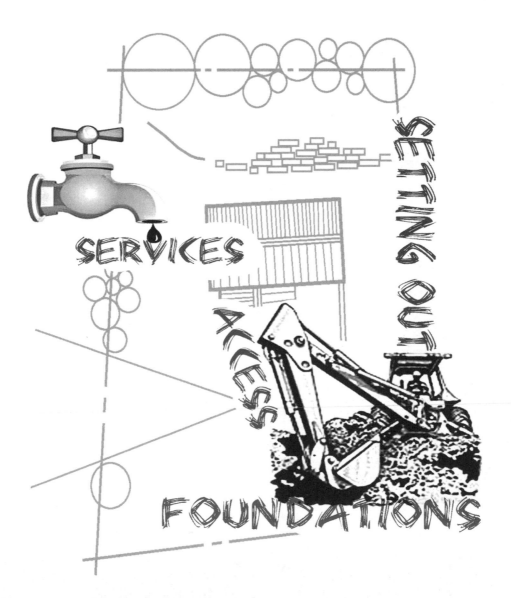

SERVICES

ACCESS

SETTING OUT

FOUNDATIONS

Chapter 11
Personal Involvement

This chapter covers:

- what work can I do myself?
- what works should I subcontract?
- time span – influencing factors
- a plan of action

Earlier in this book we asked you to examine your skills and consider how much of the construction work you might like to undertake yourself. We are now at the stage where this decision *has* to be taken. Delays and uncertainty will cost you money from here onwards so, unless you have already devised a firm plan of action, this is the time when you should sit down and create one. A plan of this nature does not have to be set in stone. It can still be flexible enough to accommodate financial or time-related problems that may occur during construction but, if you are to rely on it as a working guide, it needs to be realistic and confidently defined.

WHAT WORK CAN I DO MYSELF?

This will be determined according to the kind of skills you possess and whether they are fundamentally practical or organisational. If you are someone with bags of enthusiasm and determination, you may already have acquired new skills that you intend deploying, or perhaps you have identified a relative, friend or colleague with abilities you lack who is prepared to help. Remember that every hour you, your family and friends spend on the project will enhance the value and quality of the finished scheme and every penny saved in labour costs can be spent on better quality materials, luxury fittings or a particular item of furnishing you always wanted.

Many of the truly hands-on self-builders will tackle the construction involved below ground level. This includes setting-out, ground preparation, laying concrete foundations and the brick or blockwork up to the damp-proof course. The reason is that although they may feel certain of doing a good job, they are less confident of how it will look. But, if it is below ground or concealed, then all that matters is that the installation is stable and secure and that the work has been undertaken according to proper and rudimentary building principles. Partaking in this initial aspect of construction is also a useful testing ground. It will soon become clear whether you are sufficiently skilled to attempt other 'visible' parts of the dwelling. The 'testing' phase can also be used as a training period, where you could act in the capacity of apprentice to a more skilled friend or colleague, providing you are able to find someone willing to teach you.

Your skills might be, for example, in joinery, where a little guidance and research could help elevate a limited ability to degrees of craftsmanship. Even regardless of higher skill levels, the likelihood is that you will take much more care in completing these tasks than a tradesman you might employ, resulting in a better quality finish through attention to detail. However, some work will be beyond your capabilities, no matter how good you think you may be. This will include the installation and certification of electrical and gas fittings and central heating systems, all of which must be performed by fully trained, skilled and approved operators.

As with all aspects of a self-build scheme, safety must always be regarded as paramount and working in isolation presents its own set of problems. Once you have identified the tasks you can perform yourself, you should consider the potential each has for causing injury and establish a strategy to prevent such eventualities. Despite your best efforts, accidents can still occur and there should therefore be practical and predetermined procedures in place, ready to deal with them. Some of the more obvious health and safety issues include:

- When you work alone:
  - ✓ Carry a fully charged mobile-phone with you at all times, so you can call for help if you become trapped or are otherwise immobilised.

  - ✓ Let a partner, relative or friend know what you expect to be doing that day and arrange for them to contact you at set intervals to check everything is going according to plan.

  - ✓ Only lift materials that you are capable of lifting safely and don't overload wheelbarrows, carrying-cradles or dumper-trucks: cutting corners is never a worthwhile risk. Quite apart from the danger to your health, bear in mind that, if you become incapacitated, the work on your project will have to stop for weeks or even months while you recover.

- Invest in professional quality safety clothing, a good pair of reinforced boots, goggles, a hard-hat and builder's gloves ... and wear them!

- Whenever you operate electrical tools, *always* use a residual circuit breaker (RCB), which will instantly cut the supply in an emergency, and engage any built-in safety-guard.

- If you buy or hire equipment, read the accompanying guidance notes thoroughly and never operate plant or machinery unless you are confident you know how to control it.

- Always use scaffolding in preference to ladders, as it provides a more stable platform to work from. When ladders must be used, secure them properly at the top, use a stand-off if required, and place sandbags at the bottom to prevent movement.

- Be tidy! Most accidents occur because the working environment is left cluttered with tools and half-sawn timbers, cutting blades are left unprotected and gaps in the flooring left uncovered.

- Before you start any work on the site, prepare a good first-aid kit with emergency materials, including bandages, plasters, eye-rinse, tourniquet, splint and sling. Ensure your kit is located close by and is easy to access.

- Keep a bucket full of sand handy and another full of water. These should be readily available in the event of inflammable liquid spillage or fire. Consider the advantage of buying or hiring proper fire-fighting equipment, such as an extinguisher and fire-blanket.

WHAT WORKS SHOULD I SUB-CONTRACT?

The sixty-four thousand dollar question? The advantage of hiring sub-contractors for specific areas of work is that it will save you time (in theory) and remove the worry of taking on major parts of the construction. These are most likely going to be the tasks you simply cannot undertake yourself, either through a lack of skill or through impracticality. The disadvantage is almost entirely a financial one, though there may be a quality issue too, if you fail to hire a diligent and suitably qualified builder or tradesman.

The range of work you could sub-contract is wide and varied. You might want to employ an individual tradesman to complete a single task or an entire gang to complete the construction up to a certain stage, for example the point at which a building inspector is due to visit the site and assess progress. Alternatively, you could sub-contract the organisational and managerial part of the construction, so that someone else deals with the hiring and supervision of tradesmen and labourers, writing letters, checking plans and liaising with your architect, surveyor, mortgage company, and so on. The extent and nature of sub-contracted work is essentially up to you. It depends on the scale of the project, the time you have available to complete it, the financial package you have arranged, and the amount of work you are able and intend to undertake yourself. Perhaps the most important of all these is the time element. By identifying the point in time you want the dwelling completed, you will also be defining the rate of work and schedule of events. In turn, this may prompt you to hire skilled help to keep the project moving at an acceptable pace and within the timeframe you have set.

When employing tradesmen you should consider the following:

■ To prevent a misunderstanding arising and to protect yourself against poor quality work, always put your instructions in writing to all those you employ. Refer sub-contractors to the architect's plan or to supplementary details and make it clear what you expect of them. For major tasks, draw up a contract so that both sides know and agree what and how something is to be done, when it is to be done and how much it will cost. There are standard industry contract forms available to architects, builders and project managers or you can buy them direct from the Building Centre, 26 Store Street, London WC1E 7BT. Telephone: 020 7692 4000. Website: **www.buildingcentre.co.uk**

■ Check that electricians are suitably qualified and experienced to undertake the work you employ them to do. They should be registered and approved by the National Inspection Council for Electrical Installation Contracting (NICEIC). You can contact the NICEIC to locate an electrician or to check their registration is up to date. Write to them at NICEIC, Vintage House, 37 Albert Embankment, London SE1 7UJ. Telephone: 020 7564 2323. Website: **www.niceic.org.uk**

■ The installation of gas pipes and appliances, including central heating boilers, must be undertaken by a CORGI registered engineer or fitter, and the work must comply with the gas regulations. CORGI stands for The Council for Registered Gas Installers and they can be contacted at 1 Elmwood, Chineham Business Park, Crockford Lane, Basingstoke, Hants RG24 8WG. Telephone: 01256 372200. Website: **www.corgi-gas.com**

■ The Department of Trade and Industry has a 'Quality Mark Scheme' for builders and associated trades, including plumbing, heating and roofing. It maintains a public register of independently assessed builders and tradesmen who are good, fairly priced and local. All the contractors in the scheme will provide you with a proper quote, a contract and a warranty against poor workmanship and insolvency lasting six years. To access the list telephone 0845 300 8040 or visit the website at: **www.qualitymark.org.uk**

■ The Office of Fair Trading (OFT) exists to protect consumers' interests by eliminating unfair trading practices and tackling unscrupulous traders. Contact them on 08457 224499 to check whether complaints have been received about tradesmen you intend employing. You should also obtain their free leaflets, *Need A Plumber or Builder...?* and *A Step-By-Step Guide to Getting Work Done on Your Home*, as these contain valuable advice and information, and list contact addresses for trade associations and professional bodies. Telephone the publications department on 0870 6060 321 or visit their website at: **www.oft.gov.uk**

■ In 1997, Cockerill and Scott produced a report *Training, Skills Provision and Multi-Skilling in the Construction Industry* and found conclusive evidence that the sector was characterised by 'a pronounced lack of certification and of qualifications'. It was, they said, 'a rather gloomy picture'. The situation is a little improved today, but it remains as difficult as ever to find a good, honest, qualified and experienced builder who consistently produces impeccable work at a reasonable price. The National Federation of Builders (NFB) offers a glimmer of hope by providing enquirers with a list of qualified and reputable local builders and also an insurance-backed Benchmark Plan. You can contact them at Construction House, 56-64 Leonard Street, London EC2A 4JX. Telephone: 020 7608 5150. Website: **www.builders.org.uk**

■ The Health and Safety Executive (HSE) are one of the most useful authorities you can contact prior to setting up your construction site or employing tradesmen. They have an entire series of free, easy-to-read and informative leaflets on subjects of interest to the self-builder. These include *Safety in Excavations*, *The Absolutely Essential Tool Kit for the Smaller Construction Contractor*, *Construction Fire Safety*, *Working on Roofs* and *Construction (Health, Safety and Welfare) Regulations 1996*. They also publish (HSG150) *Health and Safety in Construction* priced £9.95, which provides general guidance on health and safety for everyone involved in construction, refurbishment, maintenance, repair and demolition work. You can contact the HSE at Caerphilly Business Park, Caerphilly CF83 3GG. Telephone: 08701 545500. Website: **www.hse.gov.uk**

■ The Construction (Design and Management) Regulations 1994 (known as the CDM regulations) play an important role on all building sites. They are designed to protect the health and safety of personnel involved, and severe penalties exist for site managers and employers who fail to implement them. The CDM Regulations are complex and extensive with rules and procedures for every stage and variation of the construction process. The Health and Safety Executive (HSE) publish a number of guidance books on CDM including: (HSG224) *Managing Health and Safety in Construction: Construction (Design and Management) Regulations 1994: Approved Code of Practice and Guidance*, priced £9.50. Contact details for the HSE are given above.

The CDM Regulations do not apply to all self-builders. The HSE advise that those building their own home with the intention of living in it at completion can disregard most of the conditions. However, anyone constructing a dwelling where the intention is to sell it at completion must comply with the whole of the CDM requirements (because they will be deemed to be undertaking the work for business purposes). Self-builders who use contractors to assist them in the construction need only concern themselves with Regulation 7 (Notification of the Project) and Regulation 13 (Designers' Duties). Free leaflets describing these and the notification form for Regulation 7 are obtainable from the HSE. Full details are also available on their website at **www.hse.gov.uk**

TIME SPAN – INFLUENCING FACTORS

The time period involved in completing a self-build project is determined by many things and, not least, the tenacity of the builder to finish on target. Some will have a strict, defined and uncompromising date, which they intend meeting at all costs. Others may be much more relaxed about the process, seeing the entire project as one that will evolve and gradually reach a conclusion at some unspecified future date. In fact, most will fall in the middle ground between these two extremes, completing within two years. However, self-builders are often idealists, and the conception and planning stage can take up most of a lifetime before the vision becomes a tangible reality.

Once construction begins, there are two major influences: cash flow and the time of the year that certain phases are planned to be undertaken. Thousands of man-hours are lost in the building industry each year due to inclement weather. When it rains, builders sit in their site-sheds while trenches flood and newly built walls get soaked. In the commercial sector, these interruptions are inevitable and usually anticipated, but the self-builder can find them immensely frustrating and stressful, because he has a vested interest in the site. A day lost to the weather is a delay he can well do without and, if too many days are lost, the project can face financial problems.

In an attempt to remedy this situation, self-builders should consider the fact that there are only a couple of advantageous periods during our four seasons when certain tasks can be undertaken with reasonable confidence. Firstly, site excavation and pouring concrete for foundations is best done during long periods of dry weather, when the ground is firm. Far too often this is attempted in winter, just as the plot turns into a sea of mud. The second target is to aim for a weathertight shell by the autumn, because this will allow work to continue inside, regardless of the weather.

The rate of cash flow is always going to be a difficult problem and a likely stumbling block, regardless of how well you plan the project. Careful cost projections and a continual analysis of expenses will help, particularly as your time becomes more labour orientated. The 'plan of action' at the end of this chapter is intended to assist you in this regard. It provides a vital framework through which you can determine exactly when staged loan payments will be required and also when injections from personal funds may be opportune.

For the plan to work, you will need to estimate, with a high degree of accuracy, how much and when finance is going to be needed (and available) and fit the stages of construction in, so that they harmonise with each other. These elements will depend on the nature of your project, which might be self financed from, for example, an inheritance, and take several years to complete; or at the other end of the scale, it could be largely financed through a staged loan with the dwelling itself being delivered in kit-form on the back of a lorry, erected in days on slab foundations and be ready for fitting out before the weekend. Whatever route you choose, it is worth noting in your 'action plan' other influences that may affect you progressing towards completion. For many, this will include the stages when the local building inspector will be required to examine the work and confirm that construction to that point complies with the regulations and any conditions that may have been imposed. It is important you observe these statutory requirements, and developing a good working relationship with the building inspector can prove helpful in keeping the project on course. The least number of stages requiring notification include:

- at commencement, when the inspector will make their first site visit following excavation of the foundations and prior to concrete being poured;

- at damp-proof course level and prior to the pouring of any concrete floor slabs;

- at the preparation and instalment of drainage systems;

- at completion of the dwelling.

These stages should be fully explored and discussed at your first meeting with the building inspector. If you intend sub-contracting the work, make sure the builder is made aware that he will be responsible for ensuring all work undertaken conforms to the building regulation standards ... and never assume anything to be a fact unless you have received confirmation in writing.

A PLAN OF ACTION

The example plan of action (figure 11) sets out the timescale for your programme of work. We have listed it in simple numerical terms as '1 – 2 – 3' etc., and these can be altered as required to represent your chosen intervals (weeks, fortnights, months, and so on). The periods you choose will depend on cash flow and, critically, when staged-releases from any loan are expected. The first column contains details of the projected work phases and, again, these can be modified so they relate to your own specific project.

The second column, 'skill input', is an important one, as it enables you to control the building work. Enter here the aspects of construction you intend completing yourself. The plan can help identify areas requiring further research or additional practice and, by charting them now, you will have a ready reminder of what needs doing and when. The items remaining are those you will need to 'buy in' and these can be distinguished from the others by using a different colour of ink or an appropriate symbol.

The third column identifies the 'cash intensive' work stages that are beyond your skill level and require programming to provide time for the arrangement of competitive quotes. Advance planning is essential when outside tradesmen are going to be employed. You must be able to give them plenty of warning of when you will need

Figure 11 Plan of action (typical example)

CASH FLOW	£20,000 > > >	▨▨▨▨▨▨

WORK STAGES	SKILL INPUT	CASH INTEN-SIVE	LABOUR INTEN-SIVE	TIME PERIOD								
				1	2	3	4	5	6	7	8	9
GROUNDWORKS & SUB-STRUCTURE				→	→	→	→	→	→			
❏ Create access	SELF		✓	▨								
❏ Shape site and form levels for excavations	SELF	✓	✓	▨	▨							
❏ Setting-out	SELF		✓		▨	▨						
❏ Excavate for foundations	SELF		✓			▨						
❏ Set up reinforcement and cast foundations	SELF		✓				▨	▨				
❏ Build brickwork/blockwork up to damp-proof course	EXT	✓						▨	▨			
❏ Form service entry points to meter positions	EXT	✓						▨	▨			
SUPER-STRUCTURE												
❏ Construct walls to 1st floor involving setting out of windows and door openings												
❏ Joinery ground floor 1st fix												
❏ Joinery 1st floor 1st fix												
❏ Build walls up to roof level												
❏ Wall plates and roof setting out												
❏ Construct roof timbers												
❏ Felt, batten and tile roof												
❏ Flashings to chimney stacks, wall abutments, etc												
❏ Window frames & glazing												

Figure 11 Plan of action (typical example) *continued*

CASH FLOW											

WORK STAGES	SKILL INPUT	CASH INTEN-SIVE	LABOUR INTEN-SIVE	TIME PERIOD									
				10	11	12	13	14	15	16	17	18
SUPER-STRUCTURE (CONTINUED)												
❑ 1st fix electrical: bring in supply, run cabling and install back-boxes												
❑ 1st fix joinery: external door frames & temporary doors, door linings, cills & staircases												
❑ 1st fix plumbing: bring in supply and main pipe runs												
❑ Plaster out												
❑ DRYING OUT (the longer you allow the building to dry out, the better - use this time to consider interiors)												
❑ Early 2nd fix joinery: door frames, skirting, architraves												
❑ Early 2nd fix electrical: face-plates for lighting and sockets, temporary light fittings												
❑ Construct the main features: fireplaces, decorative ponds & pools												
❑ Wet trade finishes such as terracotta												
❑ Dusty trades including ceramic tile cutting, stone features, etc. (dust screening is useful to isolate particular rooms)												

Figure 11 Plan of action (typical example) *continued*

CASH FLOW											

WORK STAGES	SKILL INPUT	CASH INTEN-SIVE	LABOUR INTEN-SIVE	TIME PERIOD								
				19	20	21	22	23	24	25	26	27
SUPER-STRUCTURE (CONTINUED)												
❑ Cleaning: encourage sub-contractors to clean 'as they go'. Keep rooms free of plaster dust and debris so they are ready for decoration												
❑ 2nd fix plumbing: taps and all drainage connections, pumps, boilers and radiators												
❑ 2nd fix joinery: staircase handrails and ballustrading, kitchen units, fitted wardrobes, internal doors and main entrance door (beware of any potential damage by outstanding work)												
❑ 2nd fix electrics: to a level complying with regulations (temporary light-fittings can be exchanged for superior ones as the interior design takes shape)												
❑ Painting and decorating												
❑ External works: garden landscaping, hard surfaces												
❑ VAT reclaim												
❑ Carpets and ceramic flooring												
❑ Curtains and other soft furnishings												

them and for how long, so they can keep this period free and plan their other commitments around it. In addition, you will need to know when payment of services provided by outside agencies and individuals is likely to become due, so that your cash flow keeps pace with any loan release. The most frustrating position you could ever find yourself in is where tradesmen refuse to work for you because they have not been paid for an earlier task, and a mortgage company won't release any more funds until you have reached the next stage of construction. Work effectively stops through a lack of funds and funds stop because there is no work being done! It is the worst manifestation of the 'Catch 22' scenario, and one you must strive to avoid.

The more labour-intensive stages are identified in column four and these are important, because they slow down the rate of cash flow. In theory, the only spending during these periods should be on low-cost labour and materials. Further savings can of course be made by undertaking the labour yourself, and this will also add value to the project as a whole.

Along the topmost line of the action plan, write the amount of finance you will need and when you will need it. For example, to illustrate how to use the plan, we have entered an amount of £20,000 as the sum estimated will be needed by period '6' to complete the 'groundworks & sub-structure'. If the required amounts were not available from personal funds or from a loan advance by period '6', the plan would have to be altered to accommodate it. By extending the time period to coincide with a loan release date, the matter would be resolved and work could proceed.

The action plan should be reviewed at regular intervals, as new information becomes known. Continuous assessment is probably going to be required for complex or large-scale self-build projects and any that are to be conducted over a long period of time.

Summary

■ Identify the construction tasks you will be undertaking yourself.

■ Consider the safety hazards of working alone and implement procedures that will help prevent accidents or deal with any that might occur.

■ Decide which tasks are beyond your level of skill and consider the number, type and cost of tradesmen you need to employ.

■ Giving regard to your own personal circumstances, determine the length of time you intend spending on the construction of your property. Identify each stage of the process and the approximate start and completion dates.

■ Prepare a 'plan of action' taking into account cash-flow, loan release dates, personal and external skill input, the work involved in each stage and the anticipated cost of completing it.

■ Review your plan at regular intervals and amend according to changing circumstances, financial limitations and the work entailed.

USEFUL INTERNET WEBSITES

www.theweatheroutlook.com
Although most news channels give good short-range weather forecasts, self-builders need to know what the weather is likely to do over the next few weeks so they can plan their schedule for exterior work. This site provides detailed regional forecasts lasting up to 28 days.

www.city-and-guilds.co.uk
Learn useful constructions skills in advance of starting your self-build project. The City & Guilds website gives details of courses available and these include bricklaying, plastering, joinery and roofing. The site also shows you where your nearest college is located and how to contact them.

www.portakabin.co.uk
Unless you are happy about tradesmen and labourers ploughing cement and mud through your temporary on-site accommodation, you are going to need to hire portable toilet facilities. This website provides contact details of local portaloo suppliers, including map references.

Chapter 12
Preparing the Site

This chapter covers:

■ creating a suitable access

■ shaping the site

■ dealing with the problem of nearby trees

■ 'setting-out' the house

There is a choice given to all self-builders who reach this penultimate stage in the preparation of their site. They can sit back and allow external forces to shape it ready for construction or they can intervene and actively determine the house form and access onto the plot. Neither will necessarily get them what they want and it could be that both routes will actually lead them to exactly the same position. However, as the saying goes, if you don't try you will never know, so if time and motivation are available in sufficient quantities, the best course of action is to get involved and explore the possibilities.

Early discussions with the planning authority will undoubtedly have supplied you with considerable guidance on the design and position of your plot access; 'sight lines' are always of major concern to planning officers. These refer to the degrees of visibility seen in all directions from the access point by you and your family, pedestrians crossing the entrance and traffic passing it. The 'sight lines' could be restricted by the angle of the plot, trees, boundary walls and the curvature of the road, and these could all be exacerbated by the flow and speed of traffic. The planning authority will take these factors into consideration and demand you adopt the safest option at the planning application stage. However, if a dropped kerb already exists, then the position of entry onto the plot may have been predetermined. Getting permission to vary it is unlikely, unless you have considerable evidence that an alternative access route would improve the safety aspect for all concerned.

Once you have established the position where your vehicle crosses the pavement to enter the site, you can progress on to the secondary measures needed to initiate construction.

CREATING A SUITABLE ACCESS

From a suitable vantage point, consider the most appropriate access route to the intended dwelling and identify areas for parking. The planning department will already have stipulated the minimum hard standing for vehicles, but you may wish to expand this to park additional cars, a boat, caravan or trailer. The arrangements you plan now will have a significant impact later, particularly if you wish to conceal vehicles on one side of the building or to the rear. With the access and parking positions decided, you can then think about how you intend joining the two up to create a driveway.

Much depends on the nature of your plot. If it slopes away from the road, you could find that a parking area is best fitted into the scheme at an elevated position, so the drive stays reasonably level. This can be a considerable advantage in the depths of winter, when snow and ice might otherwise impede access. Perhaps your site has enough room to accommodate a turning circle, which would prevent you having to back out of the drive (important if the road outside is a busy highway).

This is also an opportunity to unleash the garden designer inside you and begin planning the main cultivation and recreational areas. Once you begin excavating, there will be a great deal of ground material available that you could use to create an interesting and varied landscape. This will utilise an otherwise wasted commodity and save you a small fortune in transportation and tipping costs.

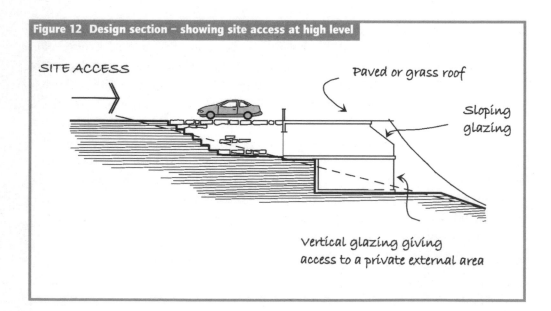

Figure 12   Design section – showing site access at high level

SITE ACCESS

Paved or grass roof

Sloping glazing

Vertical glazing giving access to a private external area

SHAPING THE SITE

During the house design stage, you will already have decided whether to build a single or a multiple-level dwelling. This impacts on the depth and spread of the foundations, which will be specified by your architect in consultation with the planning and building control authority. In any event, there will be a considerable amount of excavation required. As mentioned above, topsoil is a valuable asset; it should be stripped from the surface carefully and stored in a convenient position ready for later use. The underlying strata of coarse material can also be usefully employed, for example to shape up the site.

Bear in mind that, once the house is built, you may not be able to get excavation machines or tippers to certain parts of the plot. With careful advance planning, you can mould these garden areas now, using earth-moving equipment, rather than spend weeks of backbreaking work with a spade and wheelbarrow at the end of the project. A minimum of 15cm of topsoil is usually required to blanket a garden. By distributing it now, you will release space on your plot where the mound of earth would otherwise have to be stored and, as time will prove, space is going to be at a premium, once the construction gets under way.

One of the first purchases you will need to make is economical hardcore, which should be used to form a base for the main access so that heavy delivery vehicles can get onto the site. The hardcore can also be deployed in other areas, for example where you intend storing building materials. It may seem obvious, but *don't* buy hardcore in bags from your local DIY store, as it is far too expensive for this purpose. Instead, look in *Yellow Pages* under 'Builders' merchants' and buy loose by the 10 or 20 tonne load. Alternatively, buy clean hardcore from the small ads in a local newspaper.

Laying hardcore is not an extravagant indulgence but an absolute necessity. It provides a firm surface and keeps the site accessible for deliveries without which your self-build project would grind to a halt. The hardcore should not be discarded at the end of construction, as it can be retained for the sub-base of a driveway, patio or paved area.

DEALING WITH THE PROBLEM OF NEARBY TREES

In Chapter 9, we discussed felling trees that might be in the way of your planned dwelling and the situation for those protected by a tree preservation order, but these are not the only circumstances where trees present a problem for the self-builder. Whether living or dead, trees that are too close to the construction area can cause extensive damage in the future and you may not become aware of it until it is too late.

Trees draw moisture from the ground, and in the summer months they can shrink the surrounding soil by 40mm or more. This is exacerbated with clay soils and causes the surface area to rise and fall as the seasons change. Far from curing the problem, a felled tree can make things even worse because it is no longer drawing moisture from the root area. In clay soils, the ground can swell by up to 150mm, jeopardising the stability of foundations and any drainage systems nearby. Dead tree stumps and their roots will also eventually rot and cause a depression affecting structures and any hardstanding above ground, as well as causing a shift in the soil substructure below ground, which could weaken load-bearing foundations.

The proximity of trees to dwellings is covered by British Standard 5837, which suggests that the anticipated tree height *at maturity* should equal the minimum distance measurement to any strip-foundations (see Figure 13). Where trees are planted together and in rows, the minimum distance should be increased by another 50 per cent. The most comprehensive long-term answer is to remove such trees and their roots below ground, then fill and compact the prevailing cavities with suitable material consistent with the ground around it. But this is an enormous task and only the most meticulous self-builder should consider it. An alternative course of action will be suggested by the building inspector and this might include taking special precautions, such as piling the foundations. 'Piling' involves the installation of long sections of steel or concrete that penetrate deep into the ground to support and strengthen the foundation layer.

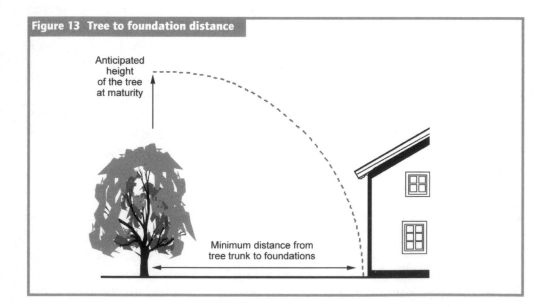

Figure 13 Tree to foundation distance

Anticipated height of the tree at maturity

Minimum distance from tree trunk to foundations

'SETTING-OUT' THE HOUSE

If you have elected to sub-contract the groundwork, the foundation line-boards will now be positioned and you will see the full-size shape of your new home for the first time. This is an exciting moment. You can actually walk inside the dwelling layout and start imagining what it will be like, once the walls are built. 'Setting-out' is a fairly straightforward task and one you may opt to undertake yourself. To complete it, you will need:

- a 30 metre canvas tape-measure;

- some 50mm x 50mm softwood stakes;

- several lengths of floorboard about 900mm long;

- a sledge-hammer;

- a tenon-saw;

- a builder's spirit-level;

- a spade;

- a builder's 90-degree angle;

- ground-marking paint (available from builders' merchants);

- plenty of line-band (also available from builders' merchants);

- good copies of the architect-drawn and planning authority approved construction plans;

- excavating machinery you have hired.

A flask of coffee, dry weather and willing volunteers to help you, are all optional extras well worth considering. The challenge is to draw your house at full scale on the ground. This will involve crossing lines to pinpoint the corners and widths of the walls, foundations and 'sleeper walls' for ground floor joists. However, the initial task is to set out lines for excavation and, to achieve this, it is important you refer to the plans to find an accurate and convenient starting point. By checking the distances from a landmark, such as the plot boundary, you should be able to identify the position on the ground of a significant corner from your dwelling plans. Use a stake to flag this spot, then go back and re-check your measurements.

Although the approved plans will have all the dimensions you need to accomplish the work, your architect will be happy to provide additional setting-out and foundation drawings to assist you. Explain your level of involvement in the construction and always seek advice if you are uncertain about how to proceed.

With your starting reference-point identified, you can now begin setting-out line-boards (see Figure 14). This involves two ground stakes and a cross board. On top of the boards you need to mark-out the thickness of the outer leaf, cavity and inner leaf walls, and the interior and exterior extent of the foundations. Carefully make an appropriate number of saw-cuts through the edge of the boards and run line-band between these cuts, denoting the positions of the inner and outer walls and the foundations. Check all your measurements again, then fix the boards in place using timber stakes. Accuracy is everything at this stage! Take your time to get it right, even if it involves procuring second opinions from every friend in your social circle. Once you are confident that the dimensions and positions precisely reflect those on the plans, you can prepare the ground ready for excavation.

String out the full widths of the foundations and use these as guides to stain the ground with marker paint. Keep the boards *in situ* because these will be needed as fixed reference points throughout the duration of the work. Now bring your excavating equipment in ready to start digging, but be careful not to damage the boards. If this is the first time you have used a commercial digger, take some time to practise

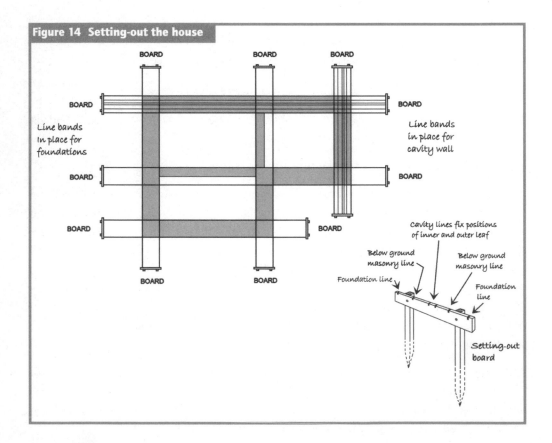

Figure 14 Setting-out the house

operating it in a secluded corner of your plot. Once you are confident you can manipulate it properly and are able to dig with accuracy, start excavating the foundation trenches to a depth detailed on the approved plans. Clean out the bottom of the trenches with a spade and check the dimensions are accurate at the base and up the sides. If the sides of the trenches are weak, you may need to install some temporary timber support, before the concrete is poured.

The pre-concrete pouring stage is usually when the building inspector will make their second site visit; make sure an appointment is booked well in advance. This will also give you time to calculate the amount of concrete you are going to need and place an order with a suitable local supplier. It is important to note that the specification of the concrete mix must conform to what is stipulated on the approved plans and architect's drawings. You will need to order the correct type and required quantity in cubic metres. There is a handy program you can acquire as a download to your personal computer, which converts any size and dimension into the appropriate volume (see 'Useful Website Addresses' at the end of this chapter). If the building inspector approves the trenches, plan the pouring of your concrete the next day to prevent any potential damage to them being caused by inclement weather, and make sure you have enough labour and machinery to enable the pour to be carried out.

Smooth and tidy up the surface of the concrete sufficiently to enable the first course of masonry to be laid level with a good bed of mortar. Accuracy is again important here because the aim is to achieve a standard and equal level throughout the foundation run, with any discrepancy resolved by the bed of mortar. The foundation can now be used, interestingly, as the first stage to setting-out the roof, because it mirrors it on a flat plane. However, the roof's three-dimensional design is likely to be quite different. The roof structure will sit on the wall-plate timber which, in turn, will sit on the top of the inner leaf you plotted with line-bands earlier. Using these as a template, you can now plot out the hips and valleys and the position of ridge tiles by angling line-band at 45 degrees from each walled corner. The value of this preliminary roof check is that it will indicate in advance when to stop building walls. It may be rudimentary, but it could help you explore any potential problems and assist in the calculation of brick quantity supply.

As the concrete foundations set (together with the sun, if it has been a particularly long day), it is worth reflecting on what has been achieved and what yet needs to be done. The layout of your new home is now engraved on the plot. Your self-build project is under way and, perhaps for the first time, you can see a tangible consequence of the hard work and money you have invested. With the foundations in place and a roof check undertaken, all you now have to do is link the two up by stringing the wall positions. Take pride in what you have achieved so far: you deserve it!

SUMMARY

- Prior to planning the foundations and setting out the shape of the dwelling, prepare the access with hardcore and use excavating equipment to move soil for landscaping.

- Assess the impact of trees on your proposed dwelling and deal with them in consultation with the building inspector and planning authority.

- Set out the walls and foundations of your home using line-band, giving careful attention to the dimensions and positions detailed in your approved plans.

- Excavate for the foundations and invite the building inspector to assess your trenches prior to pouring concrete.

USEFUL INTERNET WEBSITES

www.canfixit.co.uk
A useful site that concisely explains how to go about laying strip-foundations.

www.diydoctor.org.uk
This site provides more detailed information about setting-out and laying foundations, including a reference table of strip-foundation minimum widths.

www.meracl.com
Download the 'Meracl Multiconverter' from this site and install on your personal computer. This handy program converts length, volume, area, mass, time and temperature, from one unit into another ... and it's free!

Chapter 13
The Substructure

This chapter covers:

■ bringing in or diverting services

■ the building inspector

■ damp-proof course

■ building the walls to ground level

Before moving on to the next stage of your self-build project, it is important to gather information and undertake a little additional research. You have already laid the foundations of your home and it is time to examine what will be built on and around them. Good planning now will help prevent you from making critical and costly errors over the following few days or weeks of construction.

When preparing to bring in services for electricity, gas, water and drainage, there are a hundred ways of getting it wrong and only one way of getting it right! Time spent discussing these aspects with your architect is an investment you will not regret. Make sure you understand what groundwork is involved and the appropriate materials to use. It is not possible for us to detail the various methods and materials here, as they are simply too vast, and entirely dependent on the style of individual construction, the nature of your plot's soil structure, and the mandatory criteria of the specific service provider.

The following information is based on a standard build and should be considered as general guidance only. In all circumstances, you must check what is required for your own construction, following discussions with your professional advisor and the service providers' technical installations officer.

BRINGING IN OR DIVERTING SERVICES

During the design stage and whilst creating plans for your property, you and your architect will have considered the issue of energy consumption and meters and their location inside or outside the dwelling. Service providers' individual connection arrangements vary and it is wise to contact them at the earliest opportunity to acquire instructions and guidance. Most will give consent for all mains services to be provided via a single trench, and supply information about the minimum distance they must be from one another.

Electricity

Examine your approved plans and identify where the first electrical intake point should be located. This will be at the foot of the wall on which the electrical distribution board will eventually be positioned. A service trench needs to be dug out from the plot boundary where the mains service is located (without interfering in any way with the mains service itself), to the foundation entry point of the dwelling. Take advice from your architect or deal direct with the service provider about the size, depth and preparation required for this trench.

Position the appropriate ducting into the dwelling, bringing it in below the finished ground level, and raise in a slow bend upwards, above the concrete slab or sub-slab. Once the floor slab is cast, a secure and waterproof temporary housing can be constructed for the electrical supply, and it is at this stage that you can ask the electricity authority to lay their armour-clad cable from outside your property boundary. The cable will drop into the open trench, through the ducting into the building, and connect into an electricity meter installed by the provider. Two double sockets inside the temporary meter cupboard should be sufficient to run the innumerable items of equipment and tools you will need over the coming months.

Water

The second most important service to bring onto the site is the water supply. Most providers now require water to be metered and they will deliver and install water to a meter position just within the boundary of your plot. The remaining sections of installation are your responsibility. It is best to undertake your part of the work involved first, then the water provider can make the connection to both sides of the water meter.

The usual entry location for mains water into a dwelling is at the kitchen sink and it is customary to terminate the supply pipe at this point. Builders' merchants sell blue 'alkathene' pipe with a range of compression joints, and this should be laid in the same service trench as other utility ducting, running up to the foot of the dwelling (providing all service providers agree to this arrangement). Always aim to install the longest possible sections with the fewest number of joints.

At this stage, it is useful to consider the exterior facilities you might want to install in your garden and then lay water supply pipes ready for them. For example:

- a concealed sprinkler system might be ideal, if you plan to have vast areas of lawn;

- water features and fountains are good focal points for a garden and these will need an independent water and electrical supply;

- a large greenhouse might benefit from a built-in watering or misting system, as might rows of exterior hanging-baskets, tubs and containers.

At the very least, you will probably need an outside tap for convenience when washing the car or watering plants and, of course, initially you will require a builder's tap for mixing cement and mortar, rinsing off boots and washing hands. To accommodate this, take a 'T' junction off the blue alkathene pipe to a convenient position away from the actual construction. Bring the pipe up a short timber post and connect a temporary tap. Insulate the pipework above ground level and build a secure housing around it.

The entry point to the kitchen sink will also require a duct with a gradual bend in it, to allow the supply pipe to curve up into the building. Terminate the blue supply pipe half a metre above the intended finished floor level with the relevant compression cap. Future connections can be made with internal copper or plastic pipes as required.

Care must be taken to bring all the service ducts into the 'footprint' of the building, above the top surface of the foundation. Install a lintel for protection where the ducts penetrate the brickwork below ground. The arrangement must be appropriate, to prevent any pressure on the ducts or the service pipes inside. Traditionally, even gas pipes were brought in this way, but it is now preferred and much safer for the mains gas feed and meter to be installed externally.

Gas

The choice of housing for the gas meter is likely to be limited because the service provider will insist on it being wall-mounted, recessed into a wall or partially recessed into the paving. From a design point of view, it needs to be unobtrusive, but it should also be easy to access by meter-readers and conveniently located for connection out of the dwelling and into the back of the meter box. The easiest arrangement is usually to have the housing for the meter backing onto an external wall of the dwelling.

Unlike the provisions required for water and electricity, there is no need to prepare an actual entry point into the dwelling for mains gas installation. All you need at this stage is a suitable open trench and a gas meter box positioned appropriately. As before, you will need to discuss the relevant specifications with the service provider, to ensure your groundwork complies with their policies.

Telephone service & cable television

While you have an open trench, most telephone and cable television companies will provide you with link-up sectional duct piping to install in it. These should run from the boundary of your plot and terminate in a slow-bend rising against the dwelling's exterior wall. A robust (the rather disconcerting term used is 'rat-proof') pull-cord needs inserting through each section of the duct as you progress. This will enable the companies to pull their wires and optic cables through, once the property is complete.

With all the mains pipes, cables and wires in place, the trench(es) can be backfilled to ground level. Remember to leave the boundary end open so that final connections can be made. It is also important to protect the surface of the trench from heavy vehicle traffic, which might otherwise disturb or damage the duct piping underground.

Careful planning enables these crucial services to be available to you and those you employ right at the very start of construction. They will improve the building process considerably and make it easier and more rewarding to work on the site. Caution should be applied where service trenches are likely to conflict with excavation lines for drainage or areas where the operation of heavy machinery is expected. In these situations, it is better to delay the installations rather than risk damaging them.

THE BUILDING INSPECTOR

This is an opportune stage to remind you about the importance of the building inspector and explain what they do in more detail. There is often confusion between the planning officer and the building inspector, despite the fact that their roles are quite separate. Planning officers are concerned with your use of the land and how it will impact on other people, nearby buildings and the environment in general; whereas building inspectors are concerned about the building work itself and whether it is consistent with the approved plans and complies with Building Regulations.

There are effectively two different types of inspector. The first are those who enter the profession with a wealth of prior experience and knowledge about the construction industry because they were once themselves a builder or were indirectly involved in the trade. These inspectors are often able to advise you about practical solutions to difficult problems. They can help you to overcome obstacles and build your dream home within the bounds of the relevant legislation. Some will even see a major problem as a professional challenge, going all out to resolve it for you, rather than face defeat. The second type includes academics who, with college or graduate training, become inspectors despite having very limited or no on-site experience. Although the latter may have an equal desire to be helpful, their lack of 'hands-on' practice means they may be less able to devise solutions to the same problems. Nonetheless, a solution will probably exist, but it *will* invariably be down to you or your architect to identify it.

The inspector's service is not free. The local authority will charge for the time given for advice, plan vetting and site inspections. It is wise, therefore, to discuss any proposed works on scheduled inspection dates, rather than contact them with different issues on different days. For example, at the pre-foundation stage you could consult the inspector on the type of damp-proof course recommended and any tips they might have on installation techniques.

It is interesting to note that some construction experts and commentators advise the least possible contact with building inspectors. We can only imagine this must be borne out of a particularly bad experience. On the contrary, we have found inspectors to be usually informative, experienced and helpful; the more involved they are in the construction, the more likely they are to offer good practical advice about building methods and materials.

DAMP-PROOF COURSE

To discuss this subject before starting the actual wall-building may seem as if we are putting the horse before the cart, but it is essential to prepare for it, as varying techniques and mediums can affect the form and modes of installation. As always, advice from your architect and building inspector are vital, if you are to get it right.

Water penetration and the resulting problems of dampness are the foremost cause of deterioration in all buildings. The presence of excess moisture encourages the growth of mould, wood and brick-rotting fungi, which can invade a house with such vigour that they literally eat away the structure. To counteract this, the Building Regulations require that dwellings are designed with prevention in mind and British Standard 8215: 'Design & Installation of Damp Proof Courses in Masonry Construction' sets out the key criteria. There are also essential references contained in BS 8102 'Protection Against Water from the Ground', BS 5628 (Part 3, s3) 'Movement Joints' and 'Exclusion of Moisture'.

The principal considerations when choosing materials for a damp-proof course (DPC) are durability, resistance to stress, pliability and compatibility. The DPC must act as an effective barrier, stopping water from rising up out of the ground and through the brickwork. There are two main types of established DPC membrane material: PVC and bitumen. The latter is more expensive and usually only specified when the circumstances demand extra protection. The installation height of all DPCs is required to be 150mm above the *finished* ground level. It is therefore important to decide exactly where the ground level will be, once the garden and any paving have been established, because levels are likely to differ from their current height.

The other significant factor is that the effectiveness of a DPC can be compromised by careless workmanship when building the walls both below and above ground level. If excess mortar and other building debris are allowed to rest in the cavity, they can provide a bridge which moisture will use to traverse the DPC and continue its journey up the walls. By keeping mortar lines neat and cavity floors clear of building debris, you will be helping to maintain the efficiency of the DPC installation and reduce the chance of damp penetration for years to come.

BUILDING THE WALLS TO GROUND LEVEL

The Egyptians were probably the first to devise sound construction methods and much of what they invented still survives today in various forms of building technique. They used crude but effective versions of line-band, plumb-bobs, straight edges, levels and a fixed right-angle to check corners and columns. They also conceived the principle of using a 'ranging rod', which is a lath long enough to set out the brick and block courses with joints from the top of the concrete foundation to the underside of the damp-proof course (see Figure 15). Adopting the same method, you can use a 'ranging rod' as a measuring stick for any point around the building.

First, build the corners as indicated in the illustration below. Check the levels from corner to corner around the building, using either sophisticated levelling equipment, which you can hire, or a builder's level available from most good building suppliers. These masonry walls are best constructed with reject engineering brick, concrete foundation blocks or a stronger block specified by a structural engineer at the building approval stage. Regardless of the material used, the principle remains the same.

Typically, the base sections are cross-bonded and brought up to support the thickness of walls above it. There are load-bearing calculations involved here and your architect will have used the appropriate formula when they entered details on your approved plans. Use line-band to join the corners and anchor them in place with course irons (available from a building supplier) or weight them with loose bricks. Next, lay each course of brickwork to join the stepped corners. Keep an eye on the quality of your trowel-work and keep the brick faces clean. Practise your pointing and bedding and continually monitor the accuracy of each vertical and horizontal plane.

At the end of this exercise, you may be bursting with confidence and pleased at having acquired a new skill. Alternatively, you may have decided the quality of the work undertaken below ground level lacks visual appeal and now consider it prudent to get competitive quotes for someone else to construct the remaining shell. In any event, it is another task completed and you can feel more reassured about the whole project having reached ground level.

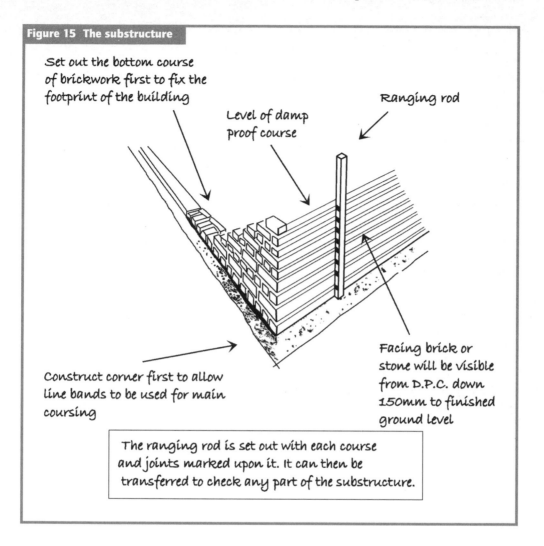

Figure 15 The substructure

Set out the bottom course of brickwork first to fix the footprint of the building

Level of damp proof course

Ranging rod

Construct corner first to allow line bands to be used for main coursing

Facing brick or stone will be visible from D.P.C. down 150mm to finished ground level

The ranging rod is set out with each course and joints marked upon it. It can then be transferred to check any part of the substructure.

SUMMARY

■ Contact the service providers to acquire their specifications for trenches, ducting and meter housing and compare these to any details entered on your approved plans. Discuss any discrepancies with your architect prior to undertaking any installation.

■ Fill the trench(es) carefully and leave the boundary end open for access by the service providers, so that final connections can be made. Protect the trench route from heavy vehicle traffic, which might otherwise damage the pipes and ducting underground.

- Check the type of damp-proof course required and assess where the ground level will be when all building work is completed.

- Build the walls up to the damp-proof course, keeping the cavity clean of mortar and other debris. Check that the walls are level both vertically and horizontally.

USEFUL INTERNET WEBSITES

www.diyfixit.co.uk
Lots of tips and walk-through guides covering all aspects of home building.

www.bsonline.techindex.co.uk
Register and access up-to-date summaries of any British Standard and, if desired, buy the documents online.

www.uswitch.com
Once services and meters are installed and you have opened an account with the service provider, you can consider switching suppliers to get the best possible deal. This is just one of many sites that compare all major suppliers' prices, identify the most competitive and then allow you to apply online to switch from one provider to another. Saving money has never been so easy!

Chapter 14

Constructing the Shell

This chapter covers:

■ solid or timber floors?

■ setting-out the walls

■ constructing the walls

■ supports for the first floor

■ setting-out the first floor

You will have realised by this point in the book how initial design decisions can affect the entire shape, form and structure of the dwelling. In turn, these decisions enhance your eventual enjoyment of the property and can transform something mundane and conventional into a much more exciting home for you and your family. It is at this juncture that both exterior and interior design plans force tangible repercussions on the finished product.

Such consequences are never more obvious than when gauging the type of flooring to install and materials to construct exterior walls. The first influences the level of comfort and design, whilst the latter affects the overall visual appeal of the building and its ability to combat weather conditions.

SOLID OR TIMBER FLOORS?

The two major forms of floor construction are 'suspended' and 'solid'. Suspended floors are usually made out of quality or economical timber boards or waterproof chipboard sheets fixed on top of joists. They can also be constructed with concrete plank or post and beam. Solid floors have a more substantial stone and sand sub-base, cast in concrete and with appropriate insulation and a damp-proof membrane. There are variations on these two themes, but the choice really depends on the kind of eventual floor finish you want in your home.

When the intention is to lay carpet, suspended timber floors offer greater comfort, because they 'give' slightly and produce a softer walking surface. High quality timber tongue and groove flooring can be left uncarpeted, if the desire is to create a stylish and contemporary home. Alternatively, flooring quality chipboard tongue and groove sheets are the cheapest material, and the preferred choice of commercial developers keen to maximise profit. The main problem associated with economical materials used for suspended timber floors is that they quickly deteriorate. Central heating causes them to expand and contract and, before very long, the gentle 'bounce' effect can become a frustratingly audible creak and squeak. Pinning, screwing and even gluing floorboards down has become a regular chore amongst new homeowners up and down the country. Though excessive noise is often the result of inferior materials compounded by poor installation, a suspended chipboard floor should only be considered when cost and design practicalities have priority over more stable and durable alternatives.

Suspended floors require firm regular support from sleeper walls positioned below the damp-proof level. These will be set out on the approved construction drawing and should be built at the same time and together with other sections of the sub-structure.

A solid concrete slab is the perfect base for laying ceramic floor tiles, slate, stone, marble or terracotta in kitchens, dining rooms and hallways. Other rooms requiring a softer feel can then be carpeted with a quality underlay to improve the level of comfort. It is worth noting that a compromise between the two constructional forms of flooring exists in the form of a suspended concrete floor. This helps maintain a completely dry sub-base through continuous air circulation and venting in the void. It can also be set low to allow insulation and underfloor heating to be included within a top screed, which could then be completed with distinctive ceramic floor tiles. This arrangement is typically Mediterranean in structure and form, being cool in summer, warm in winter and elegant in style.

Concrete floors, unless suspended, are laid on a sub-base incorporating a damp-proof membrane and insulation. The building inspector will need to assess this type of floor before the slab is cast so, once the damp-proof course and membranes are ready, book an appointment so they can attend the site to examine the installation work. Unlike the foundations, concreting of the floors is limited to small, individual areas and therefore the volumes are much easier to handle. However, levelling of the surface needs to be done with greater care, because it will be a base for decorative materials. A long, straight piece of timber worked from side to side helps to create the level and a wooden float is then employed to smooth out any irregularities. A mechanical power float finish should also be considered.

Refer to the approved plans for the size of timber floor joists required. These must be 'tanalised', a process in which timbers are impregnated under pressure to drive tanalith-oxide preservative deep into the cellular structure. This is designed to protect the joists against wet and dry rot, woodworm and other insects for at least 20 years. Set out the joists on top of the damp-proof course, space according to the architect's drawing and ensure cambers (if any) face upwards. Nail a lath across the joists to temporarily hold them in position. Using a long straight-edge and a spirit-level, check the timbers in both directions and pack the joist ends as necessary, until they are completely level. Finally, wall the joists into the inner leaf to permanently secure them.

Setting-out the walls

Unlike the situation where, having bought a new home, you then find that nothing will fit into the room dimensions, when building your own home you can *guarantee* that everything will fit. That is, providing you check the appropriate measurements and construct solid wall sections of the internal and external shell accordingly. It is at this stage you need to also examine all window, door and archway openings and confirm that:

■ the desired number and size of kitchen units will fit along the walls;

■ bathroom suites will sit comfortably in the planned layout, leaving enough manoeuvring space around baths, basins, WCs and shower-units, so these facilities can be used easily;

■ fitted wardrobes will fill appropriate walls neatly, and doors will open while someone is standing in front of them (remember to include the desired size of bed and its position, radiators or alternative wall-mounted heating units, and other immovable objects).

It is critical that all external openings are set out accurately, particularly if the over-all appearance of the dwelling is to be recreated from the drawings. When the outside leaf of the structure is to be constructed in brick, every dimension must be based on a standard or specified brick size and a standard mortar joint width. This provides the best possible prospect for all drawing dimensions to be duplicated in true, three-dimensional form. The first facing course of brickwork is the most impor-tant, because this sets out the continuing shape of the vertical wall. It is also crucial that the door and window openings fit the brickwork dimensions and, equally, that the first course over the openings reflects accurately any prior and all onward layers.

Doors and windows are available in standard, modular sizes, and these will generally fit neatly into your scheme, but special care needs to be taken with any unusual or bespoke units manufactured in a different style, size and material. Internal doors are also produced in standard dimensions but, because the thickness of partition walls is likely to vary, the width of door linings will need measuring on site after construction. When preparing the openings in the blockwork to accommodate internal doors, allow sufficient width for the type and size of door you choose, plus a rebated and sub-stantial door lining. Chimneys are easily constructed by using standard flue liners (usually 225mm diameter). The overall dimensions for hearths and fireplace openings will be marked on your drawings, but don't forget to consider the design of this major feature from a position within the room where it will eventually be seen.

Once the horizontal position of every brick and block contained in the first course around the building has been established, you can start building upwards. Consideration of the self-build plan is now starting to switch from a flat two-dimensional layout to a three-dimensional one, and with it comes a whole new set of influences.

If you began using standard size materials, then the remaining structure will fit together in a fairly straightforward, modular fashion. For example, standard window heights relate to standard brick courses; standard door heights relate to standard internal blockwork courses; and standard room heights relate to standard staircase units. Materials are manufactured in this way to make the architect and developer's life as easy and cost efficient as possible. Things are designed to fit together in an orderly manner and this is fine, providing your desire at completion is to have a 'standard' house. But self-builders are rarely creatures of convention and it is more likely that there will be an urge to stray from standard shapes, dimensions and materials. The good news is that you remain in total control, deciding when the standard component solution is appropriate or when to produce a unique picture window, sweeping grand staircase or split-level living room.

In addition to flair and individualism, there may also be practical reasons for moving away from the expected, standard shape and size of materials and customary building methods. For example, a double-fronted, extra height entrance door doesn't just add impact but makes moving large items of furniture in and out of the house much easier; low ceilings may be more economical for room heating but they prevent the installation of pendular light-fittings; mezzanine levels and galleries can transform wasted voids into additional living space.

Before proceeding to construct the walls, there is one final check to be made. How are the first floors going to be supported? Bear in mind that the more substantial the walls supporting the first floor can be made, the less noise and vibration will be transmitted from children's bedrooms to living areas below. Now is a good time to plan beefing-up supporting cross walls or bed several courses of dense concrete or engineering brick to create a more stable seat for the joists. But remember that only by creating a more generous foundation can a more generous wall be built upon it. Joist ends should be well placed and firmly bedded to provide a good solid first floor. Further enhancements can be made later, and after the structure has been made weathertight, which will improve the stability of the floors even more.

Load-bearing internal walls should be bonded into the outer walls. Although the minimum thickness and density of blockwork will be described in detail on the approved construction drawing, you could decide to improve on the basic standard.

A thick wall with deep door linings can turn the act of passing through one area to another more tangible and make a particular room beyond the doorway seem something very special. These are also the aspects of quality rarely experienced (though often complained about) by modern home owners and are the elements that turn the self-built house into a much more attractive and valuable commodity, regardless of whether your intention is to live in it or sell it at completion.

CONSTRUCTING THE WALLS

The blockwork can now begin. Constructing the walls using large blocks gives an advanced sense of progress because you can see the results of your labour within a very short time. A useful and economical measurement guide (a storey lath) can be made from roofing lath timber, available at all good builders' merchants. Cut it to room height size and inscribe on it the blockwork courses, window and door heights (see Figure 16). The 'storey lath' will assist you to set the position of lintels and any padding stones that may be required, if large spans or heavy loads are involved. These should all be detailed on the plans and drawings and, as always, referring to them is essential.

Wall-ties fix the inner and outer leafs of the external walls together and their position will depend on the type and size of structure, the materials used and the

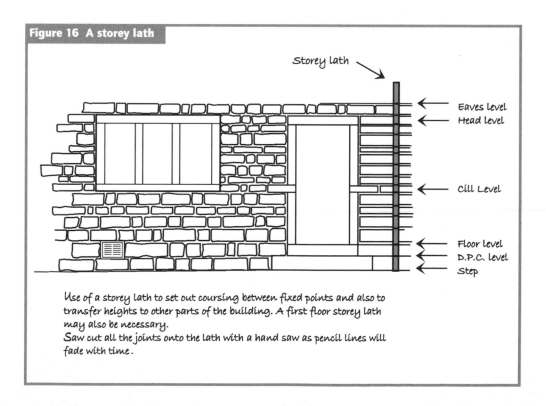

Figure 16 A storey lath

Storey lath

Eaves level
Head level

Cill Level

Floor level
D.P.C. level
Step

Use of a storey lath to set out coursing between fixed points and also to transfer heights to other parts of the building. A first floor storey lath may also be necessary.
Saw cut all the joints onto the lath with a hand saw as pencil lines will fade with time.

construction method. The appropriate number to use and the spaces between them horizontally and vertically will be given as instructions in your approved plans.

Using the same method as you did with the 'below ground' work, start constructing the longest walls by building the corners first, then use line-bands or a long straight-edge to complete each course in between. Remember to check the walls diagonally whilst the mortar is wet as this will allow you to straighten blockwork in both directions should it be necessary. Continuously check vertical accuracy with a long spirit-level and only build two or three courses of blockwork at a time to prevent the courses below sliding out of true.

SUPPORTS FOR THE FIRST FLOOR

The first floor position of single and split-level dwellings will in fact be the roof level and consequently, because the load-bearing weight is much lighter than with floor joists, less restraint is required. However, if another storey is to be constructed, then joists must be properly secured and your architect will have taken this into consideration, when they created your plans. The approved drawings will give the minimum size of joists needed and how they should be spaced, suspended and fixed. Unless you have requested otherwise, the specification will be a standard one and you may wish to improve on it, particularly if you want to use the roof space for storage or for a conversion project later on.

Load-bearing walls brought up through the first floor to support the roof will offer adequate support for joists. Any lightweight partitions at first-floor level will need supporting within the confines of the first-floor construction and this won't pose a problem, providing walls cross the joists at right angles. But walls that run along the length of a joist will need extra support and this is usually achieved by doubling-up the joist timbers.

SETTING-OUT THE FIRST FLOOR

Set the timbers out along the top surface of the walls again with any cambers facing upwards, and nail a lath across them. Level them and then pack the ends where necessary, as you did with the ground floor. Check again that they are level in both directions, using a spirit-level and straight-edge. Finally, build the walls up to secure the joists in position. As with the ground floor, the joists at this level will be cross-braced and made firmer, once the roof is put on.

Scaffolding is essential for working on this type of project at these heights. Although it can be hired, there are financial benefits in buying it, particularly if the construction is expected to continue for a prolonged duration. There is always a good market for second-hand scaffolding and, once the building has been completed, you will probably sell it for more or less the same amount you bought it at. Ladders and hoists will also be needed to make lifting materials to the first floor and roof sections easier. Great care should be taken when working at these heights. You should not only be aware of your own safety but that of others on the ground. Make sure that family members and any visitors are aware that they must not pass through any area where someone is working at high level. Children, particularly, should be warned of the dangers and kept under close supervision.

The more you work at this height, the more comfortable you will become and, after only a short period, you will find yourself moving around with balance, poise and agility. The danger is that you will become over-confident and stretch too far or fail to use adequate safety precautions. Always keep this in mind and maintain a strict site safety code. When working across joists, planks can be put down to act as a walking platform but never, ever, leave the plank ends overhanging a void.

Lightweight, non-supporting walls are usually constructed as a softwood frame with plasterboard cladding. These are very easy to assemble, though assistance might be required to manoeuvre the heavy plasterboard sheets until they are pinned to the frame. The construction drawings will detail the minimum standard size and, as before, these could be increased to improve rigidity. It is particularly beneficial to double the timbers around door frames, as this can help prevent walls vibrating and plaster from cracking.

Before you proceed to brick-up the walls, construct another storey lath, which will enable window and door head heights to be transferred around the building. Follow the sections on your construction drawings to close off the cavity at the top of the walls and prepare a level seating for the wall plate. This will be strapped down into the cavity. All required sizes and positions will be specified on the plans. The next task is to complete the shell by putting the roof on and then make the entire structure weatherproof. Your days spent working outside are gradually coming to an end.

SUMMARY

- The type of floor you have chosen will dictate how you begin constructing the shell. Be aware that the building inspector will need to assess the damp-proof installation for solid floors before concrete is poured.

- Final checks should be made to ensure fitted furniture, bathroom suites and kitchen cupboards will fit snugly along the walls you are about to build.

- Be aware that a standard design is likely to produce a standard house and materials quoted in the construction drawings are usually of 'minimum' quality. There is always an opportunity to improve the standard as you build.

- As you proceed, check and double-check that brick courses are level along horizontal and vertical planes and that joists are held firm and flat.

- Install wall-ties between interior and exterior load-bearing walls as instructed by the approved plans.

- When working at height, remember to employ safety precautions and make certain others are aware of the dangers.

USEFUL INTERNET WEBSITES

www.hotline-chimneys.co.uk
Lots of advice and information about installing chimneys and flue systems so you can enjoy a real or artificial fire in your new home. The company offers a useful service of providing specific guide notes once issued with detailed construction dimensions. And if you don't want a chimney but still want a real fire, visit **www.the-fire-place.co.uk** for details on powered flues.

www.rmc.co.uk/diy/pages/diy.asp
Information on bricklaying and a source for ready-mix mortar products and cavity insulation.

www.igltd.co.uk/standard.html
This company produces a wide range of lintels for every conceivable residential construction. It also has a useful automated online service for identifying the right size and type of lintel for a specific purpose.

Chapter 15

The Roof

This chapter covers:

- roof types

- DIY or sub-contract

- felting the roof

- battening

- tiling

- making it weatherproof

The design of the roof and preparation required to secure it to the main structure will be detailed on your construction drawings. The roof was first considered when foundations were poured, and it was at that very early stage that the importance of wall

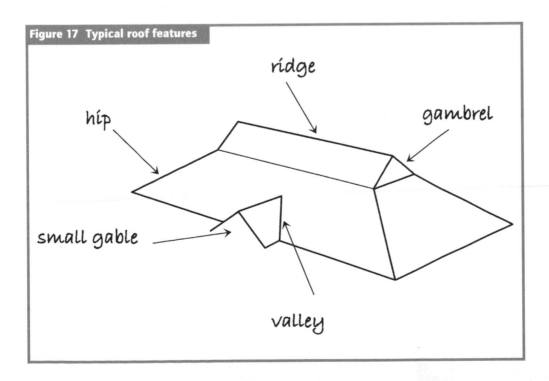

Figure 17 Typical roof features

ridge

hip

gambrel

small gable

valley

strengths and their relation to the roof became apparent. That initial assessment should have enabled you to arrive at the current stage of construction with a suitable and solid base on which the roof can now be placed.

ROOF TYPES

There are two main types of roof and the one you have chosen to build is likely to reflect how you intend using the space it will provide (see Figure 18). Traditional roof designs offer greater flexibility because they are constructed with substantial timber beams, whilst the lightweight trussed rafter type is easier to lift into place, but supplies

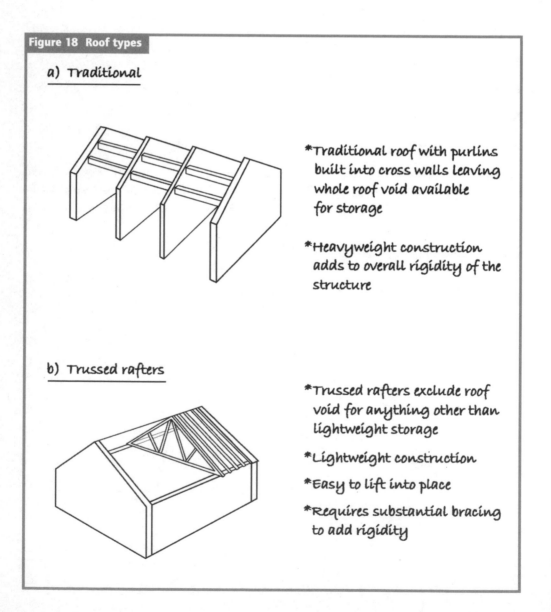

Figure 18 Roof types

a) Traditional

*Traditional roof with purlins built into cross walls leaving whole roof void available for storage

*Heavyweight construction adds to overall rigidity of the structure

b) Trussed rafters

*Trussed rafters exclude roof void for anything other than lightweight storage

*Lightweight construction

*Easy to lift into place

*Requires substantial bracing to add rigidity

a void that cannot be exploited. The roof can be a major feature of the dwelling, comprising different levels, hips, slopes and valleys, or it can be a simple watertight cap for the structure formed out of a single ridge line with equal pitches on either side.

The basic principle of the traditional roof construction is to bring load-bearing cross walls up into the roof space to support horizontal running purlins (see Figure 19). These are large section timbers onto which the rafters are fixed at regular intervals, to support the roof coverings. When large spans are involved, the purlins can be replaced with lightweight steel beams, and timber is then placed on top of these, so that rafters can be fixed.

A trussed rafter roof is the lightweight alternative, and ideal if the void is only going to be used for minor storage. This type of construction relies on an array of small bracing timbers, rather than large single beams. The amount of timber involved virtually fills the void, making it fairly useless, but the frames can be lifted into position easily. Once seated on top of the walls, the frames are connected using galvanised metal plates, and diagonally braced according to the manufacturer's instructions.

Roof frames can be created in a plethora of different shapes and materials and each one will have its own set of pertinent calculations for load bearing and fixing. Your architect will have recommended a particular type of construction based on cost, style and function, in accordance with local planning restrictions and building regulations. The profile of your roof may therefore already have been determined by earlier limitations or constraints forced upon you by external authorities.

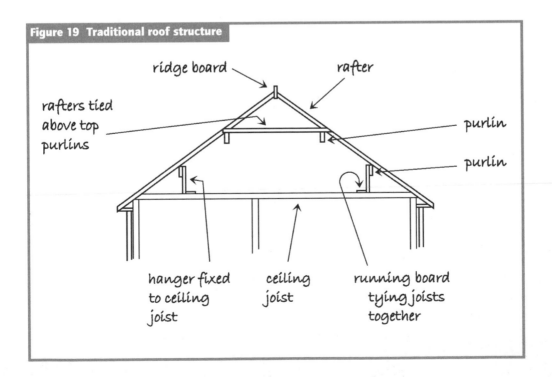

Figure 19 Traditional roof structure

DIY OR SUB-CONTRACT

The real question is: 'How have your skills developed?' Do you feel confident about tackling the entire roof structure, which in many ways, is a quite separate exercise from foundation laying and shell construction? Creating the structure of the roof and fitting it into position is only one part of the process. There is, in addition, battening, felting and tiling or slating, all of which involve different skills and trades.

If you have developed a forte for joinery, you might want to produce the main framework and then leave the installation, felting and tiling to an outside agency. Alternatively, if you have found working at height uncomfortable or you are under pressure to complete the dwelling before winter sets in, you might prefer sub-contracting the whole of the roof. To find a qualified roofing contractor in your area, contact the National Federation of Roofing Contractors at 24 Weymouth Street, London, W1G 7LX or telephone them on 020 7436 0387. They also have a useful website at **www.nfrc.co.uk** that includes a wealth of information, technical advice and manufacturer details for roofing products and systems. Whichever route you choose, the following explanation of roof assembly stages and the work involved should prove helpful.

With a traditional roof, it is essential that the wall plate, purlins and ridge section are parallel with each other and level. To achieve this, check the Building Regulation approval for a description of how to bed and strap the wall plate down along the top of the finished walls. If any hip work is required, the wall plate will need to change direction, and plates should be strapped across the corner with a length of timber, so as to resist any outward thrust.

The construction drawings will indicate whether 'pad stones' are required for seating the purlins into position. These will help to spread the weight and, by using heavy-duty straps, the timber ends can be tied into the gable walls. The purlins must be level throughout their entire length and, as with joists, any curved edges must always face upwards. The rafters will have a tendency to slide down the roof slope, and it is important you prevent this by cross bracing above the highest purlins or notching the rafters over the purlins and/or the wall plate. All the relevant sizes for timber spacing and position will be detailed on the construction drawings. The size of rafters will also be described and, where they meet along the ridge at the topmost part of the roof carcass, a ridge-board needs to be installed, into which all the top ends of the rafters can then be secured with nails.

Cutting the upper parts of the rafters is best done on the ground before fixing them into position. Each saw-cut will be identical, so a template can be made and used to mark the position for subsequent cuts on each timber length. The lower end rafter cuts are more difficult because the timbers will already be fixed onto the roof structure. It is common practice to employ a line-band running along the edge of the rafters and then use a plumb-line to mark the vertical saw-cut position. It is essential all vertical cuts are equal and level because the fascia-board will be fixed onto the cut ends, thus providing a firm base on which guttering can be installed.

The method of bracing into gables and framing for eaves boards will all be indicated on the drawings. Builders will not normally require any additional information, as these aspects of the structure are not subject to building control inspection approval and the likelihood is that the builder will have undertaken this kind of work many times before. However, if you are an inexperienced self-builder, you probably *will* need more detailed guidance and your architect can supply it, providing they are made aware at an early stage that you intend doing all of the work yourself.

FELTING THE ROOF

Once the timber carcass is complete, you can felt the roof. This is most definitely not a task you should undertake on a windy day. Despite felt being a heavy material, it is easily caught by a gust of wind and, if you happen to be in the way, it will take you with it to the ground below. The four ingredients certain to produce disaster are felt, height, wind and you!

Choose a dry, calm day to carry out the work and double-check your scaffolding, making certain it is secure and at the appropriate height to walk around the wall-plate section of the building. Before you start felting, practise walking up and down the roof slope until you feel confident and safe. Rather than add to the risk by carrying a hammer and felt-nails, buy a slater's pouch to wear around your waist and don't forget to use goggles, a hard-hat and gloves for further protection against splinters and flying debris.

Roofing underfelt is manufactured as either a hessian or plastic-based material, which is light enough to carry but strong enough to take the weight of a man walking on it, once fixed in position. When you take delivery of the required quantity of felt rolls, make sure you keep the original wrapping covers, as these will contain essential instruction data which you will need to refer to later.

Check your construction drawings and follow them when installing the fascia board and a tilting fillet behind the fascia board, which will continuously support the roofing felt and allow any trapped rainwater to run out from behind the roof tiles. Roll out the first run of felt horizontally along the lower edge of the roof frame, nailing it down and pulling it tight as you go. Some types of felt have a non-degradable edging strip of about 75mm to 100mm which should project beyond the roof, draping into the rainwater gutter. Others are totally non-degradable, and the decision on which to use is likely to depend on cost and the desired quality of your build.

The pitch of the roof will determine the amount of overlap for the next run of felt. This is usually 100mm to 150mm, but the actual dimension will be given in tabular format on the original wrapping. Generally, the lower the pitch, the greater an overlap is required. Think of the underfelt as a totally weatherproof membrane and you will appreciate what is needed to secure it as you progress. The pitched verges, for example, will need special attention and a sufficient overhang of felt (check your drawings for full details). Keep in mind that any rainwater driven under the slates by wind or from a broken tile, needs to drain down the roof and out into the gutter.

Chimneys also need careful attention and felt should be used to dress them vertically, to ensure penetrating rain is properly contained. The construction drawings will have details of the specifications for under-boarding around the chimneystack. Refer to them and build accordingly. The same goes for felting up wall abutments and coverage of the tilting fillet behind the fascia board.

BATTENING

With the underfelt on, we now need to prepare for battening. The space between battens is crucial to ensure an accurate alignment of and support for the roof tiles. The pitch of the roof again plays a part in this calculation and so does the type of tile you intend using. Check your construction drawings and read through the tile or slate manufacturer's literature before starting. Although there is a wide range of batten timber available, don't settle for anything less than 50mm x 25mm tanalised softwood, if the tiles are to be nailed down. Galvanised steel nails should be used to secure the battens in place through the roofing felt and into the top of the rafters.

Setting out the battens is an important task, because it will determine where the tiles are eventually positioned on the roof. It is not advisable to trim preformed tiles to fit because it alters the way they lap onto each other and reduces their weatherproofing qualities (but see 'varying length' of tiles below). Consequently, the number used need to slot exactly into the space available up the pitched side of the roof face, from gutter-edge to just below the ridge, leaving enough space for ridge-tiles or lead flashing at the apex. Help in achieving this precise exercise comes in the form of a 'ranging lath'. As we mentioned earlier when setting out the walls, laths can be usefully converted into measuring guides because they are long, slender and economical lengths of timber that are easily cut to an appropriate size.

First, measure the distance from the apex of the roof to the lower edge and cut the lath down to meet this size. You can now work on the flat at ground level, using the lath as a representation of the pitched section of roof. Consult your construction drawings to identify where the first and last row of tiles will be positioned, bearing in mind that sufficient space must remain for the ridge tiles or flashing. Mark the position of the uppermost and lowest rows of battens on the lath at the appropriate

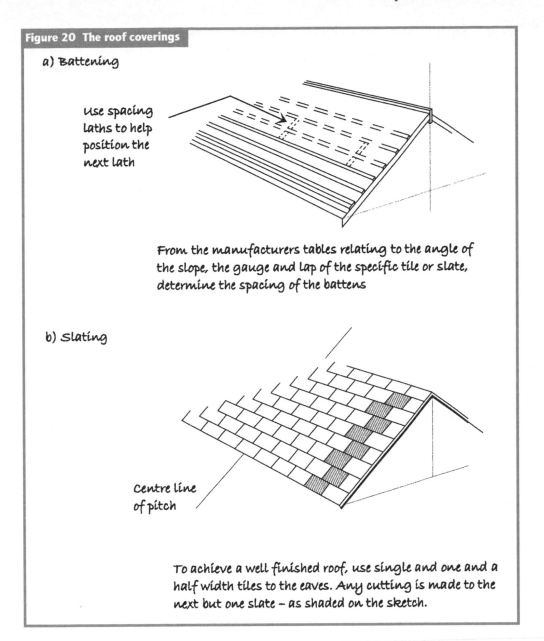

Figure 20 The roof coverings

a) Battening

use spacing laths to help position the next lath

From the manufacturers tables relating to the angle of the slope, the gauge and lap of the specific tile or slate, determine the spacing of the battens

b) Slating

Centre line of pitch

To achieve a well finished roof, use single and one and a half width tiles to the eaves. Any cutting is made to the next but one slate – as shaded on the sketch.

points. You can now lay tiles along the lath to identify the remaining batten positions. It is likely that slight adjustments will be needed to reduce the gaps between battens, so that a perfect run of tiles up the roof slope is achieved.

Once the 'ranging lath' has been created, measure the gaps between the batten positions precisely and cut a second lath into spacing guides. These should be numbered for identification. You can now go onto the roof with the ranging-lath, spacers and battens, to complete the task (see Figure 20). Fixing the rows of battens in their appropriate positions should be a fast and straightforward operation, culminating in the production of a wall-to-wall ladder of timber over the entire roof area.

It may have been your earlier intention to employ a slater to complete the remaining roof structure but, having successfully achieved the tasks so far, you should now feel much more confident about the skills you possess. With the scaffolding in place and everything prepared for tiling ... why not have a go at the last part of the job and save yourself even more money? It is not difficult and you have already proved yourself more than capable of tackling it.

TILING

The techniques involved in tiling or slating a roof depend on the type of product being used. Some tiles simply hook over the batten with every fourth row nailed down, whereas slates have pre-drilled holes so that every course can be secured with nails. Tiling is invariably 'material specific' with regard to fixing, cutting, trimming and flashing. Manufacturers always produce installation guidance notes to accompany their products and these should be followed with due care and attention. Despite this, once the express form of roof covering has been decided, there are some basic principles that apply in almost all situations.

The first consideration involves finding out how the first run of tiles is to sit on the roof at the lower (gutter) edge. This in turn will provide you with a suitable starting point and allow the first tile to be fixed in position. Mark the centre of the first batten and then loose lay a row of tiles on top of it. Do the tiles fit snugly and finish neatly in the appropriate position at each end? If they do, consider yourself very lucky indeed, as this is more likely the result of good fortune, rather than good judgement. If you are not so lucky, centre a gap between two tiles on the bottom edge of the roof and spread tiles in each direction, reducing the gaps very slightly to create a perfect fit.

Tiles and slates are generally produced in a wide variety of sizes. The intention is to make life easier for builders and roofers, who prefer to have a range of pre-cut materials that will fit almost any structure shape, rather than have to spend time and energy trimming materials to fit. Tiles with varying lengths help make battening a straightforward task because the spacing required up a roof pitch can be equal, except for the last batten, which will take the reduced length of tile. Similarly, varying widths allow tiles to be positioned from the centre outwards, finishing equally and appropriately at the roof verge on either side. There are often variants beyond the normal width as well, for example many manufacturers produce a one and half width tile to help achieve a suitable overhang.

When tiles must be cut for the row to fit neatly, the trimmed tile is usually placed at the next-to-last position along the row, thus allowing the last tile to have a preformed edge at the verge. To ensure the finished roof looks properly balanced, always start fixing the first row of tiles at the mid-point of the batten, with the first tile centred (or joint-centred, if it is found two tiles are better taking the central position). If tiles need trimming, you will need to undertake it at each end (next-to-last) to maintain the roof's symmetrical appearance (see Figure 20). Subsequent rows are fixed upwardly, with staggered joints lapped according to the manufacturer's instructions, and alternate courses identical in layout.

MAKING IT WEATHERPROOF

The design, composition and size of the roof tile you use will determine the type of flashing you install at junctions, hips, abutments and chimneystacks. The best guide on this subject is the Lead Sheet Association (LSA), who produce excellent publications covering every possible variation and situation. They can be contacted on 01892 822773 or by e-mail at **leadsa@globalnet.co.uk**. The handbooks are produced in three volumes: (1) Flashings, (2) Roof Cladding and (3) Weatherings. They also have an *Installers Pocket Guide*, which is more economically priced and includes extracts from all three volumes. You may find the books are available from your local library or they can be purchased direct from the LSA's website at **www.leadsheetas-sociation.org.uk**

If you opt to employ a plumber to make the flashings for you, he will advise on the appropriate design and construction of support boarding for the lead work. These will apply to concealed gutters, the skirting around chimneystacks, wall abutments, hip details, valleys (where the roof may change direction) and verge trims. Not all plumbers are familiar with this type of work, so thoroughly vet any preferred tradesman before employing them. Ask about the level of knowledge and experience they have, and use someone who has been recommended whenever possible.

Your architect will advise you about the work involved in making the structure weathertight. Obtain details from them about finishing the verges, pitch and gable ends. It may be normal practice in your locality for verges to over-sail the ends of buildings or alternatively they might have to be capped by stone slabs (termed 'tabling'). The more likely option in some areas is for the verges to be trimmed and pointed with a hard mix of sand and cement mortar. Some man-made tile manufacturers produce preformed verge-closure sections, which conveniently slot into the gap, and ridge tiles in matching colours and textures. It all comes down to the original choice you made about roofing material and an early appreciation of the fundamental principles.

Once the structure has been made weathertight, you can afford to stand back and breathe a sigh of relief. The major labour-intensive construction work to the exterior shell is complete and you can now turn your attention to the interior aspects. This is a pivotal moment, when you move away from the *perspirational* and walk towards the *inspirational*.

Summary

■ Prepare the top of the walls so they are ready to accept the roof frame.

■ If you employ a roofing contractor, make sure he is suitably qualified and experienced.

■ Construct the roof carcass according to the details supplied in your approved plans. Consult your architect for advice and guidance if you are in any doubt about how to proceed.

■ When felting the roof, remember to use safety equipment and never undertake the work in windy conditions.

■ Be aware that the type of slate or tile you use to cover the roof will influence the number and position of battens and the manner in which the tiles are laid and fixed.

■ The work involved in creating and installing lead flashing is a skill not all plumbers possess. Check that your preferred tradesman has sufficient knowledge and experience to complete the task to a professional standard.

■ It is crucial to ensure your newly constructed shell is watertight. Consult your architect about how to properly close off all verges, pitches and gable ends.

Useful Internet Websites

www.clear-skies.org/technologies.htm
A site dedicated to green energy alternative systems, including solar panels for roofs, water turbines and wind power. There are also details about the household grants that are available to those who buy and install them.

www.rooftiles.co.uk
This website contains details of everything you could ever wish to know about roof tiles, including links to thousands of different designs and colours.

www.trustedservices.co.uk
A site whose aim is to provide details of tradesmen throughout the country. The unique element here is that, to be listed, the tradesmen must have been recommended by ordinary homeowners who have employed them. The list includes contact details for electricians, plumbers, builders and roofers.

Part Three
Internal Works ...
The Fun Part!

Interior Design Sample Board

Chapter 16
Major Features

This chapter covers:

- designing the main elements
- the staircase and changes in level
- focal points
- fireplaces
- the kitchen
- the bathrooms
- feature lighting
- feature surfaces
- fixed and fitted furniture

The main advantage of reaching this stage will become obvious if constructing the exterior shell has been undertaken during periods of inclement weather. You will be dry and, perhaps for the first time in the entire build to date, enjoy shelter from the wind. This welcome improvement in the level of comfort should enthuse and fill you with optimism, as you forge towards completing the interior aspects.

DESIGNING THE MAIN ELEMENTS

The first considerations involve establishing walkways and the installation of temporary lighting throughout all major room areas. These two elements will allow you to visualise each room in detail and plan what needs to be done and when. This is an enjoyable phase and should not be rushed! Remember that the quality of the finished product depends on your ability to establish a good design scheme and then stagger the work required to accomplish it in priority order.

The priority may, of course, depend on many things, and having sufficient funds available is likely to be one of them. Cash flow may have been put under a considerable strain in recent months, and this is a useful point in the construction to give

Figure 21 Typical set of details of a major feature – elevation

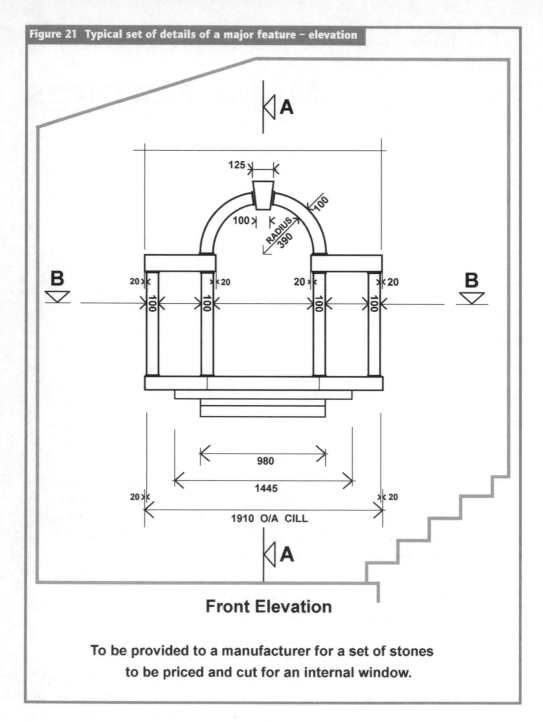

Front Elevation

To be provided to a manufacturer for a set of stones
to be priced and cut for an internal window.

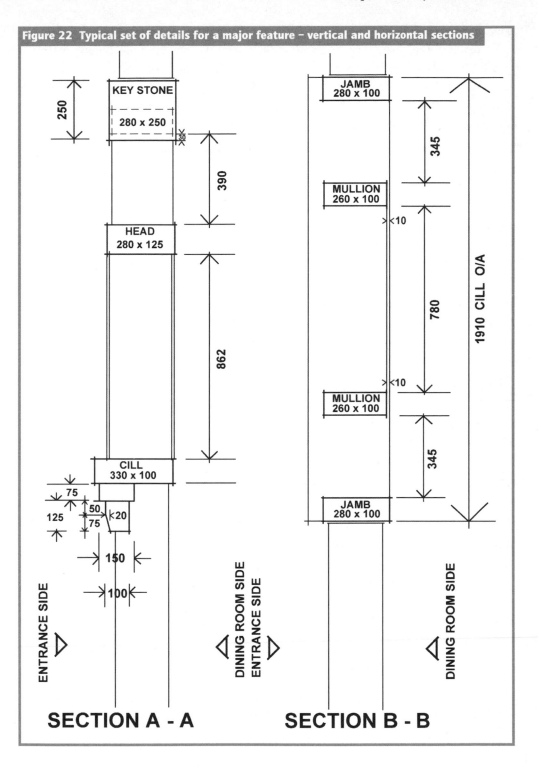

Figure 22 Typical set of details for a major feature – vertical and horizontal sections

attention to other (low expenditure) matters which will allow your finances time to catch up. If you already have the materials, you could, for example, begin creating a grand staircase or luxurious kitchen and spend your time on the labour-intensive aspects involved. Alternatively, you might decide to take time out for research, sketch 'dream schemes' for living areas and bedrooms or explore the pages of all those interior design magazines you have been collecting.

At the very least, you should discuss your ideas and aspirations with your architect and/or interior designer. They will help guide you in directions you could not even conceive, and supply information about innovative products and materials new to the market. This is also a good time to go out and about. Visiting new development show homes, architectural warehouses and public or trade exhibitions will cultivate inspirational ideas for your new home. The Internet is also useful as it delivers information and images about products throughout the entire world right into your home. There are thousands of fabrics available, automated heating and lighting systems, carpets and tiles, beds and fitted wardrobes, light-fittings and kitchen goods – all in a multitude of styles and designs, colours and textures. Use this period to explore the endless variety of possibilities that are now open to you.

THE STAIRCASE AND CHANGES IN LEVEL

The arrangement and location of rooms and their levels and interlinking landings will have been decided at the outset, but it is only now, with the model constructed at full size, that you can see and measure out every aspect of the original design. The entrance into your dwelling and staircase leading you up and through it are major features, and the approach to their design and character will determine the remaining parts, whether historical and traditional, modern and contemporary or simply functional.

With regard to the staircase itself, the range of dimensions that can be used in the design of balconies, balustrading, handrails and step sizes, will be limited by Building Regulations. These have come about through safety considerations, which have evolved over many years. Beyond these limitations, the remaining design of the staircase is entirely up to you. Important and influential matters to consider include:

- The position of the staircase and whether it will be freestanding, linked only by the ground and upper floor, or supported by a wall.

- The material used to construct the staircase, treads, balustrade and handrails. Timber is the obvious choice for many, but polished metal or a combination of the two can enhance a contemporary design.

- The layout of the staircase is crucial. Half and quarter turns with a variety of treads can increase the available space remaining in a hallway whilst straight, sweeping and curved flights can be grand and imposing. When considering stair-flight turns, be aware that enough room needs to be created so that heavy and bulky items of furnishing can be manipulated around them.

■ Building Regulations restrict the widths and heights of treads, but the remaining design is usually open to interpretation. Closed treads are commonly used when carpeting is intended. Open treads are less intrusive and a valuable option when natural light needs to pass through to reach other areas. Cut-string is a more decorative form of timberwork and provides an impressive staircase for an open hallway.

There are off-the-shelf systems that can be purchased from builders' merchants and adapted to suit your particular self-build project but, if funds are available, there is nothing more magnificent than a handcrafted staircase built by an experienced carpenter. The cost of timbers will probably depend on whether you intend painting, staining or lacquering them upon completion. It may seem obvious, but we will state it anyway: there is little point paying the additional price for beautifully grained hardwood, if it is going to be hidden under a layer of paint.

Remember that the design of your home is not limited to the horizontal plain. Split-levels, mezzanines and galleries really can turn an ordinary dwelling into something quite extraordinary. There are always opportunities to exploit a given space in all directions and the creation of different levels generates interest and character. Care must always be taken to construct within the terms of the building regulations and advice from your architect is essential in this specific regard. In addition and where the available space is limited, split-levels *can* cause an area to appear cumbersome and constricted, particularly if barrier-rails and balustrades become obtrusive. However, with good planning and adequate space, living areas can be interlinked with minimal visual intrusion, producing a unique and interesting home with rising and falling levels and a variety of positional viewing points.

Focal points

Certain rooms, such as kitchens, dining rooms, bedrooms and the main living room, lend themselves to a focal point. Consider a fine farmhouse kitchen and you immediately think of a vast cooking range, copper ventilation hood, open-faced brick and stonework and natural, 'wholesome' materials. These are all character building, emotive elements that revolve around a central theme. They give purpose and provide identity.

Dining rooms can have a prominent table and subtle or pendular lighting to create a suitable atmosphere. In bedrooms, the bed itself may provide the focal point or, alternatively, it may be a richly decorated wall or an ornately framed and colourful picture. Living rooms always benefit from a fireplace, whether traditional or modern, real flame or artificial. The fireplace is, as it has been for centuries, the key focal point for family members and friends to gather around whilst deliberating the day's events or just relaxing in quiet contemplation. Such emphasis and importance is given to this particular element that we describe it separately and in more detail below.

FIREPLACES

An open or gas-flame fire satisfies all of our senses. It is something tangible we can see, feel, hear, touch and smell. It is comforting, relaxing and inspiring. Even the most minimalist and contemporary of room designs can benefit from a fireplace interpreted into its simplest form – flames captured within pure shapes and boundaries. They are no longer just a primary source of heat but are also highly decorative and innovative in the materials used to fabricate them. The conceptual variety of design is boundless and includes everything from big Victorian and Edwardian surrounds to chic steel and chrome 'hole-in-the-wall' models, well vented but defying the confines of a traditional style.

The choice is truly subjective and, as many who built slate and granite varieties know only too well, fashions can change very quickly. Bear in mind it is not always wise to create a fireplace that reflects the decorative nature of the room, because this is likely to change several times as opinions, tastes and styles come in and go out of vogue. Remember that the fireplace will probably remain long after the decoration and furnishings have been changed.

To further explore the vast range available, Internet users might wish to visit the following websites:

www.antiquefireplace.co.uk	**www.fire-power.co.uk**
www.designfireplaces.co.uk	**www.galleryfireplaces.co.uk**
www.fireplacemagic.co.uk	**www.stone-essentials.co.uk**

www.nfa.org.uk (The National Fireplace Association)

THE KITCHEN

The kitchen often lies at the very heart of family life and will invariably serve as a meeting-point for the home's occupiers. In recent years, fashion has created a compulsion to change fittings repeatedly, but the central feature of a quality cooking range or hob and oven combination remains constant. It is an inescapable visual anchor for the room and an important focal point. It is also a very practical consideration because, after all, the fundamental purpose of the room is to cook food. Once the type of equipment is chosen, you will need to think about associated installations, such as ventilation, extraction and the power source.

Whatever style of kitchen you choose, be it Provençal or Mediterranean, Spanish, Mexican or South American, Middle Eastern or Far Eastern, traditional, cosy, industrial or contemporary, the next most important consideration should be the floor. Like the cooker, the floor finish is likely to be a more permanent fixture than the units and must be easy to maintain, hygienic and, above all else, versatile enough to harmonise with future changes of colour, style, decoration and fittings.

Much depends on the type of floor you choose. Terracotta, African slate, Yorkshire stone and ceramic tiles will all need a substantial sub-floor and the preparation involved should allow for the finished level to equal that of doorway carpeting in adjacent rooms. Screeding, mortar or tile adhesive and the floor slab or tile thickness will raise the sub-floor level considerably and an accurate estimate will need assessing prior to installation. Solid floors of this nature can be both costly and labour intensive, but the finished result will mature and last a lifetime.

The style of kitchen units comes and goes, but it is often the quality of the worktops that dictates a time for change. Inferior worktops deteriorate rapidly due to water damage around sinks, scoring from knives, laminate chipping, heat, grease and de-bonding of the laminate surface from the timber below. More robust materials such as marble, laminated hardwood or some of the very best quality solid resins, can rectify this lack of durability. They will not only survive well beyond the period when other 'off-the-shelf' solutions have failed, but will probably outlive the base-cupboard carcasses as well.

Remember that the quality and style of a kitchen is a primary and significant element that people take into consideration when buying a new home. So if you are building for profit with the intention of selling at completion, plan and install a kitchen that will make an impression, rather than one that will necessarily last for decades to come.

THE BATHROOMS

Self-builders can unleash their wildest fantasies when creating bathrooms and en-suites for their new home. These are areas that can be truly experimental. Basic concepts can be expanded without restriction to produce miniature Roman spas or Hollywood suites complete with sauna, Jacuzzi, steam-room and pool. The bath itself can descend into the floor or rise up from it on a stepped plinth, surrounded with mirrors and subtle lighting. Walls and floors can be clad in luxurious marble, the most ornate ceramic tiles or even industrial sheet metal for a futuristic look. Showers can take the form of entire waterproofed rooms with direct drainage through the floor.

There is an unlimited array of themes and design concepts to consider and these range from Victorian reproduction all the way through to sparklingly modern schemes. You could even have different bathrooms with different themes or, instead of just having 'his' and 'her' bathrobes, how about 'his' and 'her' bathroom suites? Inspiration might come from a hotel you stayed at whilst on holiday, a glossy society or celebrity magazine or even a single ceramic tile used as a base for your scheme. There are fittings to satisfy every taste, style and concept. A well-planned, sumptuous and spacious bathroom can truly help fulfil the 'dream home' objective.

When planning the layout and interior aspects of these rooms, remember that the four most important basic installation elements will need professional attention. These include:

- comprehensive and long-lasting 'wet' area waterproofing;
- electrical fixture, switching, power-point and cabling safety;
- a hot and cold water supply for all planned fittings;
- the adequate drainage of waste water out of the building.

With these elements uppermost in your mind at all times, you can devise a scheme to suit purse, purpose and preference.

Feature lighting

Standing on your temporary walk boards, looking at unfinished walls and raw ceiling constructions, it may be difficult to envisage the type of desirable lighting effects you want for each room. Indeed, you may think, 'Why bother when it can all be done after the main building work has been completed?' The fact is, once walls have been plastered, it will be much more difficult to conceal cables and alter the position of fixings. Doing the basics now simply makes the entire installation much easier later.

For every focal point, every dramatic view of one room from another, for every corner and alcove and even for every picture hung on a wall, there is the opportunity for enhancement through feature lighting. Traditional switch, dimmer controls and bulbs can be replaced with ultra-hi-tech systems, touch sensitive pads and low-voltage micro-fittings. These are not only energy efficient, but convenient too. Automated systems have built-in security programmes that mimic normal family life, switching lights on and off as if you were there, moving around the house. This can be very useful whilst you are away on holiday or simply out for the evening. Other systems alter several light fittings in a room with the press of a single button, changing the effect and mood instantly from 'party time' to 'relaxation' and everything in between.

Lighting outside the property can be planned at the same time and cables installed and accommodated whilst trenches are available. The additional installation of infrared movement sensor switching will also add a security defence element to the garden illumination system. This is all very simple to arrange at this stage and cost effective too.

Using a spare print of the house plan for your electrician, mark up the actual position of fittings with dimensions from walls or any other fixed point. He can then plan his part of the work and advise you about any specific building preparation, for example where conduit is needed so that cables will eventually be concealed.

FEATURE SURFACES

We have already discussed bathrooms and the feature flooring of kitchens, but what about other areas of the house? Dining rooms or a conservatory might also benefit from a solid floor with decorative tiling. A living room may lend itself to having a feature stone chimneybreast or timbered wall. This kind of embellishment is usually installed prior to any plastering, so plan it now and slot it appropriately into the schedule of works.

Stone cappings to low dividing walls, stone windowsills, brick arches and slate skirtings will also need fixing prior to plasterwork commencing. Remember that an allowance must be made for the considerable thickness claddings require where they adjoin other surfaces, including door frames, timber skirtings and finished walls.

FIXED AND FITTED FURNITURE

Fixed furniture will require a screed on walls prior to plastering. For example, any fixed seating will need properly secured battens to enable sound and strong anchoring. Kitchens can greatly benefit from lining-out prior to plastering. Indeed, for kitchen units to withstand heavy use, it is wise to mark out on the brick walls the position of every base and wall unit and the extent of any tiles.

With regular and deep fixture points, line these areas with 22mm block board, allowing the tiles and tops of wall units to lap over the edge by 5mm to 10mm. When the room is plastered, bring the walls out to the same thickness as the block board and allow to dry out. This will provide the most positive, rigid fixing for your wall and base units and service runs passing behind them. Bear in mind that electrical socket positions will need marking and cutting out for back-box fixing, prior to attaching sheets to the wall.

SUMMARY

■ Although you may have planned the position of the staircase in advance, you should consider carefully how it will be constructed and the materials that will be used.

■ Focal points are essential. Consider the main feature for each room in turn and then plan to install it at an appropriate stage of the internal work schedule.

■ Most self-builders choose to have an open fire in addition to more convenient heating systems. The form it takes, whether real flame or artificial, and the design of the fire surround, are crucial considerations.

■ The floors and walls of bathrooms and kitchens will need special attention to ensure they are waterproof and adequately prepared prior to any ceramic tiling. Bathroom suites and other fixtures will also need careful planning, if a luxurious concept is to be realised.

■ Lighting installations, feature surfaces and fitted furniture can be planned and prepared at this early stage. This will guarantee firm and concealed fixings prior to plastering.

USEFUL INTERNET WEBSITES

www.simplyautomate.com
Extraordinary home automation systems for security, lighting, heating, blinds and curtains. There are also systems that can be operated remotely by telephone or computer links whilst you are away from home.

www.electriclightcompany.co.uk
Online shop with a good range of contemporary, innovative and exciting light fittings for the home. The site also has other unusual accessories rarely seen on the high street.

www.designsearch.net/glass.html
Glass brick walls and partitioning is becoming increasingly fashionable. This site offers links to every conceivable use of glass in the modern home. Examples include glass floors and walls, kitchen work surfaces, stained glass, toughened and curved glass products.

Chapter 17
The Floors

This chapter covers:

- flooring materials

- cable and pipe runs

- soundproofing and insulation

- installing timber floors

Every installation from this stage onwards has the effect of closing-off sections of the building and this certainly applies to flooring. Once the floors are fixed down in position, it will be much more difficult to lay sub-floor pipes and cables or correct the anchor points and subsequent rocking of joists. That said, the flooring *must* be installed prior to fixing doorframes, skirting, covings and plastering the walls.

In general, a compromise between fully installing the floor and accessibility has to be made. This may take the form of carefully planned and well-positioned hatches, which will allow work to continue in the sub-floor void, albeit with some restriction and inconvenience. The content of this chapter follows standard practice and points out some of the benefits and pitfalls involved. As with all construction projects, an assessment of how and when to install flooring should be taken after careful consideration of your own specific dwelling requirements and following advice from your architect.

FLOORING MATERIALS

We have considered in detail the many types of specialist floor finishes, but the majority are likely to be timber. Economical chipboard is fine, providing you don't expect too much walking traffic and accept that it has a fairly short lifespan in comparison to more substantial solid timbers. Hardwood planked tongue and groove is, without doubt, one of the best flooring materials and provides warmth, durability and a beautifully grained surface suitable for all room types. More than this, natural timbers mature and improve as they age and are easily maintained and refurbished. Old floors can be stripped, sanded and re-lacquered as required but, even when they are left scratched and distressed, a simple sand-down and coat of varnish can bring them back to their former glory.

Many will probably decide to compromise between the choice of superior hardwood and economical chipboard, settling on an installation of softwood tongue and groove. This provides a good floor and the soft grain ensures adequate fixing to the joists without the timbers splitting. It is also easy to create service hatches, once additional support has been given to the joists below. Softwood flooring can be lacquered or carpeted and, with an additional layer of fixed plywood and adequate adhesive screeding, it can also be prepared sufficiently to accept vinyl or ceramic tiles (though solid concrete floors remain the best long-term solution for this type of finish).

This is an appropriate point to mention one of the most unique ranges of vinyl floor-coverings we have come across whilst writing this book. They are suitable for almost any application, but look particularly striking in bathrooms and kitchens. An attempt at describing in words the concept of a 'dry water', 'perfectly flat pebbled' or 'soft metal mesh' floor is probably absurd and at best paradoxical, but thankfully the company have a website where these extraordinary products can be viewed. Go to **www.marley.com** and examine the 'x-photographic' and 'x-water' range. Samples and brochures can be obtained online or by telephoning Marley Floors on 01622 854040.

CABLE AND PIPE RUNS

Most standard constructions have cables and pipes running in the sub-floor void fixed to or cut into joists. This arrangement means water pipes are concealed from view, except where they rise from the floor to radiators, bathroom and kitchen taps, toilet cisterns, water-tanks and shower units. Electric cables rise from the floor in a wall conduit, which is attached to the brickwork, for sockets, and down from the ceiling for light switches. Although drainage from baths and showers is usually installed above the floor level, sometimes this too needs to enter the sub-floor void, if the normal gravity incline from floor to fitting is inadequate.

Good access needs to be provided so these installations can be undertaken after the flooring has been fixed down. This involves creating hatches in appropriate and convenient positions. Service hatches will not only be used for the initial laying of pipes and cables, but also for repairs, maintenance, alterations and additions in the years to come. Good planning and robust construction of access hatches is essential to ensure the floor remains solid and secure. There is nothing worse than a squeaky, badly supported afterthought cut through a new floor, as many homeowners will testify.

Service hatches should be established throughout the dwelling but, on the upper floors, easy access can be provided for the initial installation of pipes and cables by delaying the construction of ceilings. With a little forethought, plumbers and electricians can complete tasks from beneath the upper floor without constraint and, once their work is finished, the ceilings can then be installed.

This is also a useful opportunity for self-builders to consider other system installations involving cables, which would benefit from concealment. For example:

■ If you ever wanted to make taking a bath a more rewarding and relaxing experience, how about a cabled music system with speakers built into the bathroom ceiling?

■ You could run television aerial and satellite cables throughout the house to sockets in each room, providing everyone with their own independent home entertainment facility.

■ This is a good stage to consider hiding all those unwanted burglar-alarm and other security-system cables, such as CCTV, which could be linked to control-panels and viewing screens in appropriate rooms.

■ Telephone wires, computer cables and devoted Internet lines can be easily cable-managed and hidden under the floor, making the completed dwelling a much tidier home.

When cables are situated within the sub-floor void, it is often wise to run small ducts, which will keep them safe and dry. Plastic overflow piping available from most good DIY stores is ideal for this purpose and can be attached to the joists. Always remember to keep cables well away from and underneath hot-water pipes, as the heat generated can cause some cables to become brittle and crack over a period of time.

SOUNDPROOFING AND INSULATION

There are two types of noise generally produced in the average home. Ambient sound is generated within the space of rooms from mechanical and electronic devices, such as hi-fi systems and televisions, and from adults and children talking. Other reverberated noise, such as footsteps, is transferred from floor surfaces through to the rooms below. There are simple and economic solutions to these irritating problems that the self-builder can provide for himself and his family.

The easiest and most comprehensive method is to install acoustic insulation in the void between floors and a soundproofing damper-mat underneath carpets. This absorbs most noise and provides a much improved level of comfort for all concerned. But what about situations where carpet is not going to be used? Solid and laminate timber flooring has become very popular in recent years, but one of the major drawbacks is the incessant noise created by walking on it, which can be extremely irritating to occupiers in rooms below. The answer is to install acoustic matting between the joists and floorboards that will cushion any vibration (see Figure 23). There is a wide range of materials available for both void and sub-floorboard sound insulation and all have different applications and specifications. Internet users might wish to explore these further by visiting **www.customaudiodesigns.co.uk**, **www.domesticsoundproofing.co.uk** or **www.soundreduction.co.uk**, who offer reliable solutions to most residential noise problems.

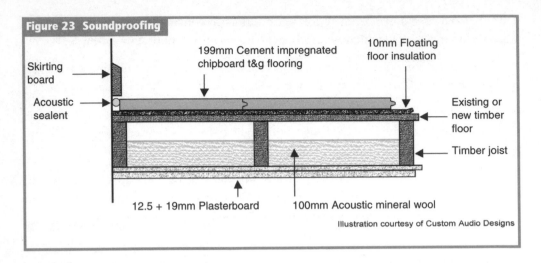

Figure 23 Soundproofing

Skirting board

Acoustic sealent

199mm Cement impregnated chipboard t&g flooring

10mm Floating floor insulation

Existing or new timber floor

Timber joist

12.5 + 19mm Plasterboard

100mm Acoustic mineral wool

Illustration courtesy of Custom Audio Designs

INSTALLING TIMBER FLOORS

First, consider whether to install finished timber boards or an economical and temporary floor, which can be lifted and replaced after plastering. Plastering is a dirty, dusty and wet process that can ruin top-quality hardwood timbers. At best, the cleaning-up task will take days if not weeks to complete, whereas simply lifting inexpensive chipboard sheets can be undertaken in an afternoon. The alternative is to ensure there is adequate protection available for the flooring surface once planks are fixed down, but this can be problematic if contractors fail to leave it in position whilst they work.

The procedure for fixing traditional tongue and groove flooring is quite simple and easy to perform. Check one last time that the joists are secure and there is no 'twisting' along their lengths. Ground floors can be 'nogged' with short lengths of floor joist to tighten-up the mooring and further blocked against partition walls. First-floor joists must support a level floor and carry a smooth underlining of plasterboard for the ceiling below. The principle here is to block the outermost floor joists against the brickwork, then cross-brace at 1.8m to 2.0m intervals. This produces rows of bracing that square-up each joist in turn (see Figure 24). Leftover softwood timber cut into 25mm by 36mm struts is ideal for this job or there are proprietary metal braces available from builders' merchants.

You will need a pair of floor-cramps when you start laying your tongue and groove planks. This is a special piece of equipment, not unlike a vice in appearance, and it enables the boards to be firmly tightened into position. Cramps can be purchased from a builders' merchant or hired from suitable outlets. Purchase also a box of 50mm floorboard nails. Some builders use ordinary nails or even screws, but neither live up to expectation and will eventually allow the boards to work loose. Floorboard nails are designed for the job and haven't changed their shape in centuries, being tapered with a hooked head and stamped out of sheet metal. More old adages apply ... *Never change something just for the sake of it. If it isn't broken, don't try to fix it!*

Both hardwood and softwood timbers should be left to settle and dry out for as long as possible inside the structure, before being fixed into position. Damp or unacclimatised planks will contract excessively, causing unsightly gaps to appear between the timbers. This can be cured with infills of flexible substances specially designed for the purpose, such as silicone or even timber splints if an immaculate finish is required, but it is better to prevent the need for such work by simply giving the boards time to condition themselves.

Lay the first board against the wall and double nail into each joist crossing it. Hardwood planks will benefit from small pilot holes being drilled to prevent any splitting. Place the next board alongside, cramp to the joists, then insert two short pieces of board into the groove of the next board to tighten against it. This will close the second joint tight against the first, whilst protecting the groove from impact damage. Once it is nailed down, you can move onto the next board, working across the floor, closing each joint in turn. The final couple of timbers will need to be dropped into place and forced into position from the wall. Before nailing these down, use a floorboard lever, which is 'L' shaped, to pull the joint together as tightly as possible.

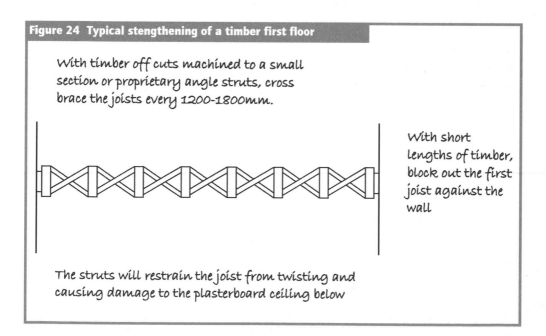

Figure 24 Typical stengthening of a timber first floor

With timber off cuts machined to a small section or proprietary angle struts, cross brace the joists every 1200-1800mm.

With short lengths of timber, block out the first joist against the wall

The struts will restrain the joist from twisting and causing damage to the plasterboard ceiling below

SUMMARY

■ Consider the position and fixing of pipes and cables in the sub-floor void before flooring is nailed down. Prepare suitable access hatches where required.

■ Decide the type and quality of flooring you intend laying according to the room 'use' and final floor finish material, for example ceramic tiles or carpets.

■ Before laying the floorboards, think about reducing noise by installing sound-proofing material in the void and beneath the floorboard timbers.

■ Leave the installation of ceilings until your plumber and electrician have finished laying water pipes, drainage and cables.

■ Leave the floorboard timbers in the building for as long as possible before they are fixed into position. This will help them to acclimatise properly and prevent joints opening up in the coming months.

USEFUL INTERNET WEBSITES

www.diynot.com
Good general advice on all DIY aspects, including floor types, materials and products.

www.englishtimbers.co.uk
Examine different timber grains and colours, access technical guidance and identify solid timber floor products to suit all tastes and applications.

www.woodenflooring.co.uk
View a vast range of both solid and laminate timber flooring, with advice and information about how to lay them.

Chapter 18
The First 'Fix'

This chapter covers:

- electrical work

- plumbing and heating

- waste pipe connections

- joinery prior to plastering

There is something very satisfying about a smooth, newly plastered wall. It appears pristine and feels like velvet to the touch. The matt, terracotta-like surface begs for colour to be applied and, if truth were known, self-builders who arrive at this stage are usually itching to unpack paintbrushes and wallpapers.

To find yourself in a position where you have to chase into the plaster, to move or extend a cable or make a patch repair around a hole for a forgotten pipe run, will leave a scar that is impossible to remove. It is therefore imperative that a great deal of care is taken to plan thoroughly for electrical, plumbing, heating and joinery installations, before the wet trades move in.

ELECTRICAL WORK

The installation of a dwelling's entire electrical system can seem quite daunting. The best way forward is therefore to explore individual sections of it and then gradually build it up, until you have the details for a complete project. Consider how each room will function. This is a task all the family can get involved in, as each member will have something to contribute.

Chalking-up ideas and the positions for sockets and switches on the walls will help, but always make secondary and more comprehensive notes on a spare set of plans; these can then be labelled as the *Electrical Layout Plans*. Position all light switches, wall lights and ceiling lights on the drawing. Consider where you would like double power sockets, and then add another spare socket to make cleaning the room easier. Identify the position for telephone and data faceplates, television aerial sockets and intruder system movement detectors.

The next question is whether to wire the property yourself or get an electrician to do the job for you. If the former, there are a large variety of excellent DIY guides available and now is a good time to acquire one from a bookshop or local library. Study the book you choose carefully and refrain from starting any electrical work until you are certain you understand the high degree of safety protocol involved.

Once you have decided exactly where all your 'end cable points' are going to be, fix the back-boxes for switches and sockets. The deepest available galvanised boxes, with an earth connection in the back corner, are advised, as they make the physical process of connecting the wires much easier. It may be necessary to chase these into the blockwork, so they only protrude as far as the finished face of the plaster, typically 18mm, but this will depend on how true the wall is.

Establish from your electrical guidebook the size of cable for the load and distance of each circuit, allowing spare capacity for an additional spur or light fitting which you could wish to add at a later date. With cable sizes for ring mains and lighting circuits known, buy reels of 50 or 100 metres at a time as bulk buying is much more economical than purchasing by specific length. You will also need plastic sheathing or trunking to cover the cables prior to plastering the walls. Some builders prefer chasing out a groove in the block work to accept cables, but this runs the risk of cracking the lightweight block material and is best avoided.

Remember to use rubber grommets for every entry point into a back-box and leave sufficient cable protruding so it can be shortened, stripped and fixed at a later stage. As a temporary measure and to assist the plasterer, curl cables inside the back-box to prevent them getting coated with plaster. Even this precaution will not stop plaster getting into the box and, once the work has finished, you will need to scrape out all excess material from inside the box and around cable entry points.

Use appropriately sized clips at recommended intervals to fix the cables to joinery, under the floor and within roof voids. Resist making any dramatic changes in cable direction, as sharp turns can cause the wires or their protective sheath to break. Low-voltage and high-intensity fittings will require transformers to reduce the voltage. Great care must be taken to assess and select the appropriate size of cable running from a transformer to the light-fitting, because the distance from one to the other will be an influencing factor and, in all situations, the accompanying manufacturer's guide should be followed.

You have now literally designed your wiring layout from first principles to full installation. You have assessed the number of circuits your home requires and the size of distribution board (always add 20 per cent extra capacity so that additional circuits can be installed later if required). It was once the duty of the electrical provider to test the system prior to connection to the national grid, but this is no longer the case. It is now the responsibility of the installer. Despite following your electrical installation guide to the letter, we strongly advise you hire a fully qualified NIC registered electrician (see Chapter 11) to inspect and test your work and make the final connections to the distribution board and mains supply. Once the final electrical work and tests have been completed, ask the electrician for a report and safety certificate, which you should keep for future reference. If they tell you everything is fine, it will be an enormous confidence boost; if they tell you there is a problem, it will be a relief to know you did the right thing in getting them to check everything. Either way, their expertise will prove invaluable.

The 'first fix' is almost complete. You should have all your cabling in place, transformers in accessible positions and lighting circuit wires run and coiled ready above ceilings. When plastering is completed, a tiny hole can be cut through the ceiling for a recessed fitting and the cable will be lying ready to be pulled through and connected. All the back-boxes and sheathed cables should also now be in position, ready for the plasterer to finish off. Circuits should be returned to the site of the distribution board, and everything should be properly clipped and labelled for easy identification later.

An indelible, fine-nibbed pen is useful for writing the circuit type and the intended fixture or fitting to be connected, along each cable. It is important to mark every cable and wire clearly with information about where it has come from and where it is going. For example, the two tails for a ring main should be referenced together, and cables for a switch should be noted in the same way (from a junction box to a specific light-fitting). All this information will be very useful later, when the 'second fix' is undertaken. Keeping a separate written plan with circuits shown in different colours, so as to distinguish them from each other, will also prove worthwhile.

PLUMBING AND HEATING

There is a logical approach to the 'first fix' of plumbing, which is very similar to the 'first fix' electrical installation. The three main aspects to consider are:

- the domestic hot and cold water system;
- the central heating system;
- the waste pipes drainage system.

Again, assess these issues, room by room, and the task will become much easier. Identify all the items, fittings and fixtures that require piped water feeds from the domestic water system. It is customary for the hot water supply pipe to be positioned on the left hand side of a fixture, even when a mixer tap is going to be ultimately connected. It is good practice, and a compulsory requirement, to terminate the pipe above the floorboard with an isolation valve, to enable the system to be pressurised at an early stage. This is, in effect, a stop-tap for the individual fitting and very useful, should you wish to change or modify it in the future.

It is vital to fit the appropriate size of copper pipe, to ensure there is no resulting loss of pressure through the system. Time then for you to make another trip to the local library or a good high-street bookshop, to acquire a comprehensive DIY plumber's guide. One of the fundamental decisions will be whether or not to use soldered or compression joints. A little practice will soon have you producing soldered joints with ease. Simply heat the joint, just enough for a silver coloured line to appear between the pipe and the joint. Overheating it will drain the joint of solder and cause it to leak.

All pipe runs should be adequately clipped and supported below ground floors and in first floor voids, whilst maintaining good and easy access via hatches in the floor construction. Sleeves can be incorporated into the block work to avoid sand and cement getting into contact with the copper. Your local builder's merchant will advise which products best suit the purpose. The entire system should be taken to the hot water storage tank and the cold water mains entry point. It is important you provide an isolation valve at the point of entry into the building (your mains stop-tap), so that the whole house can be protected in the event of leakage.

Assess which pipes would benefit from insulation. These will usually be contained within the roof space, those below the ground floor structure and, of course, any that exit the outer shell into garden or garage areas. Finally, make provision for additional floor hatches above joints, as these positions are going to be more susceptible to failure in the future.

The central heating system is likely to follow a similar process as has already been undertaken with the domestic hot and cold water. The flow of water needs to run and return to a fixed position, progressing through the boiler, pump, radiators and water tank. Pipes under ground floors should be lagged to ensure the heat transfers efficiently into radiators and is not lost in transit. At upper floor levels, they do not have to be insulated, because the gradual release of heat will actually benefit these areas.

The size of boiler and radiators can be calculated from your plumber's guide. The capacity of the boiler in comparison to the number and size of radiators is crucial and, unless you fully understand the principles involved, it may be prudent to seek assistance from a heating engineer. He will design a system for you, giving due regard to any specific requirements or preferred products. Once the system is designed on paper, you can install the major pipe runs through walls and floors, leaving other items and final connections for the 'second fix'. You will need to fix skirting after plastering but before radiators, tanks and boiler connections.

One very important point – in this section we have detailed the water pipe system *only* and *not* the pipes required for gas. The fitting of gas appliances and systems *must* be carried out by CORGI registered installers (see Chapter 11) and for very obvious reasons. It is one thing to have a badly fitted and leaking water pipe, but quite another if the pipe is carrying gas!

WASTE PIPE CONNECTIONS

Every sink, bath, shower, toilet, bidet, washing machine and dishwasher or any other water-fed appliance or fitting, will require a UPVC drainage system. These are 'push together' pipes installed and connected to the main drainage. Although most of them will be fitted at the 'second fix' stage, you must make sure that parts which will be concealed are installed before plastering and brought up through the floor, through internal walls and partitions or through external walls into gullies positioned around the building.

JOINERY PRIOR TO PLASTERING

Door linings should be cut to size and fastened together with spacing laths across the bottom to provide stability, before being drilled and packed vertical and fitted into the block work door openings. Double fix to at least four points up each side, checking as you proceed that the head is level and the lining frame remains square. Linings should project beyond the block work to a depth that allows for plastering. To ensure perfect stability, it is advised you use sand and cement to point around the frame prior to plastering. Although the plasterer will inevitably fill around the door lining, this measure makes certain the timber is held rigidly in place.

Windowsill boards can now be fitted to the backs of the window frames and the more substantial these are, the better. They should be drilled, packed and plugged into the block work, checking that they are level as you proceed. There will shortly be an enormous amount of moisture introduced to the internal aspects of the structure through plastering and this will cause flimsy sill timbers to curl. The greater the thickness of sills, the less detrimental the effects of plastering will be.

With the staircase lifted into place, check that treads are level and the flight is firmly held, with substantial fixings at both the top and bottom. If the staircase adjoins a wall, fix through the adjoining string into the blockwork, as this will provide additional stability. You may need to pack timbers out slightly to allow for plastering or, depending on the staircase design, the string could be plastered in. The latter works well, if a hardwood facing is going to be added at a later stage. Having the staircase fixed into position will be a great help because, at last, you will be able to remove those temporary ladder-links to the upper floors.

Timber partition walls are one of the easiest house elements to construct and here, as with all other aspects, there is the opportunity to erect them stronger and better than would normally be provided with a standard build. How often have you heard it said that when a door slams the whole wall shakes? Well, don't let it happen in your case. By increasing the thickness of timbers you will be creating a firm and solid framework that will withstand all amounts of door slamming. A soleplate or bottom rail is the first part in the partition wall fixture. This sets out the wall and floor positions and can also be used to set out all the vertical rails. The framework should be positioned at 400mm centres, with timbers crossing the vertical stands at 450mm centres. This arrangement allows substantial opportunities to fix plasterboard sheets, prior to skimming.

Summary

- Design your electrical circuit scheme carefully, ensuring all requirements are fulfilled for the household. Make a detailed written plan, using different colours for different circuits.

- Buy or borrow comprehensive professional electrical and plumbing installation guides. Read these through several times to achieve an acceptable level of confidence and knowledge, prior to starting the installations.

- Once all the wiring and back-boxes are in position and appropriately fixed, hire an electrician to assess your work and to make any final connections prior to testing.

- Install water pipes, drainage system and tanks according to the appliances, fittings and fixtures required. Prevent heat loss or likely damage by insulating appropriate pipes.

- Erect door linings, install windowsills and partition wall framework, and take the opportunity to improve the minimum standard where desired.

USEFUL INTERNET WEBSITES

www.foe.co.uk/campaigns/biodiversity/resource/good-wood-guide
We should all aim to be more environmentally aware and this site from the Friends of the Earth helps you choose 'green' timbers for your construction. By using the 'right' timbers, you will be protecting our natural resources and helping prevent waste.

www.dcd.co.uk
The Building Research Establishment demonstrated that the DCD Controller is a capable unit with the ability to manage both the domestic heating and hot water services to a high standard and provide substantial energy savings. The manufacturer claims it is so intelligent that it teaches itself how to manage your system.

www.smarthome.com
An American site, but well worth a visit. It claims to be the world's largest retailer of home automation products. There are details on every conceivable system ... there is even a touch-free automatic soap-dispenser! More practical products and applications include wall-mounted remotes, home theatre systems, and electronic probes for the automation of lighting, heating and water. Many of these require 'hard-wiring', so check their compatibility with UK voltage prior to purchase.

Chapter 19
The Wet Trades

This chapter covers:

■ plastering

■ concrete floors and floor tiles

■ screeding for vinyl coverings

■ the 'drying out' period

Unless you have had a long-held desire to appear in a Laurel and Hardy slapstick, don't even consider attempting the first part in this series of tasks: plastering is a skill like no other. Not only is it messy, it also involves a race against time to apply the mixture to the wall, level it and achieve a good even finish, before it turns from liquid to solid. Plasterers tell us that 20 per cent of their work comes from undoing the calamity caused by DIYers' attempts at plastering walls, or (even worse) a ceiling. It is rare for a novice to succeed in this particular assignment and, more often, the finished wall is as even as the frown on the self-builder's brow.

PLASTERING

While plastering is an art form only truly recognised after being tried (and botched), constructing the base for it is something anyone can undertake. Plasterboard sheeting is likely to form the sub-base for ceilings, partition walls and, in some cases, the internal cladding for structural walls. First, there needs to be an adequate and rigid frame made up of timber battens, onto which the sheets are then fixed.

In the case of ceilings, fix 'runner boards' made from spare lengths of tongue and groove flooring along the tops of the joists, to stiffen the ceiling from side to side. This will provide ease of access in the roof void and will be useful for supporting electrical cables. If roof trusses have been used (check your construction drawings), every truss will be braced to support (hang) the ceiling underneath. Where a roof has been built using purlins, the ceiling joists should be hung with 25mm x 75mm softwood hangers from a purlin line above. Along the base of partition walls, moisture within the plasterboard can result in bowing and it is useful to run a second line of timber above the soleplate to prevent this. The timber will enable a top fixing through the skirting board to trap and hold the plasterboard straight and it will pull the skirting straight as well, if needed.

The range of plasterboard sheet sizes available makes it relatively easy for one person to do the job, but four hands are better than two and enable bigger sheets to be fixed. A simple footlift can be made from a spare section of softwood and used to lever boards up against vertical framework (see Figure 25). Dry-lining screws are used to attach the boards and, once erected, the joints should be covered with joint-ing-tape – both these products are available from a builders' merchant. Care must be taken to stagger the joints as much as possible and all edges of partition sheeting should be securely fixed down. The rolled paper edges of the plasterboard should be used to span the joists of ceilings. Cut holes around sockets and switch-boxes before fixing the sheet into position. First score the paper surface with a Stanley knife, then peel back and cut the plaster section out.

Once all the walls and ceilings are boarded, use jointing-tape to finish off and secure all corners where the walls or walls and ceilings meet. This will bind the whole surface together and, combined with earlier joint taping, it will help prevent the finished plaster-skimmed surface from shrinking and cracking. You can now install corner-beads and cut templates for curved sections, so the rough plaster has a boundary to adhere to and the finished skim will be neatly formed. This final task prior to plastering could be left for the plasterer to complete, if required. Bear in mind that it is the finished quality of these surfaces that you will see for years to come and they must therefore be created competently and with precision.

Once plastering has been carried out, the spaces you devised in your early plans transform into real rooms for the very first time. There are lots of 'wow' moments involved in self-building – but this is probably one of the most memorable and satisfying!

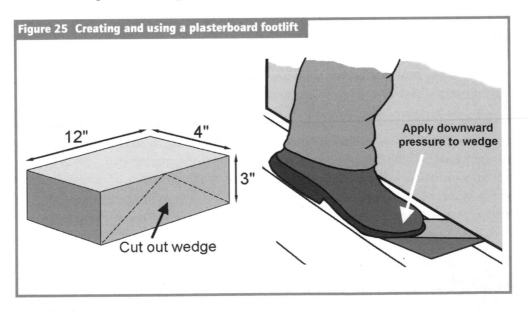

Figure 25 Creating and using a plasterboard footlift

12"   4"   3"

Apply downward pressure to wedge

Cut out wedge

CONCRETE FLOORS AND FLOOR TILES

Concrete slabs laid earlier will have dried by this stage. However, if you intend finishing them with terrazzo tiles, stone, marble or slate, they are about to get wet again! Wetting the concrete prior to laying these materials is essential, otherwise the bedding screed, mortar or adhesive will dry out too quickly and will shrink and crack. This results in the materials failing to bond together properly and, over time, they will detach completely.

The type of material will determine the composition of the bedding medium required. Whilst a simple waterproof mortar mix is sufficient for some, others will need a specific adhesive recommended by the manufacturer. Always check the accompanying instructions or consult your dealer to identify the correct type. When laying the bedding, bear in mind the depth of the material, which will raise the overall floor height. Use a plumb-line and a straight-edge to achieve a smooth level with the height of floors in adjacent rooms. Remember too that both kitchens and bathrooms should have a slight incline, so that any water spillage runs towards a drain or building exit, where it will cause the least amount of damage.

Once the floor surface is completely dry and ready to walk on, consider sheeting or boarding it for protection. Just one accidentally dropped hammer could crack a tile or chip expensive marble and that is the last thing you need to happen at this penultimate stage in the construction of your dream home. That said, by delaying the grouting of tiles until later, any that do get damaged *could* be chipped out, lifted and replaced.

SCREEDING FOR VINYL COVERINGS

The application of a latex levelling screed will achieve the best results for any concrete floor on which vinyl coverings are going to be laid. Check the floor with a long straight-edge to identify where the highest points are, then pour enough latex to cover an accessible area. With most brands of screed, you can use a float and straight-edge to help even it out. It is important not to make any sudden change of direction, as this will produce an irregular finished surface.

When the first coat is dry, check it one more time with the straight-edge and, if necessary, pour a second coat on top of it. The overall recommended thickness is usually about 8mm. There is a wide range of different screeds available and, where the floor needs greater depth, there are filler powders that can help provide bulk. Ask your builders' merchant for advice on the best product for your particular scheme.

If vinyl is intended to cover a timber floor, the installation of plywood sheeting as a floor lining is advised, so that a continuous flat surface is produced to support the tiles or rolled vinyl. The plywood should be fixed down every 10cm and pins countersunk to prevent raised heads damaging the vinyl covering. Use the biggest size of plywood sheets you can accommodate and stagger and tape over all joints.

THE 'DRYING OUT' PERIOD

With floors, ceilings and walls all ready, you will probably be bursting with enthusiasm to get on with the few outstanding jobs that need doing. But this is not a time for impatience. Rushing will simply cause more problems than it will solve. The property has been saturated by wet plaster and, though the surface may seem quite dry, there will be moisture trapped underneath which needs time to evaporate. Keeping windows open will help remove air-borne moisture, but the structure will still need about six weeks to fully dry out.

Failing to wait simply means that ceramic tiles will build up an excessive amount of water beneath them, which will bridge the gap and prevent the adhesive creating a firm bond with the wall. Tile adhesive manufacturers will not usually guarantee their product, unless the newly plastered wall has had enough time to dry. Second fix joinery will absorb moisture migrating out of the plaster, resulting in shrinkage and curling of timbers, the brass faceplates of sockets and switches will tarnish and other metal fittings will corrode. And all this because you chose to do 'something', instead of do 'nothing'!

During the drying-out period, you could find a useful distraction in, for example, building the paths approaching the house and steps into it. These are labour intensive and fairly low-cost tasks that will allow the house to progress and your cash flow to catch up.

SUMMARY

- ■ Prepare for plastering by constructing a framework on which plasterboard can be firmly fixed.

- ■ Once the plasterboard has been installed on walls and ceilings, tape over all joints and corners to prevent the finished skim from cracking.

- ■ Pre-wet concrete floors before laying decorative marble, ceramic or terrazzo tiles on an adequate and appropriate bedding material. Leave grouting until later, in case any of the tiles become damaged.

- ■ Pour levelling screed on concrete floors that are to be vinyl covered. Check the first coat is level, before applying a second one to bring the depth up to about 8mm.

■ Once the walls and ceilings are plastered, leave the entire structure for at least six weeks to completely dry out. Open windows whenever possible, so there is a regular change of air inside the building.

USEFUL INTERNET WEBSITES

www.silvertrowelplastering.co.uk
This company promote a product that acts like plaster when being applied, but looks like marble when it hardens. It can, therefore, be used to produce almost any flat, curved or angled interior surface. View their gallery for the array of colours and patterns that can be created.

www.technosolution.co.uk
Follow the links to 'plastering' and you will find a very comprehensive DIY guide to the entire subject. But are you brave enough to attempt the task?

www.readersdigest.co.uk/athome/walls.htm
A great little site from the famous *Readers Digest* DIY manual. This section includes a full step-by-step guide, showing you how to dry-line a wall ready for plastering.

Chapter 20
The Second 'Fix'

This chapter covers:

- electrical work

- heating and domestic pipework

- joinery

- ceramic tiles

- the main entrance

You might imagine that the 'second fix' is the final one, since there is no mention of a 'third fix', but in fact, it is just another recognised stage in the construction process. The important thing to remember is that, although final fittings *can* be installed during this phase, there is good reason to consider using temporary items in some cases, because these can then be removed and replaced later, when all decorative works have been completed.

For example, if you install an expensive and fragile light fitting to a ceiling, it could be damaged as you fit out and paint the rest of the room. It would therefore be better to plan for installation of the fitting, by making sure all connectors and timber fixing points are in place but, for now, fit a simple pendant flex and bulb holder. Other fixtures, such as boilers and ceramic tiles, can of course be fitted into their final positions and will have to be, so you can complete other aspects of the internal spaces.

This is also a money-guzzling phase, when costs can easily run out of control. There will be a temptation to invest in fittings to adorn your newly built house, although most can wait until later when you have more disposable funds available. Prudent self-builders often choose to employ the VAT reclaim element, made available at completion, for purchasing the more extravagant fixtures and fittings. Now is a good time to think about priorities – what is it you *really* need that will enable you to proceed?

ELECTRICAL WORK

We have already mentioned how a simple flex and bulb-holder can be a temporary but very economical alternative to a spectacular fitting you may wish to fix later. The same applies to sockets and switches. White plastic are the cheapest you can buy and these are available from all good hardware stores, though you should always try to buy in bulk from a builders' merchant, as the cost per item is considerably reduced. Once funds are released at completion, these can be replaced with more expensive coloured metal, chrome, satin finish, brass or any from the vast range available to suit your design scheme.

The only permanent feature light-fittings you should buy at this stage are those that will require recessing into the fabric elements of the building or that, because of the nature of the fitting, will be difficult to install later. Ceiling spotlights, concealed strip-lights and flush-mounted floor-lights all fall into this category. It is important to remember that these units may need to be unclipped and disconnected over the next few weeks, to allow for the decoration of walls and ceilings. Always aim to buy products that are flexible enough to fit, remove and return as required, because they will make your workload lighter and easier.

HEATING AND DOMESTIC PIPEWORK

Your newly plastered kitchen, main bathroom, en-suite shower, guest bathrooms and utility room, will have pipework protruding through walls and floors, waiting for final connections to be made. Facilities, materials and fittings you need to install include:

- baths, basins, WC pans, cisterns and taps;
- shower bases, cubicles, electric-pumps and power-consoles;
- heated towel-rails;
- ceramic tiles and other fixed solid-sheet or panel wall-coverings;
- boilers, tanks and pressure-maintaining water-pumps.

These smaller rooms are often the first to be decorated and finished, so that sanitary ware, towel-rails, toilet-roll and toothbrush holders, cupboards and cabinets can be fixed into place. It is here too that initial experiments with colour schemes can be attempted. Many of these rooms are modest in size and will only be visited occasionally by guests, so designs can be created to be as daring and dazzling as you like. You could splash them with vibrant Mediterranean blues, yellows and terracotta or use glass fittings, metallic fabrics and silver paint for a bold contemporary feel.

Abandon subtlety, but keep an eye on how different elements harmonise with or complement each other, to achieve a spectacular and lasting impression.

Decisions now need to be made with regard to the kitchen and utility rooms, so that the boiler, sinks, dishwasher, washing-machine, cupboards, work surfaces and tiles can be fitted. The sizes, shapes and designs of these items will require consolidating, so they unite in a pleasing and orderly fashion. Laundry and dishwasher appliances do not necessarily have to be bought at this stage, but their dimensions and specifications need to be known, to ensure they correspond with the gaps created beneath work surfaces and between kitchen units.

The radiator positions in all rooms will have been determined during the first-fix and these can now be installed. They can either be temporarily fitted with easy drop-down connections which will allow the radiator to be lowered into its final position once decoration has taken place, or permanently fixed with a grilled housing to complement the interior design of the room.

If you have decided to supplement your energy requirements with one or a combination of the various alternative and renewable methods of generation, provision must be made for their entry into the building and the creation of adequate space for storage. For example, solar-panels and windmills often require a bank of batteries for energy to be stored and these will need housing in a properly ventilated room. Other forms of energy recovery include the utilisation of heat-pumps and the recycling of waste to produce methane gas. These are much more experimental and, although fully tested documented systems exist, there are very few ready-made versions available to the self-builder. We suggest you undertake thorough research and contact various environmentally conscious organisations to explore all the possibilities and implications.

JOINERY

With the main flight of the staircase in position, it is now time to fix the handrail and any balustrades to landings. The vertical newel posts provide the handrail with its strength and these are at their most vulnerable when freestanding, for example at the foot of the staircase. Make sure these upward timbers are properly anchored by taking them through the floor and bolting them rigidly to the side of a floor joist.

If the staircase has been bought as a standard package, all the sections of it will be prepared with suitable cuts and joints ready to assemble. The handrail and balustrades should slot neatly together with adhesive, pins and screws, according to the manufacturer's instructions, but some minor adjustments may be required to fit the sections into their final position. On the other hand, if the staircase is a unique grand design and one created for you by a master joiner, he will probably already have tested off-site that

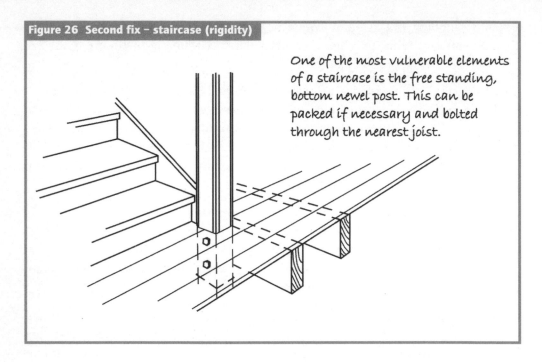

Figure 26 Second fix – staircase (rigidity)

One of the most vulnerable elements of a staircase is the free standing, bottom newel post. This can be packed if necessary and bolted through the nearest joist.

everything fits together perfectly. In theory, it should slot into its final position even better than a ready-to-assemble off-the-shelf variety because it has been made to fit the space you have created yourself in the entrance hallway.

Skirting and architraves were traditionally fixed to timber plugs inserted into the mortar line of walls before plastering. It is now modern practice to plaster first, bringing the plaster out to the front edge of door linings and then fix skirting and architrave, after it has thoroughly dried out. Central heating can cause skirting to curl away from and between their fixings, simply because they are long sections of timber with little depth. To remedy this, a quality adhesive should be applied between the plastered wall and the back of the timber, bringing it up to the top edge of the skirting.

Standard skirting and architrave are available from most good timber suppliers, but never be afraid to design your own, if you want something unique. This can be achieved by producing a sketch, which your local timber merchant can machine-up for you. The advantage of this is that you get to choose the type of wood, shape and height for the finished product and the additional cost involved is usually quite minimal. It is an ideal solution, where skirting and architrave need to match fixed, fitted or freestanding furniture in particular rooms.

When planning the timber detail of your home, it can be useful to use older dwellings as a point of reference. Traditionally, skirting was much bigger and architrave had much more detail than their modern counterparts. This was because the room heights were greater and skirting needed to reflect this to remain proportionately in keeping. In addition, because decorative timbers were made up of stained and varnished hardwood rather than painted softwood, ornate detail was added to indicate a certain quality and style. It is important you examine the internal aspects of your new home carefully to determine:

- the most appropriate style of skirting and architraves, without losing sight of the fact that it is a newly built house;

- whether traditional heights and materials proposed will sit comfortably with the height and design of rooms and the furnishings placed in them;

- whether skirting and architraves would be better painted to suit the room's colour scheme or left unpainted to display their natural grain and colour.

Once final joinery sections are fixed into position, there is a considerable liability introduced into the workspace. Protect them as much as possible and be very careful not to scratch or impact them with materials and tools used for outstanding construction work. Above all, resist the temptation to hang internal doors for now, as these will almost certainly get damaged.

If you took our advice to go beyond the minimum standard when building up the walls, you will now find it paying dividends and particularly as you come to install hefty curtain-poles and pelmets. Bear in mind that the simple action of drawing weighted curtains back and forth every day will have an effect on the fixings for poles and runners. Over time (sometimes mere months), these fixings can work loose and will need repairing or replacing. The answer to this problem lies in providing secure and substantial fixtures at the outset. A timber batten attached to the actual brickwork within the depth of the plaster is always better than attempting to plug and screw through it. The pelmet hangs and is fixed on top of a facing batten. The curtain-pole is attached with long fixings through the plaster and into the concrete lintel behind. When done properly, curtain-poles will stay firm for years to come regardless of use or the weight of fabric hung on them.

CERAMIC TILES

Ceramic tiles are available in an immense range of patterns, colours, finishes, textures and sizes. The type chosen is entirely subjective, but it is prudent to remember that, because fads and fashions change quickly, the more 'in vogue' your selection, the sooner it will date. Whilst classic simple colours and patterns may not be so awe-inspiring, they are more enduring and will be enjoyed over a much longer period.

The way tiles are set out greatly affects their appearance and, unless preference dictates, there is no reason why you should follow customary horizontal and vertical lines. Smaller sized tiles and mosaics look exceptionally good when twisted on their axis and presented as a diamond. Although this will involve more cutting, there are an array of cutters and edge-trims available to make the task easier.

Where a standard horizontal grid layout is desired between the underside of kitchen cupboards and above worktops, it is the way tiles are placed against electrical sockets and switches that can make all the difference. Rather than adopting a general build approach, where they are placed randomly, try instead to achieve a recognisable rhythm with logical clean lines. For example, by following the horizontal top edge of a socket through along the wall and the vertical right edge up and down, a grid is created, with the sockets and switches falling methodically into the tile pattern. This produces crisp clean lines that will greatly improve the overall appearance. Bathrooms often benefit from some of the larger Mediterranean sized tiles. The added bonus here is these slabs will cover a vast expanse of wall space quickly and neatly, hiding any slight imperfections that may exist in the plasterwork below.

The general principle for tiling a whole wall area is really quite simple and logical. The first determination is, of course, the unit size of your tile and the best joint width. Most DIY shops sell a range of plastic spacers to suit different sizes of grout lines and these make the entire task much easier and neater. If friezes are going to be

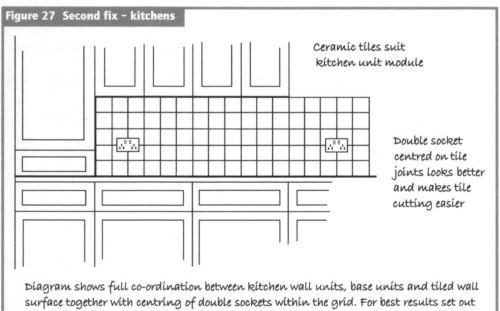

Figure 27 Second fix – kitchens

Ceramic tiles suit kitchen unit module

Double socket centred on tile joints looks better and makes tile cutting easier

Diagram shows full co-ordination between kitchen wall units, base units and tiled wall surface together with centring of double sockets within the grid. For best results set out all this prior to cutting out for the electrical back boxes.

incorporated into the tile pattern, establish whether these tiles will alter the general flow of the grid and, where they do, mark the positions full-size on the wall, so the rest of the grid can accommodate them. Horizontally centre the tiles on the wall, leaving equal sized margins to the extreme right and left. These outer tiles will probably need cutting to fit, but this arrangement provides for a much more balanced finished result.

Next, consider the vertical setting-out of your wall surface. There are several possible approaches you can take. If the wall is to be fully tiled, follow the same principle as you did for setting the horizontal line, that is, centre the tiles with equal top and bottom margins. If, however, you propose bringing the ceiling colour down the walls as a frieze, the topmost run of tiles will need to be full ones. They must be carefully marked out, so that the run of tiles up and down are calculated and positions established prior to fixing.

The floor should be considered before setting-out the bottom course of tiles. If it is also going to be tiled, find the lowest point of the floor and measure up the wall one-tile height. Draw this horizontal line level around the room. Each tile can now be measured around the room and trimmed to fit down to the floor, where appropriate. From this level starting point, the whole wall surface can quickly grow until all walls are fully tiled. Be certain to use fully waterproof (not water resistant) adhesive and grout, as anything less will eventually absorb water, grow mould and decay.

Once the bathroom has been completed, you can fix towel-rails, toilet-roll holders, wall-cabinets and mirrors, and position and fix sanitary ware. Use the same logical approach to this task by fixing at tile-joint, horizontal, vertical or centred positions, to achieve a more harmonious effect.

The main entrance

The main entrance is the first and last area seen by you, your family and guests, and as such creates an initial and a lasting impression. Early considerations about design and the space afforded to it will now be instrumental in determining the quality and extent of further enhancements. Much will also depend on your interior design scheme (see Chapter 21) and the floor finish, colours, fabrics and fixtures you choose to employ. Bear in mind that, although an entrance hallway is rarely used as a sitting or living space, it is one room that everyone passes through numerous times a day and its presentation should therefore be treated with due care and attention.

Hopefully, you have not yet succumbed to hanging your new front door, because there are still lots of opportunities when it could get damaged. Keep the temporary one until all work is complete, tradesmen have left and all major deliveries made.

Summary

■ Prepare for final electrical fittings, but install economical alternatives where possible for now, to prevent expensive ones getting damaged.

■ Fit boilers, tanks, pumps and radiators and plan layouts carefully, so that sanitary ware, sinks, baths and showers can be connected.

■ Complete any last sections of joinery, including staircase handrails and balustrades, skirting, door architraves and curtain-poles and pelmets. Where possible, protect delicate unfinished timbers against knocks and bangs.

■ Tile bathroom and kitchen walls according to the style, colour and pattern of choice. Plan these surfaces carefully, giving due regard to the fact that quality counts and fads change

Useful Internet Websites

www.mfi.co.uk
Design your new kitchen online. Handy tips and guides on how to measure and plan it properly. Also includes ideas and examples on traditional, classic and contemporary styles.

www.focusdiy.co.uk
Lots of design ideas for bathrooms and kitchens together with DIY tips and product reviews. The site also has a very handy ceramic tile calculator, so you know the quantity needed for any size of room.

www.homedesign-online.co.uk
Nothing if not unusual, this site brings 'Blue Peter' techniques to your desktop with cutout models helping you create 3D versions of rooms. In addition to room design packs, there is also a software program available.

Chapter 21
Interior Design

This chapter covers:

- design flair

- basic themes

- room character

- loose furniture

- soft furnishings

- colour scheme

- interior design services

Your efforts have now delivered you to a wonderfully creative phase in the self-build project and you should feel rightfully proud of the achievement. Gone are the limitations imposed by building regulations, planning officers and inspectors. You are now free to express yourself and to be as original or as conventional as you like.

DESIGN FLAIR

It can sometimes be difficult finding the starting point, when there are no limits restricting you. The best advice is to begin with your own aspirations. Try to identify the combined elements that make up your own personal 'wow' factor. What kind of interior style attracts you? What are you comfortable with? Always remember that you are creating a home for you and not one designed purely to impress your guests, so go for concepts *you* like – not ones you think others will find appealing!

Interior design is an exceptionally self-orientated philosophy. There may be something you have seen in a hotel reception, a restaurant, a new development show-house or even a friend's home, that you found impressive; but could you live with it in your own home? Only by identifying your own unique style and preferences can you hope to create an interior that will stand the test of time. It should be relaxing and meet the demands of your lifestyle, routines, finances and desires.

Design flair is an attribute we all posses, though many lack the confidence to employ it. Some prefer to adopt other people's ideas and judgements, rather than risk producing an original interior that might otherwise attract criticism. Having faith in your own vision is half the battle. The remainder is 'seeing it through' to completion without resorting to compromise or being influenced by narrow-minded and negative comments received along the way. Having the courage to complete the decor and layout within the bounds of an original concept will always produce something unique and inspiring; and if you *then* feel it truly hasn't worked, you can always alter or modify it.

Interior design inevitably involves adapting existing elements and materials to suit a particular theme. It is not just the individual fabrics, patterns, textiles, soft furnishings and colours that matter: it is when they are presented in a certain way that the final vision is revealed.

BASIC THEMES

Themes are as good a starting point as any, when trying to focus on a particular style. They involve a broad range and can be used throughout an entire home or just for specific rooms. Themes can also be employed in a methodical and precise manner or they can be softened, expanded or combined to produce a more subtle and 'homely' interior. A theme is essentially a framework on which you can build the rest of the design elements. It is the foundation, a blueprint or template you can mould and customise, according to need. Whilst the following represent a small selection of the vast range of recognised themes, you could invent numerous others by using your imagination and life experiences.

Cutting-edge

'Cutting-edge' themes are amongst the most impressive and spectacular because they are up-to-date with current interior fashion trends. They embrace styles of furniture and materials that are 'in-vogue' and, albeit for a short period of time, reflect colours and textures seen in all the best glossy magazines. The problem is, by their very nature, these elements go out of fashion as quickly as they come in, resulting in a home that requires completely refitting or one resigned to reflecting a period that has passed.

Typical examples include sculptured and patterned ceilings, which are now being plastered over; luminescent coloured walls, now being painted white; vast open-plan living spaces that have since been found too difficult to heat and keep tidy; laminated timber flooring that many are now converting to solid timber; bleached furniture, which has now given way to natural wood alternatives. In decades gone by the same was true for woodchip wallpapers, hardboard panelled doors, teak dining suites and dado-rails: all fads of their time whose existence today depict a bygone age. This is the cost of being in the spotlight, at the time.

The 'cutting-edge' approach is often best applied to individual rooms, because it reduces the medium-term expense of renewal and replacement. Bear in mind that most trends last less than five years, so you will need to budget for a new kitchen, bathroom, dining room or living room at the end of this period, if you want to maintain the theme. If you leave it long enough, of course, the theme will graduate from 'cutting-edge' to 'retrospective', without you lifting a finger or spending anything to produce it.

Minimalist

The 'minimalist' style involves clean lines, simple decor and the least volume of furnishing you can reasonably expect to live with. It produces what is perhaps the most tranquil of settings, but often the most difficult to maintain. Minimalism demands an avoidance of clutter and a preponderance of white or plainly coloured unpatterned walls. It is the very simplicity of design that produces the theme.

The advantage is that a single object or item of furnishing can become the focal point, and changing this main element and anything associated with it can produce an entirely different mood. For example, a mainly white living space might have a large brightly coloured abstract print hanging on one of its walls. The colours could also be reflected in one or more of the other elements in the room, such as a rug or the curtain fabric. By changing just these two items, the character of the entire space will transform into something completely different.

Minimalism is very straightforward and economical to create and, with sufficient discipline, it is easily sustained and renewed.

Industrial

This theme relies on mat or polished metal and metallic colours as the main elements. It produces a harsh and rather cold interior best suited to kitchens and bathrooms. The 'industrial' look can be applied to big open rooms, where imagination and inventiveness can transform ordinary living space into virtual factory floors. In smaller rooms, the reflective qualities of polished metal furnishings and fittings can help expand the space, producing an illusion that the room is bigger than it really is.

Gothic

Darkly atmospheric, the 'Gothic' theme comes into its own at night when candles cast shimmering light and shadows across richly coloured and patterned walls. Pointed arched mirrors, chunky oak furnishings and heavy fabrics combine to create an almost ecclesiastically relaxing interior, ideal for entertaining and dining. This theme has been successfully reinvented in recent years and modern versions include the use of glass tables and stone artwork to further augment the feeling of age and simplicity. Creating the impression of height is important because, traditionally, the architecture would have involved tall columns and very high ceilings. This can be achieved by using straight vertical lines in wall coverings and fabrics, and by positioning columnar-shaped objects around the room.

Continental

These themes rely on selecting colours, materials, fabrics and styles from other countries and cultures around the world. Rather than mimicking them entirely, success depends on choosing certain design elements and incorporating them into the space available. Typical examples include schemes using the rich cobalt blue and contrasting white found throughout the Mediterranean or heavily patterned tapestries and mosaics from the Far East.

Period

'Period' styles are amongst the most difficult themes to create, because their success depends on keeping all objects, patterns, fittings and furnishings within a historically accurate design setting, but not at the cost of comfort and convenience. The difficulty here is more often one of combining incongruous elements. For example, it is relatively easy to acquire quality Edwardian reproduction furniture and fabrics, but how will the television set, computer, hi-fi or compact-disc player look when placed within this design?

'Period' themes must inevitably be a compromise of the old and the new for sheer practicality, otherwise you may find yourself living in a stale museum setting, rather than a home. There are many styles to choose from and all can be adapted to suit any modern living space.

ROOM CHARACTER

Choosing the character of any particular room is highly subjective and there are a number of approaches that can be taken. The whole house could be based on a single concept or you might have each room distinct from the others around it, a technique often used by architects to lead the owner progressively through a variety of spaces. Applying the 'continental' theme above, this could produce a home where people would move from one room to another as if travelling through different countries, cultures and styles.

Alternatively, the character of the room may be dictated by its function. For example, a games room might have a large billiard-table as its main element and focal point. The colour of the table surface and type of construction timbers would then influence the colours, fabrics and materials chosen for use throughout the rest of the room. This approach succeeds by identifying a large item of furniture and building a scheme around it, to prevent the actual item itself from becoming an ostentatious exhibit incompatible with other elements in the room.

LOOSE FURNITURE

Staying with that 'exhibition piece' idea mentioned in the last paragraph, there is potential in taking a single and distinctive item of furniture and presenting it to the human eye in an uninterrupted way. With this approach, the setting created should enhance it, rather than any attempt made to hide or absorb it. Lighting can help achieve this. Try experimenting with spotlights, uplighters and concealed lighting, and explore the different effects created by natural light entering through nearby windows.

The likelihood is that you will at least have some existing loose items of furniture to transfer into the new home. Their form, construction material and colour may force you to plan rooms accordingly and, unless you intend spending a fortune on new pieces, it is important you consider these within the overall design scheme.

SOFT FURNISHINGS

The selection of colours, patterns and fabrics for curtains, seating, cushions and carpets should be made now, despite the fact that they may not be bought until funds are realised after the VAT claim is made. The reason is simple: these elements are crucial to the total design scheme and, unless they are clearly specified, it will be difficult to identify the appropriate wallpaper and paint colours to use.

Nothing can be considered in isolation when devising an interior layout. It is, in fact, the way colours, patterns and shapes harmonise or contrast that makes a scheme succeed or fail. The perfect design is one that is developed as a single picture, with all the various elements within it somehow connected. This might be by shade, colour, shape, style or pattern. Soft furnishings help bridge gaps and resolve conflicts by bringing different elements together. Their value within the overall plan should never be underestimated.

'Sample boards' are produced by professional designers to present and assess the compatibility of all the different individual elements involved. You can create your own by overlapping fabric, carpet, wallpaper and paint samples on a large piece of card. Organise them according to how they will be connected in the actual room. Add photographs of large items of furniture or samples of timber, metal and other materials, to complete the scheme's component parts. Position the sample-board under both natural and artificial light conditions and at different angles in the appropriate room, to see how the scheme performs.

COLOUR SCHEME

This is the moment things either come together or fall apart. A colour scheme is the central and fundamental element for all interior design. The problem is that it is so diverse a subject and so very personal that what satisfies one is unlikely to satisfy another. This means a compromise often has to be found and, in turn, an exciting scheme can be reduced into something quite bland.

Not that there is anything wrong with bland. After all, there is more magnolia paint sold in the UK than any other colour, and with very good reason, it creates a blank canvas against which all other colours and shapes stand proud. Dramatic furniture, striking pictures and boldly designed ornamental objects, all work better against a plain white or off-white background.

The other problem with interior colour is that it tends to follow fashion. In fact, whatever colour the clothing industry introduces this year, the wallcovering and fabric industry will launch as a new range next year. The reality is that manufacturers create fads as a means of getting us to buy more wallcoverings and paints in ever-increasing frequency. Unless you really want to decorate your home every single year, forget fashion and go with your own personal choice and taste. In other words, design according to desire ... not attire!

Colour schemes are important as they set the stage for your home and everything else inside it. The first consideration is deciding whether you want a scheme that harmonises or one that contrasts; one that is pure and simple or a rich assembly of block colours; one that complements your furnishings and fabrics or one that boldly contradicts them. All these different approaches can work, though many will depend on the strength and shade of colour chosen.

For example, planning a 'green' schemed room is fine. But what colour green? There are hundreds on the market to choose from and even more are produced with each passing year. It is very hard to imagine the breadth of single colour shades available but, as an illustration, take a long and careful look over any rural landscape – now count how many 'greens' you see. It is truly overwhelming! Moreover, this is before you have considered secondary colours existing in the room and the variety of paint finishes, fabric textures and wallpaper patterns available.

Colour schemes are, in essence, an art form requiring experimentation. It is only by testing different variations out on paper that you will eventually find the right one to reproduce on the walls and floors of your home. This is the end result and final presentation of months of hard labour, so take your time to devise a colour scheme that highlights and complements your work.

INTERIOR DESIGN SERVICES

In Chapter 8, we discussed how a professional interior designer can help you create the most stunning of rooms by giving advice on colour schemes, new materials and innovative products. An experienced and qualified interior designer will spend a portion of their committed time with you, discussing the project and assessing your likes and dislikes, before suggesting and presenting several alternative schemes for your consideration.

Independent designers maintain a vast personal library of source material. This includes a range of paint samples from a variety of suppliers, a multitude of wall-papers from different manufacturers and specification brochures for contemporary and traditional furniture. They will also have access to lighting, carpet, fabric, floor-ing and ceramic tile suppliers. Their skill lies in the ability to put these materials, colours and textures together in a way that is always pleasing, sometimes spectacu-lar and often awe-inspiring. If you wish to employ an interior designer we suggest you re-read the appropriate section in the earlier chapter, giving due regard to the advice on qualifications and experience.

Bear in mind that designers should not be limited by products manufactured or sold through a single company. Look for 'independent' professionals who operate under their own name.

SUMMARY

- Consider the variety of styles that appeals to you and devise separate schemes for individual rooms or a single theme for the entire house.

- Identify those items of furnishing and fabrics you intend keeping. Absorb these into the interior design layout by choosing appropriate paint colours and pat-terns.

- Allow single exhibit elements to become focal points by designing around them. Use textures, colours or patterns to harmonise the rest of the room with the exhibit piece.

- Prepare a 'sample board' for each room and experiment, using different mate-rials and colours, until the desired effect is created.

- Consider the advantage of hiring a professional independent interior designer.

USEFUL INTERNET WEBSITES

www.interiorstudio.com
Packed full of style ideas, creative and innovative design schemes, art resources, products and projects. There is also an interactive decorating application that allows you to select a room type and then paint or wallpaper it in different colours and patterns to test a scheme.

www.crownpaint.co.uk
Find every shade of every colour imaginable and see how different saturations and hues interact with each other. There are also lots of examples of room colour schemes available on this very useful site.

www.bbc.co.uk/homes/design/
Magazine style site with articles on home-design related subjects. Though much of the content revolves around current television programmes, there are useful resources and calculators to help you achieve that 'new' look.

Part Four
Completion and External Aspects

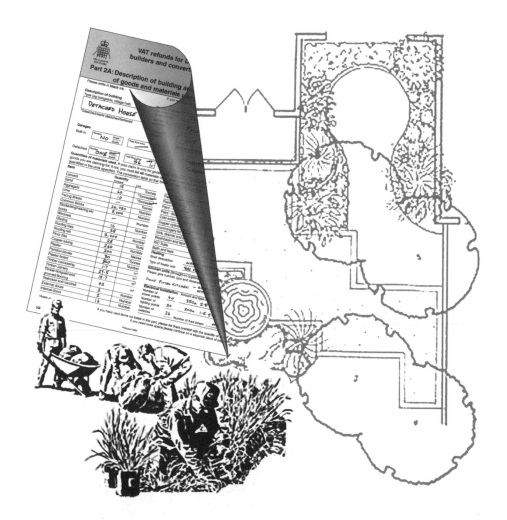

Chapter 22
Completion Notice

This chapter covers:

- signing it off
- VAT claim
- final finance issues

'Completion' means different things to different people. As far as the local authority is concerned, it is when all work described in the detailed planning application, and any subsequent conditions made at approval or from interim scrutiny, are fulfilled to the building inspector's satisfaction.

However, as is the case for most homeowners, completion from the self-builder's point of view may take an additional few months or even years. It depends on the scale of the project and when landscaping, internal decor and minor refinements have been accomplished. Avid and habitual do-it-yourselfers never truly attain completion, because there is always a new scheme to tackle, an adjustment to be made or a change to consider.

The speculative self-builder is quite a different animal. He needs to know exactly when completion is going to occur, because it will be then that he can arrange the sale of his investment. This will raise financial backing for the next venture, which he has already planned and is ready to start. The lack of emotional attachment for the first project means he can progressively move on to bigger and more profitable self-build schemes.

SIGNING IT OFF

'Signing off' is the term applied to formal completion of the dwelling. It is when the self-builder or his construction supervisor applies to the council for the 'completion certificate'. The requirements for 'signing off' will vary according to circumstances and particularly whether you have undertaken the construction yourself or have had an architect or other person oversee it.

Self-build mortgage companies usually require the certificate before any final staged payment is released. It is also a prerequisite to making final payments to a builder or sub-contractor. It indicates that they have finished their contracted work and have undertaken it competently. The certificate is an important document, because it verifies that the dwelling conforms to building regulations. It is not a warranty or a guarantee, but it *is* recognised evidence that the construction has been carried out to an acceptable standard.

As with all newly built properties, there is often a snagging period when minor defects are listed for attention. The 'contract supervision' certification process makes provision for retention of usually two and a half per cent of the cost of sub-contracted work, until a defects period has elapsed. The time period can vary according to the complexity of the project but, in domestic circumstances, it is six months (unless landscaping or a mechanical installation, such as a lift, is included).

The degree of certification is entirely dependent on the route chosen to build the dwelling and it is how the project has been financed that is particularly relevant. For example, if you chose to supervise or carry out a substantial amount of the work yourself and have been able to finance the project directly, the level of certification is quite different. In these circumstances, you will only require the building inspector's certificate. The original should be retained for safekeeping and a copy issued to your solicitor. Evidence of the certificate will be required, if you decide to sell the dwelling at a later stage.

Upon request, the building inspector will visit your project one final time. They will check the construction against the approved drawings and, if contented with the standard achieved, they will sanction the release of your certificate. Occasionally, the inspector will identify minor items outstanding and issue a description of the work required to rectify them. When these items have been attended to, they will inspect again and then authorise issue of the certificate.

VAT CLAIM

Once you have your certificate and the building project is complete, you will want to make your VAT claim (see Chapter 7). However, it is important to remember that you can only claim once and, to recoup the maximum amount, all VAT inclusive elements of external work must be finished and paid for. The claim can include the VAT for materials used to construct driveways, fencing and garages, as long as they were detailed on the original plans. The VAT claim pack gives details of eligible building materials and this should be checked carefully, to assess the specific items that can be claimed. Bear in mind that the claim must be made within three months of receiving your completion certificate.

All your receipts need to be grouped into material type and quantities used. A full list and format is given in the claim pack and set out on form 'Part 2A' (see Figure 28). In addition, every receipt needs to be listed individually, giving:

- the date items were purchased;

- a description of the goods;

- the supplier's name;

- the invoice or reference number.

Form '3' covers receipts where VAT is shown separately and Form '4' where VAT is included in the total cost. Any receipts over £100 in value *must* include your name and address.

Once submitted, the VAT application takes only a short time to be processed and, within a few short weeks (often less than 15 days), you will receive a cheque for the appropriate amount. Delays may occur if you fail to pack and list receipts properly or if there are queries about the elements claimed. The more thorough you are in preparing your submission, the swifter the response will be. If you followed our earlier advice on organising receipts and invoices, you will now find the entire claim process an easy and straightforward operation, because everything will be properly catalogued and conveniently at hand.

If your self-build scheme has been of a considerable size and cost, this will be reflected in the quantity of funds received back from HM Customs and Excise. Add to this any final, staged loan release and you may find your pockets suddenly bulging with money. After months of frugal living, when every penny mattered and had to be accounted for, there will inevitably be a great temptation to spend this instantaneous wealth on inconsequential things. Our advice would be to double-check that every last bill has been paid and every credit account settled, before considering how this sum of money could be used to your maximum advantage.

There is every likelihood that your new home will be significantly bigger than your former one and this means household bills will be greater too. You may have jumped up one or more council tax bands; new kitchen appliances will consume extra electricity and gas; more lights in more rooms means more energy is going to be consumed. Quite simply, the upkeep of your new home may increase considerably the demands on your income and, until a period has passed during which you can safely assess the level of increase, you would be wise to keep some of the VAT claim fund as a financial safety net.

That doesn't mean you should not spend some of the money: you do, after all, deserve a reward for all your hard work. A family holiday, luxurious carpets, designer curtains or a newly landscaped garden can all now be considered. Patting yourself on the back with a little indulgent extravagance can be wonderfully satisfying.

Figure 28   VAT form 2A – example of completed document

VAT refunds for DIY builders and converters

2A

HM Customs and Excise

Name of claimant (BLOCK LETTERS)

MR. A.N. OTHER

Part 2A: Description of building and quantities of goods and materials used

Please write in **black** ink.

If you make a mistake, cross it out and insert the correct details above it. The person making the claim must initial the alteration.

Description of building
Type (eg bungalow, village hall)

DETACHED HOUSE

*Detached/semi-detached/terraced

Number of storeys (Count ground floor as one storey)	TWO	Number of reception rooms	FIVE
Number of bedrooms	FOUR	Number of bathrooms/cloakrooms	THREE
Number of kitchens	ONE	Ground floor area	250 ft²/m²

Garages

Built-in   Number NO   Single/double   Total floor area ft²/m²

Detached   Number ONE   Single/double   Total floor area 36 ft²/m²

Number and description of other rooms

GAMES ROOM — 1.
SAUNA — 1.

Quantities of materials used. If your claim is only for goods used to 'fit-out' or 'finish off' the building, you need only list those goods you are claiming for. If not, you must list **all** materials used, even those you are not claiming for. Please fill in the quantities in the units specified. The conversion table on the folder will help you to do this.

Item	Quantity Amount	Unit	Item	Quantity Amount	Unit
Cement	15	Tonnes	Paint - undercoating	75	Litres
Sand	60	*Tonnes/m²	Paint - emulsion	75	Litres
Aggregate	10	*Tonnes/m²	Paint - woodprimer	10	Litres
Lime	—	Tonnes	Paint - finishing coat	20	Litres
Facing Bricks	26,750	Number	Cold water storage tank	1	Number
Common Bricks	8,000	Number	Copper cylinder	1	Number
Stocks/engineering etc bricks	—	Number	Ironmongery for doors	32	Number
Windows	16	Number	Sink, drainer and taps	1 SET	Number
Glazing	38	m²	Washbasin and taps	3 SETS	Number
Roofing tiles	3,000	Number	WC Suite	3	Number
Roofing felt	28	Rolls	Bath and taps	1 SET	Number
Floor tiles	260	Number	**Heating** Brief description WATER SYSTEM		Number of radiators
Copper tubing	200	Metres	Type of heater unit GAS FIRED BOILER		19

Item	Quantity	Unit
Plaster	30	Tonnes
Partition blocks	800	Number
Plaster-board	1·7	m³
Timber-carcassing	29·5	m³
Timber-Joinery	18·7	m³
Timber-tongued and grooved flooring	42	m³
Staircase and handrail	2	Number
External doors	2	Number
Internal doors	16	Number

Kitchen units (brought-in cupboards, worktops, etc)
Please give number, type and dimensions of each

FULLY FITTED KITCHEN   — SCHEDULE ATTACHED

Electrical installation   Amount and type of cable used

Number of power points	40	350m 2.5 t+e
Number of lighting points	20	200m 1.5 t+e
Number of switches	26	Number of fuse boxes ONE

*Delete as appropriate

If you have used items not listed in this part, please list them overleaf with the quantity of each. If you need more space please continue on a separate piece of paper.

VAT 431 (Pt 2)   Page 1

PCU(April 1996)

FINAL FINANCE ISSUES

Having moved into your new home, it is time to consider 'asset management'. This is essentially a tidying-up exercise when your possessions, materials, equipment and property can be grouped, assessed and quantified, and a decision made about whether each should be kept or disposed of.

If you have been living in an existing home until this point, you may decide now is the opportunity to sell it, so the outstanding mortgage can be paid off. Alternatively, you may consider renting out the old property to supplement your current income or to create regular and dependable finance for a new self-build project. There are two useful guidebooks, written by co-author Tony Booth and published by 'How To Books', which can help you achieve either solution and save you money along the way. Both are available from all good bookshops:

■ *Save Thousands Selling Your Own Home* (ISBN: 1857038266)

■ *The Buy To Let Handbook* (ISBN: 1857038649)

If you have been living on site in a caravan, it has probably now become redundant and will need to be advertised for sale. Return to those early references you explored when you were buying the caravan and use them to reintroduce it back onto the market. There will also be an array of tools and equipment you bought during construction and these should now be identified and assessed. List those items you wish to keep and those you wish to sell.

Finally, there is a viable market for excess building materials, including bricks, paving slabs, timber and hardcore. If these are available in sufficient quantities, you could try approaching a local builder who may offer a reasonable sum for them. Alternatively, the free advertisement section of a local newspaper is likely to reveal would-be local buyers. Although rare, some builders' merchants offer a reduced refund for excess materials still in a good condition and originally bought from them.

It is important to point out that any reimbursement received from materials sold should be discounted when calculating your VAT claim, otherwise it may be considered you have not only mitigated your loss, but also claimed a refund for it as well. A case of having your cake and eating it ... something HM Customs and Excise may find very hard to swallow!

Summary

■ Arrange the receipt of your completion certificate, once the building inspector is satisfied that all construction work has finished.

■ Prepare and submit your VAT claim, making sure all relevant receipts and documents have been packed and collated.

■ Analyse the running costs of your new home and retain some funds as a safety net before considering the amount to spend on additional furnishings, fittings, decoration or landscaping.

■ Identify to keep or plan to dispose of unwanted tools and equipment or any excess materials accumulated during the self-build construction.

Useful Internet Websites

www.ebay.co.uk
Online auctions have never been so easy. This is a great place to sell all your unwanted tools, equipment, caravan and materials.

www.mjfvat.btinternet.co.uk
A VAT specialist will take over the entire claim procedure on your behalf in return for a fee. This is just one of many such firms who operate nationally to assist self-builders.

www.readytogo.co.uk
Free advertising on the Internet where you can sell almost anything!

Chapter 23
Beyond the Threshold

This chapter covers:

■ hard landscaping

■ soft landscaping

■ preparing for winter

If you have been heavily involved in the physical aspects of construction, there will be a natural tendency to delay the completion of exterior work for a period of time. Many self-builders say they took the opportunity to have a year's rest ... and who can blame them? However, the impracticalities of living continuously on an unfinished building site will soon become apparent. The dry summer months may be just about tolerable, but a long, wet winter period can be miserable, frustrating and eventually unbearable.

The rear sections of the dwelling will be bad enough, as rain turns dusty soil into mud, but continuous pedestrian and vehicle activity at the front will transform the barren landscape into a quagmire. Imagine the effect this will have on those pristine timbered or carpeted floors of your newly finished entrance and hallway. It may be a sufferable inconvenience for you to remove and clean your shoes every time you enter the home, but requesting that children do the same is likely to fall on deaf ears, and the scenario can descend into the realms of nightmare, where pets are involved.

Then there is the problem of a family car driving in and out of the front garden area, churning mud and forming trenches in the process. Cleaning the vehicle will become a necessary, regular and annoying chore. Guests visiting you at home are unlikely to complain, though they may call to see you less frequently; others, such as the postman, who will not be so concerned about your feelings, are likely to grumble constantly about the muddy trek to your front door.

These irritations will quickly convince you to resolve the matter, once and for all, by laying a hard surface or gravel along the route from the highway to your threshold.

HARD LANDSCAPING

The temptation will be to deal with the front aspect of your property first. But this could be a mistake because, once you have laid an attractive new hard landscape at the point of entry to your site, you will realise there are deliveries of bricks, soil, sand and cement destined for the back garden that yet need to be brought in that way. By dealing with the furthest reaches of your property first, you will be preserving energy and preventing damage to materials already laid.

Hard landscaping can, of course, involve much more than paths and driveways. There are garden walls, patios, concrete slabs for a shed or greenhouse, ponds and pools to consider. It is also an opportunity to install another favourite garden feature, a rockery, the limited size of which so often makes this focal point pale into insignificance. If you took our early advice, you may have several large boulders already in position, with guests wondering how on earth you managed to get them there. You can now add smaller rocks and begin planting to complete the whole design.

As we mentioned earlier, it is both economically and practically beneficial to install the main infrastructure as part of the overall self-build scheme. The advantages are that the VAT claim can be extended to include some garden materials, and most lenders will provide funds to pay for them, as part of the total financial package.

Considerations should include outdoor services, for example trenching for the supply and positioning of an outdoor tap and for laying armoured electrical cables to sheds, garages and exterior lights along the driveway or in the garden. These installations need to be in place prior to laying hard landscaping. Advance thinking, good planning and an awareness of the total design scheme will reduce the risk of having to undo what has already been done. It is, quite simply, a labour and cost-cutting exercise, in which the basic infrastructure is installed in a logical order. Once the hard landscaping has been completed, you are then free to deal with the fine detail of your remaining garden design at leisure.

SOFT LANDSCAPING

Soft landscaping involves the installation of topsoil, plants, shrubs and trees, and the positioning of architectural structures, such as gazebos, timber arches and trellises. As with hard landscaping, this too has a coherent order to it, which if followed, will make the entire process much easier.

Think back to your earliest design concept and refer to any notes you made about plans for the garden at that time. Did you retain certain plants or trees for a particular reason? Did you plan to keep an area clear, so that unobstructed views of the horizon would be enjoyed from significant windows? When you moved large mounds of soil to specific locations, what did you intend using it for? These decisions formed part of the overall scheme and, with the main structure in place, your original vision can now be realised.

Planting will largely depend on the time of year that you reach this stage. Providing the season is appropriate, many specimen flowering trees and shrubs will benefit from being planted now, as they will then establish good roots and build up energy resources during the autumn and winter. By next spring, they will be settled sufficiently to produce their first blossom, introducing a fresh and colourful aspect to your new garden.

PREPARING FOR WINTER

The first real test of your self-build scheme will be taken as winter sets in. Driving rain, gale force winds and frost, will all try to destroy the structure you have created. However, providing your home is afforded sufficient protection, their efforts will fail to cause any consequential damage.

Checking the roof is one of the first tasks you must perform. Inspect for slipped tiles, loose flashing and felt, and any gaps in ridge-tile mortar joints. Next, check that gutters are secure and free of debris. Though plastic guttering is robust, joined sections do sometimes work loose, and any breaches are certain to cause problems later on. While the major aspects of construction are under way, it is easy to forget minor details, such as downspout and drainage covers, but these are now essential to prevent blockage from falling leaves and other garden debris.

Doors, window frames, fascia boards and all other exposed timbers, including garden fences and gates, should be carefully primed and painted or stained, as appropriate. If UPVC double-glazed windows have been installed, check that the seals remain effective and have not shrunk or pulled away from the brickwork. Finally, make sure you remember to insulate all water pipes and tanks contained in the roof space and any that extend outside the dwelling, to protect them from frost.

Once the weather deteriorates, a regular inspection is advised to confirm that the structure and materials perform as planned.

SUMMARY

- Plan to lay paths, driveways and other hard landscaping, giving consideration to any outstanding work required in these areas.

- Install major shrubs, trees and other soft landscaping elements as soon as possible, as this will allow them time to get established during the first year's growing season.

■ Batten down the hatches ready for winter. Check the roof is secure and exterior timbers have been painted or stained. Inspect at regular intervals to confirm the structure remains weathertight.

USEFUL INTERNET WEBSITES

www.gardenadvice.co.uk

If you are worried about facing an anti-climax now the main construction work is over, why not fill the void with a correspondence course on garden and landscape design. This is one of many sites available that can help you progress from building the 'dream home' to creating a 'dream garden' ... the difference is this course is absolutely free!

www.gardenlighting.co.uk

This company boasts an impressive range of exterior light fittings to illuminate your garden. They include traditional and contemporary wall, path, driveway and security lights.

www.landscapeplanner.co.uk

Even if you have several spare hours in your busy schedule, you still won't exhaust the information made available through this website. It contains links to just about everything under the 'garden' banner and is well worth browsing for help, advice, design ideas and products.

Chapter 24

Time for Contemplation

This chapter covers:

- take pride in the achievement

- enjoy the fruits of your labour

- plan the garden at your leisure

- realise the asset you have created

- recognise the new skills learned

It is said there is no greater satisfaction than creating something with your own hands. But self-building goes beyond this simple truth because, having created a new family home, you can indulge yourself by living in it. It is not just the unique sense of achievement gained by sitting in a space you invented, it is also the experience acquired during the various planning and construction stages that matter. From this moment, nothing will ever be quite the same again and, whether you choose to employ new skills learned or not, the fact is, *you do now have them!*

Much will depend on how the project went. Was it easy or difficult? Was it sometimes too challenging, or did the stages seem to fall neatly into place? Would you do things differently, if you could go back and start again? Crucially, did you enjoy the undertaking? If you did, then you may have found a new direction in life, a new occupation to be considered. There are lots of opportunities for self-builders to pursue and, as a friend once said: 'Find an occupation you enjoy and you will never have to work again!'

But these are matters for the future. For now, sit back and relax. As you gaze upon your 'dream home' ...

TAKE PRIDE IN THE ACHIEVEMENT

One of the delightful inevitabilities of construction is that it becomes progressively easier. The foundations and shell involve the heaviest and most laborious work of all; the roof, timber carcassing, floor boarding, felting and slating are much lighter aspects;

finally, work culminates with internal tiling, floor finishes and painting, which by comparison, are almost effortless. This wonderful and gradual sequence of events, from major physical effort to artistry, provides a boost to the spirit of adventure.

Once your original two-dimensional ideas turn into a three-dimensional enclosure of space, it is time to sit back and appreciate your efforts. For a while you will recall, mostly with great affection, every brick that has been laid, every timber cut to size, every nail hammered and every length of pipe fixed into place. You have built the 'homestead'. The 'dream home' is now a reality set on the ground in front of you and, as family members and friends gather for the completion ceremony (an irresistible event), the sense of overwhelming pride and personal achievement will be immense.

There will inevitably be a deluge of requests for 'private tours' from friends, relatives and colleagues who call to visit. You will find yourself narrating stories of how difficult it was to find your head for heights, what you did when three loads of concrete arrived on the same wet and windy day, and disclose the various tips and tricks of the trade you learned during construction. You will exude enthusiasm and boast about producing a standard of finish that is *exactly* how you want it.

There is nothing wrong in feeling pride in what you have achieved. This is one of the major rewards of completing a self-build project. Many may have voiced doubt in your ability at the outset and now, as you stand with them inside the dwelling, you can pat yourself quietly on the back.

ENJOY THE FRUITS OF YOUR LABOUR

There is sometimes a feeling of great trepidation and anxiety about the new home and this can manifest in a reluctance to actually move into it, until every minor detail has been completed. After living on the site in a caravan or in rented accommodation elsewhere, the sudden expanse of space and loss of familiar enclosures can be quite daunting. But this apprehension will soon dissipate as you experience the benefits. Doors that close with a gentle reassuring click, crisp paintwork and the distinctive smell of things 'new', all become recognised and enjoyable refinements.

Each of the spaces you have created provides a different range of experiences. The view from one room and one level to another, the garden and an open vista of the distant horizon from particular windows, are all of your own making. So too are the finishes, colours and materials, which you have chosen to complement the room character, mood and atmosphere. It is finally time to sit with family, friends and new-found neighbours, and enjoy the fruits of your labour. This is when you can live the experience you have created and make decisions about how each room will be used.

Plan the garden at your leisure

After moving into the dwelling and following the initial frenzy of activity to place everything in its rightful position, you will find there is time to contemplate. Early in the morning or as dusk falls, there is often a desire to 'peruse the estate' and then decisions about garden landscaping and planting can be made. If you managed to install one or two major features, whilst good access and machinery were available, the basic framework will already exist. If not, you will have a blank canvas ready for painting.

Unlike the building work, planning and creating your new garden has no predetermined timescale: you are free to undertake work at the pace you choose and spend as much or as little as you wish on the project. The pressure is off. You can visit nurseries and national garden centres at your convenience, change the planting arrangement at will and create a unique exterior design that is right for you and your family.

Realise the asset you have created

It is important to recognise that you have not only built a superb new home for your family, you have also generated a considerable financial asset as well. The investment you hold in bricks and mortar has a quantifiable value on the open property market and its capital worth will rise with each passing year.

If you built your home with the intention of living in it, you will probably not relish the idea of selling at this moment in time. However, by keeping an eye on the local, as well as the national, property market, you may recognise those occasional periods when prices surge forward before settling. This is usually the best opportunity you have for selling your home and making a good profit. It is a time of maximum capital appreciation. Bear in mind the additional value you have created over and above the baseline cost of your original empty site. For every hour spent, you have taken a basic material and converted it into building fabric. You have added up to 60 per cent to the cost of that raw material, by providing your own labour 'free'. This is an opportunity for you to 'cash-in' on the time invested.

If you sit down and work out costs against capital value, you will realise that you have probably earned much more in your spare time than you did whilst at work in paid employment. Not only that, your self-build 'work' was more challenging, uniquely rewarding and ultimately more satisfying than your normal occupation. It is often the case that self-builders actually start to doubt their own calculations, feeling something somewhere must exist to cast a shadow over the project. When scepticism sets in, visit local estate agents and make property price comparisons with your own newly built home. It is also worth considering having your home professionally assessed to determine its exact value. Following this simple exercise and with the results on paper in black and white, your sense of self-satisfaction and confidence will grow immensely.

We mentioned earlier in this book that sometimes doing nothing is better than doing something, and this can be applied to property value. Regardless of the point when you enter the property market, there is nothing more certain then that between five and ten years from now, your mortgage will have shrunk dramatically in relative terms, whilst your property value will have doubled. Moreover as your asset matures, so too does your borrowing power. If you wanted, you could now take out another loan to fund the next project or, indeed, borrow enough to fund several projects.

RECOGNISE THE NEW SKILLS LEARNED

By the end of your self-build scheme, you will realise that a considerable personal transformation has taken place. Your versatility in practical skills, the ability to organise yourself and others and oversee an entire construction project, will have provided an inner confidence. This could not have been learned in any other way and will stay with you throughout your life.

Those newly acquired practical skills and knowledge could lead in many directions and open up lots of new opportunities, both in your private life and in your chosen career. You could now contemplate a change of occupation, go self-employed, start a new business or, if you have realised a reasonable profit, even consider early retirement or moving to sunnier climates.

You could also, of course, consider starting all over again with a bigger and more ambitious self-build scheme. Our best wishes go with you in whatever path you choose to take. **Good luck!**

Glossary of Self-Build and Construction Terms

Abutment. A wall rising above the roof slope separating roof sections.

Airbrick. A brick with holes in it designed to provide ventilation.

Angle bead. Galvanised angled steel strips which are fixed to wall edges prior to plastering. They provide a continuous guide so that the finished plaster corner is straight and neat.

Architrave. A moulded frame usually made from timber, which fits around a door or window opening to hide the gaps between the door lining and the wall.

Article 4 direction. A power available under the 1995 Town and Country Planning (General Permitted Development) Order allowing the council, in certain instances, to restrict permitted development rights.

Backland development. Development of land-locked sites, such as rear gardens and private open space, usually found in residential areas.

Baluster. The vertical rails supporting a handrail. Turned or twisted baluster rails are known as 'spindles'.

Balustrade. A collective term that includes the hand-rail, baluster rails and sections of step or balcony they are mounted on.

Barge boards. Usually made of timber, these are fixed to the gable end of a roof to protect the roof timbers against wet and windy weather.

Barge foot. An additional section of timber positioned under or behind a barge board, blocking the gap where the barge board meets the soffit of the eaves.

Base slab. A raft foundation or concrete slab under a structure.

Bat. Usually half the normal length of a brick, cut to complete a wall course bond.

Batt. A slab of insulation.

Batten. A small section of timber on which sheet materials, slates and roof tiles are fixed.

Block. A masonry unit, which is larger than a brick and is designed to make the construction of walls much faster and more economical.

Blockwork. A wall built with blocks.

Bolster. A hardwood cap placed over a post to increase its load-bearing capacity.

Brandering. Battening to level ceiling joists prior to fixing laths.

Butt. To push or fit together.

Buttress. An additional bracing wall or projecting support. It is often set at right angles to the main wall and usually tapers towards the top.

Cant. The angle between two walls, less or greater than a right angle.

Cantilever. A beam fixed at one end.

Capillary action. The capacity of water and similar fluids to be sucked into narrow spaces, such as brick joints or the tiny holes of porous material. Rising damp is created through this action.

Capital gains tax. A tax levied on profit and payable to the Inland Revenue from the sale of property or other assets.

Capital growth. The increase in value of a property over a period of time.

Capped chimney. A chimney sealed to prevent birds or rainwater getting into it.

Capstone. The coping on top of a wall.

Carcassing. The timber used in structural sections of a building, for example roof rafters and floor joists.

Casement. A window hinged on one of its vertical edges.

Casing. Boards fixed in door openings to hide the wall edges and support the door.

Cavity. The gap between the internal and external walls of a building.

Cavity insulation. Ideally fitted when cavity walls are built with material usually consisting of sheets of expanded polystyrene.

Cavity ties. Galvanised metal fixings used to bond the external and internal structural walls together.

Cavity tray. A damp-proof crossing the cavity of a wall at an abutment, rising from the roof side upwards at least 150mm before passing through the wall.

Ceiling binder. A tie running between the joists or trussed rafters.

CGT. See Capital gains tax.

Charge certificate. If there is a mortgage on land, a charge certificate is issued instead of a 'land certificate' by the Land Registry. It includes the same details but also shows a record of the deed creating the mortgage.

Chase. To inscribe or cut a groove into brick, plaster or other material, usually so that a cable or pipe can be embedded into it.

Cladding. The outermost weatherproof material fixed to a wall, designed to be decorative and/or functional.

Cleared site. A plot of land that is now clear but which has previously had one or more industrial, manufacturing or other operations conducted upon it, resulting in potential contamination of the soil structure.

Completion certificate. A notice issued by the local authority after the final visit by the building inspector, confirming that the dwelling complies with building regulations.

Completion notice. A certificate issued by the architect to authorise a payment to a main contractor. The completion certificate establishes the value of retention money to be held over a defects period and a copy can be sent with the VAT claim, to enable this to be processed.

Contaminated land. Land with a prior history in which residues of toxic substances, chemical waste or manufacturing by-products are contained within the soil structure.

Contemporary design. Modern and 'of the time', using fashionable materials, shapes, colours and fabrics.

Conveyancing. The legal process involved in buying and/or selling land or property.

Coping. The topmost part of a wall, often designed with a sloping surface to throw off rainwater.

Corbel. A projection extending to support a load above it.

Cornice. A decorative addition to the top and projecting from the face of an internal or external wall.

Course. A single layer of bricks or blocks.

Covenant. An agreement to do or not do something contained in a deed. Covenants can be made by the current or any prior owner of the land, for example to maintain boundary walls or fences.

Coving. The concave decorative moulding that joins a ceiling to the walls.

Curtilage. A small area forming part of, or parcel with, the dwelling that it contains or is attached to.

Dado. Panels fixed to the lower half of internal walls.

Dado rail. Decorative and/or functional rails, usually made from moulded timber, fitted traditionally to internal walls to protect them from damage by chairs.

Damp-proof course. A waterproof membrane installed in walls and floors to prevent moisture causing damage by rising upwards through the structure. Also termed 'damp course' or 'DPC'.

DPC. The standard and widely used abbreviation for damp-proof course.

Dry joint. A brick or timber joint that is not bonded with mortar or adhesive.

Dry lined. An internal partition or cladding constructed usually with a timber frame and plasterboard.

Ducting. A system of shafts or tubes designed to carry and protect cables or pipes.

Dwarf wall. A low wall, for example one constructed to support joists under the ground floor.

Easement. A legal right to use or cross over land owned by someone else.

Eaves. The lowest section of a roof, overhanging a supporting wall.

English bond. A particularly strong method of building walls by laying bricks together in staggered alternating courses using headers and stretchers.

Escutcheon. A protective plate around a keyhole or door handle.

Fascia. Boards installed to a roof to protect the ends of trusses or rafters and on which gutters are attached.

Finial. Ornamental timber section added to the highest point of barge boards or hanging from stair newels on landings.

Flange. A flat plate at the end of a pipe or beam, through which a bolted joint can be made.

Flashing. Waterproof material covering joints between walls and roofs, usually shaped out of lead.

Floating coat. The first coat of thick plaster put on a wall to cover irregularities.

Floor plate. A plate constructed from steel or timber bedded in mortar and designed to withstand heavy loads.

Footings. The foundations of a structure.

Footprint. The 'footprint' of the building refers to those parts within the external walls.

Formwork. Temporary boards used to keep wet mixtures, such as concrete, in a particular shape until it sets.

Framed construction. A structure built with a strong skeleton frame made of timber or steel, against which a brick outer shell is added.

Freehold. Property held until the end of time.

Gable. Triangular upper part of a wall at the end of a ridged roof.

Gable end. The gable shaped canopy over a door or window or a wall topped with a gable.

Hard landscaping. Elements include paths, driveways, garden walls and patios.

Header. Brick or block laid across a wall to bond together its two sides. It also means the exposed end part of a brick.

Herringbone strutting. The type of cross bracing used between floor joists to increase stiffness.

Hip. The sharp edge of a roof from ridge to eaves where the two sides meet.

Hipped roof. A roof with sloping ends instead of vertical ones.

Infill site. The redevelopment of land that has adjacent buildings, for example along a row of terraced houses where one has been demolished or where a gap always existed.

Jamb. Vertical side post of a window or doorway.

Joist. A beam that supports a ceiling or floor.

Joist hanger. A fabricated metal slot installed in a wall to keep a joist securely in position.

Kite. The kite-shaped tread mostly used where stairs turn a corner.

Land bank. A supply of potential development plots purchased and retained by builders, which allows them to trade and construct on a continuous basis by moving on to the next plot as completion occurs on the current one.

Land certificate. A document issued by the Land Registry giving details of who owns the land. However, a land certificate should not be accepted as absolute proof of ownership as it may be out of date. 'Office copy entries' are accepted by solicitors to prove ownership.

Land-locked. A plot of land with no independent route providing access onto it and no obvious means of creating one. Examples include surplus areas of an owner's private garden.

Lath. A long slender piece of economical timber.

Lath and plaster. Old-fashioned method of plastering a wall or ceiling using slender timbers to construct a narrow gauge frame as a base for the wet plaster.

Leaf. The inner or outer wall of a cavity wall construction.

Leasehold. Land ownership restricted to a number of years and with conditions written in a lease.

Line-boards. Timber boards laid on the ground and used to mark out the widths and position of inner and outer walls and the foundations (setting-out), prior to excavating.

Lintel. Horizontal section of timber, concrete or metal, installed to the top of a doorway or window opening, designed to support the structure above.

Massing. The outline of a dwelling's external shape and form.

Mullion. The vertical sections of material that divide a window frame into smaller lights.

Newel. The main post supporting the end of a balustrade.

Nog. A wooden peg.

Nogging. Short cross-pieces of timber used to brace studs.

Nose. The extending front edge of a staircase step.

Office copy entries. Copies of the entries recorded at the Land Registry proving ownership.

Over-building. The term applies to building a structure that is inconsistent in size, quality and/or style with other buildings nearby or has excessively filled the limited amount of land space available. Also known as an 'over development'.

P.A.R. Common abbreviation for 'planed all round'.

Pane. A sheet of glass usually framed with timber.

Party wall. A wall shared between two properties, such as is the case with semi-detached houses.

Pile. A deep foundation. These are formed by creating a hole deep enough to locate solid sub-soil. The hole is usually filled with concrete and reinforced or a section of solid steel is installed.

Pink land. Land with a 'residential use class'. The term is used largely by local authority planners and originates from the ink colour used to identify residential development areas on maps and plans.

Pitch. The angle or slope of a roof or staircase.

Planning permission. Authority granted by the local council for land to be developed or additions made to an existing property, usually with certain conditions attached.

Plate. A length of timber or steel placed either on top of a wall to support the roof trusses (a wall plate) or fixed to a floor so that studs or a timber-framed partition can be installed (a floor plate).

Precast concrete. Concrete components cast in a factory or on site prior to being placed in their final positions.

Profile boards. Boards of about a meter long used to transfer the plan outline of a building onto the ground. They are held securely in place by timber stakes. Lines are stretched between saw-cuts or marks, so the position of a wall can be fixed.

Property register. One of the three parts of a land or charge certificate describing the property and rights associated with it.

Purlin. Positioned half-way up the slope of a roof, purlins are timber beams installed to support the rafters.

Raft. A firm slab, usually made from concrete, designed to spread the weight of a structure on soft ground.

Rafter. Timbers that form the main part of the roof frame going from the wall plate up to the ridge.

Ranging rod. A long slender section of timber marked to identify the position of brick and block courses or any other part of the construction. It is basically a measuring stick.

Reinforced concrete. A process of installing steel rods inside concrete beams to help them withstand stress along their length without collapsing.

Reject. Materials that do not come up to the required standard, for example, 'reject engineering brick'.

Reserved matters. The fine detail required, following receipt of outline planning permission, that will turn it, in effect, into a detailed planning application. The aspects include design, layout, access, orientation and landscaping of the dwelling.

Retrospective design. An interior scheme that reflects the immediate past and uses colours, materials and objects pertinent to that period.

Ridge. The topmost line of the roof.

Ridge tile. Preformed angled tile covering the apex of the roof.

Roll-over relief. A way of delaying the payment of capital gains tax by reinvesting profit from the sale of one business asset to another.

Sarking. Boards placed between the rafters and the roof (sometimes called the 'soffit').

Screed. A thin level layer of material usually applied to floors.

Section 106 agreement. A binding agreement regarding matters linked to the proposed development, made between the council and a developer when planning permission is granted.

Septic tank. A tank constructed or manufactured to accept sewerage when no mains system is available.

Setting-out. The use of profile line-boards to mark a plan on the ground.

Signing off. Formal completion of the dwelling.

Sleeper wall. A wall to support the ground floor, usually honeycombed in construction to provide ventilation.

Snagging. When a builder attends the site to resolve outstanding matters after the main construction has been completed.

Snow line. Considered to be 500 feet above sea level. It is the theoretical altitude at which land is expected to suffer from severe winter conditions.

Soffit. The underside of an architectural element, for example an arch or the eaves.

Soft landscaping. Elements include topsoil, plants, shrubs and trees.

Soleplate. A substantial horizontal section of timber or metal, fixed to the floor slab.

Staged loan. The total sum is released in several predetermined stages, as the construction proceeds. Payment is made either prior to a stage being reached (e.g. when foundations are going to be installed) or afterwards.

Stamp duty. A duty payable on certain documents involved in the transfer of land and property ownership. The liability falls on the buyer.

Stanchion. A vertical supporting beam usually made from steel.

Stretcher. Brick or block laid lengthways in a wall.

String or stringer. One of the parallel boards supporting the treads.

Structural indemnity insurance. An insurance policy usually required by mortgage lenders that guarantees the dwelling against structural defects for a specified term after completion.

Staged mortgage. The standard mortgage available to self-builders where funds are released in various stages (usually between three and seven) as the dwelling is constructed. Some pay sums prior to starting the appropriate stage, to buy materials or pay for labour pertinent to it; others make payment after the stage has been completed. Only a few staged release mortgages include land purchase as part of the scheme.

Strip foundation. Concrete filled trenches to support a building.

Strut. An upright roof timber connected to the rafter above it or sloping to connect another post to the rafter.

Tabling. The term used when roof verges are capped with stone slabs.

Tanalised timber. Timbers used in construction, typically for floor joists, which have had tanalith-oxide preservative driven into their cellular structure under pressure.

Tandem garage. A garage long enough for two vehicles to park one behind the other.

Taper relief. A sliding-scale allowance for capital gains tax available from April 1998 based on the principle that the longer a property is owned the less tax is payable.

Tie-beam. The main horizontal roof beam just above the wall that connects the bases of rafters.

Title deeds. Legal documents proving ownership of a property.

Trussed. Timber planks framed together to bridge a space.

Tree preservation order. Made under the Town and Country Planning Act 1990 by the local planning authority to protect trees of importance for amenity, landscape and nature conservation.

Turnkey. A self-build 'turnkey project' is one that is entirely managed on your behalf by an individual or a company (such as an architect or builder), with your own involvement limited to providing funds and design guidelines.

Underpinning. The installation of strong foundations underneath primary foundations when the latter have failed or have been found to be inadequate to support the structure above.

UPVC. A type of stable plastic used in the manufacture of double-glazed window frames, doors and cladding.

Use class. The designation of land use by the local authority, for example as 'residential'. The 'use class' determines how specific plots of land can be developed, if at all.

Vendor. The person selling land or property.

Verge. The edge of a roof at the gable.

Wall tie. A galvanised metal tie used to bond the inner and outer walls of a cavity wall together.

Winders. Triangular stair treads sometimes used when a staircase turns a corner.

Yield. The annual return on property investment expressed as a percentage.

Useful Addresses and Telephone Numbers

Association of Drainage Authorities.
Tel: 01480 411123. The Mews, 3 Royal Oak Passage, High Street, Huntington, Cambs. PE18 6EA.

Association of Specialist Underpinning Contractors.
Tel: 01252 739143. Association House, 99 West Street, Farnham, Surrey. GU9 7EN.

AXA Selfbuilders Insurance.
Tel: 01909 591652. P.O. Box 300, Lancaster. LA1 1GB.

Belmont's Self-Builder Site Insurance Package.
Tel: 0800 018 7660. Becket House, Vestry Road, Otford, Sevenoaks, Kent. TN14 5EL.

Brick Development Association.
Tel: 01344 885651. Woodside House, Winkfield, Windsor, Berks. SL4 2DX.

British Cement Association.
Tel: 01344 762676. Century House, Telford Avenue, Crowthorne, Berkshire. RG45 6YS.

British Glass.
Tel: 0114 268 6201. Northumberland Road, Sheffield. S10 2UA.

British Institute of Architectural Technologists.
Tel: 020 7278 2206. 397 City Road, London. EC1V 1NE.

British Interior Design Association (BIDA).
Tel: 020 7349 0800. 1-4 Chelsea Harbour Design Centre, Chelsea Harbour, London. SW10 0XE.

British Land Reclamation Society.
Tel: 0113 239 5600. Enviros Aspinall, Sanderson House, Station Road, Horsforth, Leeds. LS18 5NT.

British Masonry Society.
Tel: 020 8660 3633. Shermanbury, Church Road, Whyteleafe, Surrey. CR3 0AR.

British Structural Waterproofing Association.
Tel: 020 8866 8339. Westcott House, Catlins Lane, Pinner, Middlesex. HA5 2EZ.

British Water.
Tel: 020 7957 4554. 1 Queen Anne's Gate, London. SW1H 9BT.

British Wind Energy Association.
Tel: 020 7689 1960. Renewable Energy House, 1 Aztec Row, Berners Road, London.
N1 0PW.

Building Centre.
Tel: 020 7692 4000. 26 Store Street, London WC1E 7BT.

Buildstore's BuildCare Insurance.
Tel: 0870 872 0908. Kingshorn Park, Houstoun Industrial Estate, Livingston.
EH54 5DB.

Carpet Foundation.
Tel: 01562 747351. P.O. Box 1155, Kidderminster, Worcestershire. DY11 6WP.

Centre for Alternative Technology (CAT).
Tel: 01654 705950. Machynlleth, Powys. SY20 9AZ.

Chartered Institute of Taxation.
Tel: 020 7253 9381. 12 Upper Belgrave Street, London. SW1X.

Chartered Society of Designers.
Tel: 020 7357 8088. 5 Bermondsey Exchange, 179-181 Bermondsey Street, London.
SE1 3UW.

Council for Registered Gas Installers.
Tel: 01256 372200. 1 Elmwood, Chineham Business Park, Crockford Lane,
Basingstoke, Hants. RG24 8WG.

Country Mutual Self Build Insurance Scheme.
Tel: 0118 978 7000. The Studio, Broad Street Walk, Wokingham, Berks. RG40 1BW.

Department of Trade & Industry Quality Mark Scheme.
Tel: 0845 300 8040. Bay 268, 151 Buckingham Palace Road, Victoria, London.
SW1W 9SS.

Design Council.
Tel: 020 7420 5200. 34 Bow Street, London. WC2E 7DL.

District Land Registry for Wales.
Tel: 01792 355000. Ty Cwm Tawe, Phoenix Way, Llansamlet, Swansea. SA7 9FQ.

Draught Proofing Advisory Association.
Tel: 01428 654011. P.O. Box 12, Haslemere, Surrey. GU27 3AH.

Electrical Contractors Association.
Tel: 020 7313 4800. ESCA House, 34 Palace Court, London. W2 4HY.

English Heritage.
Tel: 020 7973 3000. 23 Savile Row, London. W15 2ET.

Environment Agency.
Tel: 0845 9333111. Rivers House, Waterside Drive, Aztec West, Almondsbury, Bristol. BS12 4UD.

Federation of Plastering & Drywall Contractors.
Tel: 020 7608 5090. Construction House, 56-64 Leonard Street, London. EC2A 4JX.

FE Wright 'Project Builder' (Sterling Hamilton Wright).
Tel: 0207 7165050. City Reach, 5 Greenwich View Place, Millharbour, London. E14 9NN.

Glass & Glazing Federation.
Tel: 020 7403 7177. 44-48 Borough High Street, London. SE1 1XB.

Green Energy Organisation (NEF Renewables).
Tel: 01908 665555. National Energy Foundation, Davy Avenue, Knowlhill, Milton Keynes. MK5 8NG.

Health and Safety Executive (HSE).
Tel: 08701 545500. Caerphilly Business Park, Caerphilly. CF83 3GG.

HM Customs and Excise National Advice Service.
Tel: 0845 010 9000. VAT Central Unit, Alexander House, Southend-on-Sea, Essex. SS99 1AA.

HM Land Registry Headquarters.
Tel: 020 7917 8888. 32 Lincoln's Inn Fields, London. WC2A 3PH.

Inland Revenue Stamp Taxes Helpline.
Tel: 0845 603 0135. Ground Floor, South West Wing, Bush House, Strand, London. WC2B 4QN.

Institute of Carpenters.
Tel: 0115949 0641. Central Office, 35 Hayworth Road, Sandiacre, Nottingham. NG10 5LL.

Institute of Domestic Heating & Environmental Engineers.
Tel: 01865 343096. Dorchester House, Wimblestraw Road, Berinsfield, Wallingford. OX10 7LZ.

Institute of Plumbing.
Tel: 01708 472791. 64 Station Lane, Hornchurch, Essex. RM12 6NB.

Institute of Structural Engineers.
Tel: 020 7235 4535. 11 Upper Belgrave Street, London. SW1X 8BH.

Land Charges Department.
Tel: 01752 636666. Plumer House, Tailyour Road, Crownhill, Plymouth. PL6 5HY.

Lead Sheet Association (LSA).
Tel: 01892 822773. Hawkwell Business Centre, Maidstone Road, Pembury,
Tunbridge Wells. TN2 4AH.

Men of the Stones (stone craftsmanship).
Tel: 01952 850269. Beech Croft, Weston-under-Lizard, Shifnal, Shropshire. TF11 8JT.

'MoneyFacts' Magazine.
Tel: 01603 476476. 66-70 Thorpe Road, Norwich, Norfolk. NR1.

Mortar Industry Association.
Tel: 020 7730 8194. 156 Buckingham Palace Road, London. SW1W 9TR.

National Energy Foundation (energy saving measures).
Tel: 01908 665555. The National Centre, Davy Avenue, Knowlhill, Milton Keynes.
MK5 8NG.

National Federation of Builders (NFB).
Tel: 020 7608 5150. Construction House, 56-64 Leonard Street, London. EC2A 4JX.

National Federation of Roofing Contractors.
Tel: 020 7436 0387. 24 Weymouth Street, London. W1G 7LX.

National Fireplace Association.
Tel: 0121 200 1310. 6th Floor, The McLaren Building, 35 Dale End, Birmingham.
B4 7LN.

National Heating Consultancy.
Tel: 020 7936 4004. P.O. Box 370, London. SE9 2RP.

National House Building Council (NHBC) 'Solo' Scheme.
Tel: 01494 735363. Buildmark House, Chiltern Avenue, Amersham, Bucks.
HP6 5AP.

National Inspection Council (Electrical Installation Contracting).
Tel: 020 7564 2323. Vintage House, 37 Albert Embankment, London. SE1 7UJ.

Office of Fair Trading (OFT).
Tel: 08457 224499. Fleetbank House, 2-6 Salisbury Square, London. EC4Y 8JX.

Office of Water Services (OFWAT).
Tel: 0121 625 1300. Centre City Tower, 7 Hill Street, Birmingham. B5 4UA.

Planning Appeals Commission.
Tel: 028 902 44710. Park House, 87-91 Great Victoria Street, Belfast. BT2 7AG.

Planning Inspectorate.
Tel: 0117 372 8000. Temple Quay House, 2 The Square, Temple Quay, Bristol.
BS1 6PN.

Precast Flooring Federation.
Tel: 0116 253 6161. 60 Charles Street, Leicester. LE1 1FB.

Royal Corporation of Architects in Scotland.
Tel: 0131 229 7545. 15 Rutland Square, Edinburgh. EH1 2BE.

Royal Institute of British Architects (RIBA).
Tel: 0207 307 3700. 66 Portland Place, London. W1N 4AD.

Royal Society of Architects in Wales.
Tel: 029 2087 4753. Bute Building, King Edward VII Avenue, Cathays Park, Cardiff.
CF10 3NB.

Royal Society of Ulster Architects.
Tel: 028 9032 3760. 2 Mount Charles, Belfast. BT7 1NZ.

Scottish Office Enquiry Reporters Unit.
Tel: 0131 244 5649. 2 Greenside Lane, Edinburgh. EH1 3AG.

Self-build Zone Ltd. (insurance for self-builders)
Tel: 0845 230 9874. London House, 77 High Street, Sevenoaks, Kent. TN13 1LD.

Society of Garden Designers.
Tel: 020 7838 9311. 14-15 Belgrave Square, London. SW1X 8PS.

Soil & Groundwater Technology Association.
Tel: 020 7383 5393. c/o Parkman Environment, 307-317 Euston Road, London.
NW1 3AD.

Solar Energy Society.
Tel: 01865 484367. School of Engineering, Oxford Brookes University, Headington
Campus, Gipsy Lane, Oxford. OX3 0BP.

Solid Fuel Association.
Tel: 0845 601 4406. 7 Swanwick Court, Alfreton, Derbyshire. DE55 7AS.

Steel Lintel Manufacturers Association.
Tel: 01633 290022. P.O. Box 10, Newport, Gwent. NP9 0XN.

Sterling Hamilton Wright's Project Builder Insurance.
Tel: 0207716 5050. City Reach, 5 Greenwich View Place, Millharbour, London.
E14 9NN.

Stone Federation Great Britain.
Tel: 020 7608 5094. Construction House, 56-64 Leonard Street, London. EC2A 4JX.

TRANSCO Gas Emergency Services.

Tel: 0121 626 4431. 31 Homer Road, Solihull, West Midlands. B91 3LT.

Trussed Rafter Association.

Tel: 01777 869281. 31 Station Road, Sutton cum Lound, Retford, Nottinghamshire. D22 8PZ.

UK Timber Frame Association.

Tel: 01259 272140. The e-Centre, Cooperage Way Business Village, Alloa. FK10 3LP.

Water Regulations Advisory Scheme.

Fern Close, Pen-Y-Fan Industrial Estate, Oakdale, Gwent. NP11 3EH.

Zurich Municipal 'Custom Build' Scheme.

Tel: 01252 387592. 6 Southwood Crescent, Farnborough, Hampshire. GU14 0NL.

Index